PC Magazine
Guide to
Word 2.0
for Windows

PC Magazine
Guide to
Word 2.0
for Windows

Ed Jones

Ziff-Davis Press
Emeryville, California

Editor	Carol Henry
Technical Reviewer	Bruce Gendron
Project Coordinator	Ami Knox
Proofreader	Vanessa Miller
Cover Design	Ken Roberts
Book Design	Laura Lamar/MAX, San Francisco
Technical Illustration	Cherie Plumlee Computer Graphics & Illustration
Word Processing	Kim Haglund and Howard Blechman
Page Layout	Kevin Shafer & Associates and Anna Marks
Indexer	Julie Kawabata

This book was produced on a Macintosh IIfx, with the following applications: FrameMaker®, Microsoft® Word, MacLink®*Plus*, Aldus® FreeHand™, Adobe Photoshop™, and Collage Plus™.

Ziff-Davis Press
5903 Christie Avenue
Emeryville, CA 94608

ISBN 1-56276-030-0
Manufactured in the United States of America
10 9 8 7 6 5 4 3 2

**To the
Sutton family:
1991 would
not have been
half the fun
without you.**

CONTENTS AT A GLANCE

TABLE OF CONTENTS

Chapter 3: Refining Text 49

Chapter 4: Formatting with Word 91

Chapter 5: Controlling the Page Layout 127

Chapter 6: Previewing and Printing Your Document 161

Chapter 7: Working with Tables 177

Chapter 8: Working with Outlines 205

Chapter 9: Working with Fields and Form Letters 225

Chapter 10: Building Tables of Contents and Indexes 245

Chapter 11: Desktop Publishing with Word 263

Chapter 12: Working with Styles and Templates 301

Chapter 13: Using Glossaries 319

Chapter 14: Macros and Word 327

Chapter 15: Customizing Word 337

ACKNOWLEDGMENTS

A number of people deserve my sincere thanks for helping bring this book to the market. I would like to thank Cindy Hudson for giving me the chance to do this project for Ziff-Davis Press, Carol Henry for an outstanding editorial job, in spite of numerous time crunches, Bruce Gendron for a thorough and helpful technical review, and Cheryl Holzaepfel, Ami Knox, Jeff Green, Noelle Graney, and the others at Ziff-Davis Press whose hard work was essential in completing this project.

INTRODUCTION

WHETHER YOU'RE NEW TO WORD FOR WINDOWS OR HAVE SOME experience with the program, you'll find this book has something to offer you. If you're learning Word, the step-by-step explanations of the program basics found in the first chapters will provide the foundation on which you can build your skills in later chapters. If you know your way around Word for Windows, you'll find that this book is an excellent reference as well as a helpful guide to the new features of version 2.0.

You'll get the most out of this book if you already know how to use a PC and are familiar with the basics of Windows.

How to Use This Book

If you're a Word or Word for Windows novice, you should first learn the basics—begin with Chapter 1 and work through Chapter 6. Once you've mastered the fundamentals, you'll quickly be able to learn the more complex topics discussed in the remaining chapters. Explore these chapters in any order you wish, according to the topics you need to know about.

Experienced Word users will find the first six chapters useful as a refresher for the basics. Chapters 7 through 16 contain discussions of Word's more advanced topics. Each of these chapters is independent of the others, so this part of the book can be used both to learn new topics and as a comprehensive reference.

This book is written to work equally well for mouse or keyboard users alike. However, a mouse is highly recommended because it makes many tasks easier in Word.

A Quick Tour of the Chapters

Chapters 1 through 6 cover Word for Windows basics. In them you'll find helpful step-by-step explanations to guide you through the fundamentals. Chapters 7 through 16 build on the first chapters and cover Word for Windows's more complex topics. Four appendices round out the book, with discussions on topics such as program installation and Word for Windows's graphing features. Here's a chapter-by-chapter guide to the contents:

Chapter 1 is an introduction to Word, with coverage of topics such as starting the program, using Word's menu structure, using the Help system, selecting text, and quitting the program.

Chapter 2 shows you how to create different documents based on templates, how to enter and edit text, and how to print documents. You'll also learn about the different ways you can save files.

Chapter 3 explains margins, tabs, and line spacing, moving and copying text, and working with multiple documents open in different windows. A host of other word processing topics are covered in this chapter, including the use of the spelling, thesaurus, and grammar checkers, search and replace, bookmarks, revision marks, hyphenation, annotations, and adding bullets or paragraph numbers to text.

Chapters 4 and 5 examine how documents are formatted in Word. Chapter 4 examines formatting characters and paragraphs, and Chapter 5 extends the discussion of formatting to pages and to sections of a document.

Chapter 6 provides details on printing documents. You'll find tips on how you can print multiple documents with a single operation, and how you can use Word to print envelopes easily.

Chapter 7 examines Word's table feature. You'll learn how to design simple and complex tables using the Insert Table command, or the Table button on Word's Toolbar.

Chapter 8 covers Word's built-in outlining feature. With it you can create outlines, modify the contents of an outline, and add automatic numbering or a table of contents to an outline.

In Chapter 9 you'll learn how to use fields in Word to simplify a number of tasks. This chapter includes an exercise for using fields to create form letters.

Chapter 10 shows how you can automate the creation of tables of contents and indexes.

Chapter 11 provides an abundance of practical techniques in desktop publishing. In this chapter you'll see how you can import graphics into a document, how you can create drawings or business graphs directly from Word, how to insert frames that can contain text or graphics, and how you can resize graphic images within your documents. The chapter closes with numerous examples of business documents and descriptions of the desktop publishing techniques used to create those documents.

Chapter 12 details how styles and templates can be used to refine the appearance of your documents.

In Chapter 13 you'll learn how you can save frequently used text or graphics in a glossary; you can then duplicate the stored text or graphics using a simple key combination to recall the glossary entry.

Chapter 14 covers the use of macros, which are combinations of keystrokes and mouse actions that can automate many Word tasks. For example, if you must produce daily reports or perform other repetitive tasks, you can save many keystrokes with macros.

Chapter 15 shows how you can customize Word to meet your specific needs. You can add new commands to the menus, and you can add new buttons to Word's Toolbar to provide fast access to the tasks you commonly perform with Word.

Chapter 16 covers Word's file management capabilities, helping you organize your work.

The appendices include information on installing Word for Windows, using MS Draw and MS Graph, the drawing and business graph utilities provided with Word, and a handy command reference.

1

Introducing Word for Windows

WELCOME TO WORD FOR WINDOWS, A WORD PROCESSING PROGRAM that combines the power of true document processing with the flexibility of Microsoft Windows. While *word processing* is the traditional term for programs of this type, *document processing* is a more accurate way to describe Word for Windows. Designed to work with documents containing more than text alone, Word for Windows lets you combine text that has been formatted in a variety of styles with graphics, as shown in Figure 1.1. Documents in Word can include tables and framed data from other programs, such as paint/draw programs, spreadsheets, and database managers. Pictures can be placed anywhere on a page, and text can flow around the pictures.

Figure 1.1

A screen from
Word for Windows

Word lets you create templates, or models, that can be used to easily apply a certain style to routine documents. And Word has features that let you design outlines and complex footnotes, and automatically build tables of contents and indexes.

You can create links between Word documents and other programs; for example, a Word document can be linked to a spreadsheet in Microsoft Excel. Then, every time data changes in the spreadsheet, the Word document will be automatically updated to reflect the changes. Word for Windows can also read and write files that are in the file formats of the most popular word processors, including WordPerfect, WordStar, DisplayWrite, and Microsoft Word for DOS, as well as plain ASCII files.

NOTE. *Throughout this book, the name Word refers to the Word for Windows product. Word for Windows differs in operation from its predecessor, Microsoft Word for DOS. Although both programs provide powerful features aimed at document processing, Word for Windows follows the object-oriented design that is prevalent in most Windows programs. This book is written for Word for Windows Version 2.0 or above. There are significant changes from Version 1.1 to 2.0. If you are still using Version 1.1, consider upgrading to take advantage of the new features.*

The Challenge of Learning Word for Windows

Word is a complex program; hence, becoming familiar with it can be somewhat challenging. It will take time for you to learn to use Word for Windows to its fullest extent, but this book will be of great help, and the versatility you gain from the program will make the effort worth the investment. This text assumes you are already familiar with the Windows interface for which Word for Windows is designed; if you come across unfamiliar Windows terms or concepts as you work through this book, refer to your Windows documentation for assistance.

Fortunately, you can get familiar with Word in small steps. The basics of text entry and editing, and saving and printing files can be learned quickly—in fact, after working through the first two chapters of this book you will have gained a fundamental knowledge of these topics. But you should allow yourself sufficient time to explore most or all of Word's features. Because of its complexity, you shouldn't expect to learn Word as quickly as other, less powerful software.

A Note About Hardware

Word for Windows will run satisfactorily on any hardware that will run Windows satisfactorily. Windows requires an IBM-compatible PC with an 80286 or better processor, a hard disk, and a display with a graphics adapter. And though a mouse is technically not required to run Windows, you'll probably come to consider a mouse a virtual necessity. Using Windows without a mouse gives new meaning to the word *awkward*.

Remember that "satisfactory hardware" means different things to different people. Some individuals are quite content to work with Windows on an 80286 PC running at 12 megahertz; others find the relatively slow speed of such a system a major annoyance, and will consider nothing less than an

80386-based computer for running Windows. If you must run Windows on minimal hardware, consider adding a fast hard disk and/or upgrading the graphics adapter board. Because of the demands Windows places on the screen-refresh function, any memory you can add to your graphics board will make a significant improvement in how Windows behaves on your PC.

Word for Windows will operate with a wide variety of printers. Like all Windows applications, Word depends upon Windows to communicate with your printer; selecting the proper printer is a part of the Windows installation process (refer to your Windows documentation for additional details). To take full advantage of Word, you'll want a printer that is capable of printing graphics as well as text.

Starting Word

One way Word for Windows differs from Word for DOS is that you can start the Word application either from DOS or from within Windows. Starting from Windows is simpler (often involving just a mouse click on an icon), but starting from DOS lets you use command-line prompts, and include names of files to be opened along with Word.

Starting Word from Windows

When in Windows, there are two ways you can start Word: by selecting the Word icon from a Windows program group, or by choosing the file named WINWORD.EXE from the Word drive and directory in the Windows File Manager. (If you prefer to stick with the keyboard, the second method works better, although you may have to do some hunting around in File Manager to find the WINWORD.EXE file.)

The Word installation process creates a Windows program group containing Word. To start Word from this program group, double-click with the mouse on the program group to open it, and then double-click on the Word icon to start Word. Your Word icon should resemble the one shown here:

If you want to use the keyboard, open the File Manager in the usual manner, find the WINWORD.EXE file in the directory that stores Word, and press Enter to select and run Word. Or, if you know the entire path name for Word, save time by opening the Windows File menu and choosing Run; then enter the directory path, followed by **WINWORD.EXE**. The illustration below shows such an entry, assuming that the Word program is stored on drive C, in a subdirectory named WINWORD.

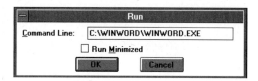

TIP. *You can start Word and load multiple documents simultaneously by entering the names of the documents after the program name in the File Run text box. Word opens the files in the order in which you typed their names. For example, if you enter*

```
C:\WINWORD.EXE ACCOUNTS MEMO1 LETTER2
```

in the File Run text box, Word loads three files (ACCOUNTS.DOC, MEMO1.DOC, and LETTER2.DOC), with LETTER2.DOC being the currently active document.

Placing Documents in Program Groups

When you use the mouse, an advantage of Windows program groups is that you can place your frequently used documents inside the program group. Doing so makes it easy to start Word and load a document at the same time; just double-click on the document itself, instead of on the Word icon, and Word will be loaded along with the document.

Placing documents in the Word program group is as simple as dragging the documents from the Windows File Manager to the program group.

1. First, open the program group containing Word. (If a program group containing Word does not exist, you can create one with the New option on the File menu; then drag the Word icon into the new program group.)

2. Drag the window of the open program group to the lower portion of your screen.

3. Open the File Manager in the usual manner, resize the File Manager so it fits on the upper portion of your screen, and get into the directory containing your Word documents.

4. Select and drag each desired document into the program group containing Word. As you do this, you'll notice that the documents are displayed in the program group with the same icon as the Word program, but with their own individual file names.

5. When you have moved in all the documents you want to include, close the File Manager.

From this point on, you can load Word along with the document you want to work on by double-clicking on the document itself rather than on the Word icon.

If you are no longer using a file regularly and the icon is cluttering your program group, you can remove it from the program group (leaving the file intact) by clicking on the file in the program group, and choosing Delete from the File menu in Windows Program Manager. Be careful: Don't select a file from the File Manager and choose Delete, or you will delete the actual file from the hard disk.

Starting Word from DOS

When you start Word from the DOS level, there are a number of different start-up options you can use. You can start Word with a blank document ready for use, or with a previously saved document already loaded, or with no document at all.

- To start Word with a blank document ready for editing, enter **WINWORD** at the DOS prompt.

- To start Word and open an existing file simultaneously, enter **WINWORD** *filename* at the DOS prompt, where *filename* is the name of the document you want to edit.

   TIP. *You can open multiple files for editing when starting Word from the DOS level just as you can from the Windows File Run text box. As you do in Windows, type more than one filename. Word opens the files in the order in which you typed their names. For example, if you enter WINWORD ACCOUNTS MEMO1 LETTER2 at the DOS prompt, Word loads all three of these files and makes LETTER2.DOC the currently active document.*

- To start Word alone, with no file loaded, enter **WINWORD /N** at the DOS prompt. (Use this option when you want to edit a file whose name you can't remember.)

Starting Word with AUTOEXEC.BAT

If the nature of your work has you using Word all day long, it may make sense to modify your AUTOEXEC.BAT file so that Word is automatically loaded when you turn on your computer. (For more information about AUTOEXEC.BAT, see your DOS manual.)

You can use Word to modify your AUTOEXEC.BAT file. *Before doing so, read the warning at the end of this section.* Then start Word, and click on Open in the File menu, or press Alt+F+O. In the Open File Name text box, enter **C:\AUTOEXEC.BAT**. (This assumes your AUTOEXEC.BAT file is stored in the root directory of drive C. If it is not, substitute the appropriate drive name for C.)

The next dialog box to appear asks if you want to convert the file from text; choose OK, and the AUTOEXEC.BAT file will appear within Word. The contents of a typical AUTOEXEC.BAT file are shown in Figure 1.2; your file will look different.

Figure 1.2

Sample AUTOEXEC.BAT file in the Word editing screen

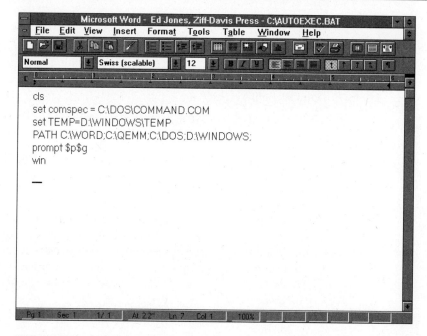

First, you should modify the PATH= statement so that it includes the name of the directory containing Word. Find the statement that begins with PATH=. There should be an existing PATH= statement (unless someone has modified your AUTOEXEC.BAT file), because the Word installation program automatically creates or modifies a PATH= statement. Examine it

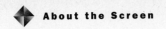

to see if it already contains entries for the WINDOWS and WINWORD
subdirectories. If these entries are not present, add them to the end of the
line. For example, an existing PATH= statement that reads

```
PATH=C:\DOS;C:\EXCEL
```

should be modified to read like this:

```
PATH=C:\DOS;C:\EXCEL;C:\WINDOWS;C:\WINWORD
```

Keep in mind that you must use a semicolon to separate all the path names.
If no PATH= line exists, add one that looks like the one shown here, substi-
tuting the appropriate drive letter for your hard drive, if necessary:

```
PATH=C:\WINDOWS;C:\WINWORD;C:\DOS
```

Next, examine the last line of the AUTOEXEC.BAT file. If it reads
WIN, change it so that it reads as follows:

```
WIN WINWORD
```

Or, if the last line contains something else entirely, you'll need to add a new
last line for starting Word, like this:

```
WINWORD
```

When your AUTOEXEC.BAT file has been edited to your satisfaction,
choose File Save As with the mouse (or by pressing Alt+F+A), select Type
(Alt+T), and be sure that Text Only is selected in the Format box; change the
file name from AUTOEXEC.TXT to AUTOEXEC.BAT, then choose OK.
Exit from Word by selecting Exit on the File menu (Alt+F+X). When you
restart your computer, Word will be loaded automatically.

WARNING! *Some resident print spoolers designed to work with Windows
may interfere with loading Windows and starting an application (like Word) at
the same time. If you get an "Unrecoverable Application Error" after modifying AUTOEXEC.BAT, it means you cannot use this avenue to load Windows
and start Word. You will have to modify AUTOEXEC.BAT to load Windows
only (make the last line of the file read WIN). After Windows has been loaded,
you can manually start Word.*

About the Screen

When Word starts, you are normally placed in a blank document, ready to
start entering text, as shown in Figure 1.3. (There are other ways to start
Word without a blank document, described earlier in this chapter.) Here are
descriptions of what you'll see on the Word screen.

Figure 1.3

A blank document
in the Word screen

Program
Control
Menu icon

Ribbon

Title bar

Menu bar

Maximize,
Minimize
icons

Style area

Status bar

Toolbar

Scroll
bar

Ruler

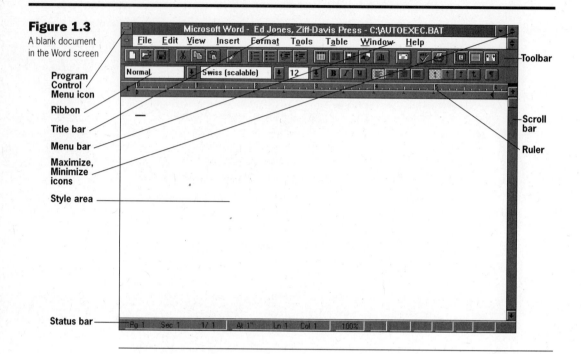

At the top of the screen is the *title bar*, displaying the program name (Microsoft Word) and the name of the document (if the document is maximized to use the entire screen). New documents that have not been saved are called Document1, Document2, Document3, and so on, in the order they are opened. The title bar also contains a *Control Menu icon* at the far left, and *Maximize/Minimize icons* at the far right.

■ The Program Control Menu icon on a blank document screen is used to open the Control Menu; this menu provides commands for changing the size or location of the window in which Word is running. You can open the Control Menu by pressing Alt+Spacebar, or by clicking on the icon with the mouse. If another document is open in a separate window under Word, it will have its own Control Menu icon, as well, for the Document Control Menu. To open the Document Control Menu, use the Alt+Hyphen key combination. Note the difference: the Program Control Menu icon is for the window in which the program (Word) is running, and the Document Control Menu icon is for the window containing the document.

■ The Maximize icon is used to bring a window to full size, and the Minimize icon reduces the size of a window.

Directly underneath the title bar is the *menu bar.* The *drop-down menus* available from the menu bar are used to apply commands to selected objects in Word, or to perform various actions. Each menu contains options related to that menu name; for example, the File menu contains various options for loading and saving files, the Format menu contains options for formatting documents, and so on.

Underneath the menu bar is the *Toolbar.* (If the Toolbar does not appear on your screen, choose View Toolbar (Alt+V+T) to turn it on.) The Toolbar is a significant aid for mouse users, as it provides access to the most often-used Word commands. Though you cannot use the Toolbar from the keyboard, you can implement the same commands through various menu choices. The icons in the Toolbar let you open and save documents, print documents, indent paragraphs, add numbered or bulleted lists, and perform many other everyday operations in Word. Because these operations relate to various tasks in Word, they will be covered in detail where appropriate throughout this text. For now, Table 1.1 shows the uses of the icons within the toolbar.

TIP. *Word's Toolbar is customizable, meaning you can replace commands available through the Toolbar with those of your own choosing. See Chapter 15 for details.*

Tip. You can hide the ribbon if you're not using it (and gain additional space to view your document) by choosing View from the menu bar and turning off ribbon.

Underneath the Toolbar is an area called the *ribbon*, which you use to control certain character and paragraph formatting in a selection of text. The ribbon contains various buttons and list boxes that you'll learn about later in this chapter. You first select the desired text, and then use a list box or a button in the ribbon to apply the desired type of formatting. Clicking on or selecting these buttons has the same effect as executing certain options from the Format Character or Format Paragraph command menus.

Because the ribbon can be used for so many different formatting tasks, it is covered in detail in Chapters 3 and 4. For now, here is a summary of how the ribbon's list boxes and buttons help you to quickly change the formatting for text you have selected.

- The Style list box at the left edge of the ribbon is used to choose a Word style and apply it to a selection.

- The Font list box, to the right of the Style list box, is used to choose a font for the selected text.

- The Points list box, near the center of the ribbon, is used to choose a point size for the selected font.

Table 1.1   **Items in the Toolbar**

Icon	Name	Description
	New	Opens a new document using default settings.
	Open	Opens an existing document.
	Save	Saves the current document under its present name. If no name exists, the Save As dialog box appears so you can name the document.
	Cut	Removes (cuts) the current selection, and inserts it into the Clipboard.
	Copy	Copies the current selection into the Clipboard.
	Paste	Pastes the contents of the Clipboard into the document at the insertion pointer.
	Undo	Reverses the last action, where possible.
	Numbered List	Numbers selected paragraphs in sequential order.
	Bulleted List	Places a bullet in front of selected paragraphs.
	Unindent	Unindents selected paragraphs (moves them to the left by one tab stop).
	Indent	Indents selected paragraphs by one tab stop.
	Table	Inserts a table. A sample table appears. Click and drag the sample to the desired size in rows and columns.
	Text columns	Formats current selection into newspaper-style columns.
	Frame	Inserts empty frame, or places a frame around selected text, table, or graphics.
	Draw	Runs the Microsoft Draw program.
	Graph	Runs the Microsoft Graph program.
	Envelope	Creates an envelope.
	Spelling	Checks spelling of current selection, or of entire document if no selection exists.
	Print	Prints one copy of all pages in current document.
	Zoom Whole Page	Displays document in page layout view, reduced to show entire page on screen.

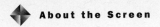

Table 1.1 **(continued)**

Icon	Name	Description
▤	Zoom 100 Percent	Displays document full-sized, in normal view.
▣	Zoom Page Width	Displays full width of page (scales document as needed to show full width) in page layout view.

- The Bold, Italic, and Underline buttons (labelled **B**, I, and U) are used to make the selected text appear in boldface, italic, or underlined.

- The group of alignment buttons, located to the right of the Underline button, control paragraph alignment of the selected paragraphs. The first button aligns flush left, the second button is for centered alignment, the third button aligns flush right, and the last button is for justified text (both sides flush with margins).

- The rightmost group of buttons lets you select types of tab stops to set—left, center, right, or decimal.

- The single button to the far right (the one containing the paragraph symbol) is used to turn on or off the display of certain nonprinting characters, such as spaces, tabs, and paragraph markers.

Underneath the ribbon is an area called the *ruler*. You can use the ruler to change indentation levels for paragraphs, adjust margins, or change the width of columns. In Chapter 4, you will learn how the markers on the ruler can be moved to change these paragraph settings. The ruler is calibrated in inches or in centimeters, depending on your Word setup. (To change the standard of measurement for the ruler, choose the Tools Options command, choose General from the Category list, and select the desired unit of measurement in the Measurement Units list box of the dialog box that appears.)

Beneath the ruler is the large *style area*, where actual typing and editing of the document takes place. Beneath the style area is the *status bar*; this provides information regarding your position in a particular document, as well as prompts and messages to you from Word.

At the far right edge of the style area, the *scroll bar* appears. The scroll bar is used to move the display to other areas of the document. Clicking on the up or down arrow in the scroll bar scrolls the window up or down line by line within the document. You can also scroll more quickly through a document, in two ways: The first method is to drag the scroll box (the smaller box within the scroll bar that doesn't have an arrow) to a position that represents your desired location in the document. For example, if you drag the scroll box two-thirds of the way down the bar, you move the window two-thirds of the way to the end of the document. The second method is to click in the area of the scroll bar above or below the scroll box, and move up or down a screen at a time.

NOTE. *Your Word for Windows screen also has a horizontal scroll bar at the bottom of the style area, for use when your lines are longer than what will show on the screen. This scroll bar is not visible unless you turn it on by selecting the Tools Options command (Alt+O+O) and turning on the Horizontal Scroll Bar option in the dialog box that appears. The horizontal bar has a scroll box and directional arrows that work similarly to those in the vertical scroll bar.*

Using Word's Menus

Tip. While a menu is open, you can move to another menu by pressing the left or right arrow keys. With the mouse, you can click on any menu and drag left or right to move to another menu.

Word's *commands*, or *menu options*, can be chosen either with the keyboard or with the mouse. Note that commands that appear dimmed on the menus are unavailable, as they do not apply to the current selection.

To use the keyboard to open a menu, use the Alt key along with the underlined letter of the menu name. For example, the F in File appears underlined on the menu; thus, pressing Alt+F opens the File menu. Once the menu is opened, you can press the underlined letter of an option to choose that option. You can perform all these related selections as a series of sequential keystrokes; for example, pressing Alt+F+S invokes the Save command from the File menu.

With the mouse, just click on a menu to open it, and drag to the desired command.

Next to the options on command menus are the *hotkeys* that also can be used to invoke the commands. These hotkeys are accessible only as keypresses, not as mouse clicks. For example, to quickly exit from Word, press Alt+F4.

Tip. Most Word commands, once chosen, can be repeated by pressing the Repeat Command key (F4).

Throughout this book, Word commands are referred to by their complete names, which include the name of the menu and the name of the option chosen from the menu. As an example, if you are instructed to use the Insert Page Numbers command, you would invoke the command by using either the mouse or the keyboard method of opening the Insert menu, and then choosing Page Numbers.

The sections that follow provide brief descriptions of the commands on Word's menus. You'll learn how to master the functions of each menu as you work through this book.

About Dialog Boxes

Menu options that are followed by an ellipsis (...), when chosen, will display a *dialog box* asking for more information. Dialog boxes contain the specific settings related to a chosen command, along with the assumptions Word has made for that command. Figure 1.4 shows, for example, the dialog box that appears when the Format Paragraph command is chosen. You can select OK (by clicking on the OK button or pressing Enter) to accept the displayed settings, or you can change any of them, as explained in a moment.

Figure 1.4

The dialog box for the Format Paragraph command

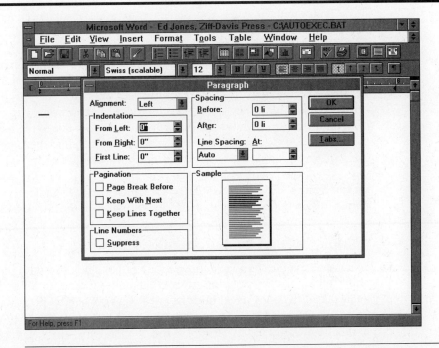

Dialog boxes vary as to the available options they contain, but they all contain some or all of the elements described in the following paragraphs.

Command Buttons These are rectangular buttons with rounded corners. They are used to implement commands or other actions, or to display an additional dialog box. Most dialog boxes contain command buttons that say OK and Cancel (or Close), which are used to confirm or cancel an action. When the term in a command button is followed by an ellipsis (...), choosing that button will cause another dialog box to be displayed. A command button labeled Options indicates more options are available if you select the button.

Option Buttons   These are buttons with rounded corners that can be turned on and off. The button is filled in when the option is turned on (enabled), and blank when the option is turned off (disabled).

Text Boxes   These are rectangles that accept text that you type in response to a prompt, such as a file name or a numeric value for a margin setting. Text boxes that accept numeric values also have double arrows at the right edge of the box; mouse users can click on the arrows to increase or decrease the value entered. Text boxes are sometimes combined with list boxes (described just below), to form *combination boxes*. In combination boxes, you can either type your selection in the text box, or choose a selection from the list box.

List Boxes   These contain lists of available choices, such as file names or font styles. Some list boxes display all possible choices, along with a scroll bar that lets you view the choices. Other list boxes are called *drop-down* boxes. These initially show just one choice; to see additional choices, you click on the down arrow at the side of the list box, or tab to the list box and press Alt+↓. A special list box on Options screens, called the Category list box, contains graphic representations of option categories.

Check Boxes   These are squares that contain an *X* to indicate when the option beside them is turned on. If the option is off, the check box is empty.

Working Within Dialog Boxes

Using the keyboard, you can move around in a dialog box with the Tab and Shift-Tab keys, or by pressing Alt plus the underlined letter of an option's name. The OK and Cancel buttons are always chosen by pressing Enter (for OK) and Esc (for Cancel). To open a list box from the keyboard, move to the list box and press Alt+↓. Once it is open, press the ↑ and ↓ keys to move within the list box. To select an option button or a check box, press Alt plus the underlined letter in the option's name.

Mouse users have it much easier—with the mouse, you simply click on any of the options within the dialog box. To turn option buttons and check boxes on and off, click on the button or box. To open a drop-down list box, click on the arrow at the edge of the list box.

Tip. To select an option and choose OK from the dialog box at the same time, just double-click on the option.

The Document Control Menu

The Document Control Menu, which is opened with Alt+Hyphen or by clicking on the Document Control icon, provides commands for sizing and choosing document windows under Word. (See Chapter 3 for details on the use of windows in Word.)

Restore	Ctrl+F5
Move	Ctrl+F7
Size	Ctrl+F8
Maximize	Ctrl+F10
Close	Ctrl+F4
Next Window	Ctrl+F6
Split	

On this menu, you have the following options:

- Use the Restore command (or the Ctrl+F5 hotkey) to restore a maximized or minimized window to its previous size.

- Use the Move (or Ctrl+F7) and Size (or Ctrl+F8) commands to move or resize an existing document window.

- The Close (or Ctrl+F4) command closes the active window, and the Next Window (or Ctrl+F6) command makes the next window the active window (when you have more than one window open).

- The Split command can be used to split the current window. This command has no hotkey equivalent, but you can accomplish the same result by dragging the *split bar*. (Unless you've moved it, the split bar resides just above the upward-pointing arrow in the scroll bar.)

The File Menu

The File menu, which is opened with Alt+F or by clicking on File in the menu bar, is divided into two parts—the first part containing the available commands, and the bottom section listing the last four documents opened by Word.

File	
New...	
Open...	Ctrl+F12
Close	
Save	Shift+F12
Save As...	F12
Save All	
Find File...	
Summary Info...	
Template...	
Print Preview	
Print...	Ctrl+Shift+F12
Print Merge...	
Print Setup...	
Exit	Alt+F4
1 C:\AUTOEXEC.BAT	
2 NEWSLETT.DOC	
3 C:\WINWORD\WORDBOOK\INS1-E.DOC	
4 C:\WINWORD\WORDBOOK\INS1-D.DOC	

- Use File New to clear the style area so you can begin work on a new document.

- The File Open command displays a dialog box from which you can pick an existing document to open.

- The File Close command closes the current document; if you have made changes to it, Word gives you a chance to save the changes before closing the document.

- The File Save command saves the current document under its assigned name. If no name has been assigned to the current document, Word will ask for a name.

- The File Save As command prompts you for a new file name for saving an existing file. (You can also use this option to save a file in a different file format, for use with another word processor.)

- The File Save All command saves all documents currently open.

- Use the File Find File command to search for a file based on its contents, or based on remarks you may have made in the file's summary (see Chapter 4 for more on this topic).

- The Summary Info command displays and lets you update the summary information for the current document (including title, subject, author's name, and comments).

- The Template command lets you change the template in use, and the options associated with a template. (See Chapter 12 for details about templates.)

- The File menu's Print Preview, Print, Print Merge, and Print Setup commands control printing operations (see Chapter 6). Use Print Preview to see an on-screen representation of what your printed document will look like. Print displays a dialog box for printing a document. Print Merge, explained in Chapter 9, is used to print form letters or labels based on a file of names and addresses. Print Setup shows you a dialog box so you can choose your desired printer and select options such as paper size and orientation.

- The File Exit command is used to exit from Word. If you choose Exit and have not yet saved your revisions to a document, Word prompts you to save the changes before exiting.

The lower portion of the File menu contains the names of the last four documents you opened from Word. You can quickly reopen any of these documents by selecting the file name from the menu, or by typing the underlined number beside the name.

The Edit Menu

The Edit menu contains various commands used when editing documents. (These will be covered in greater detail in Chapters 2 and 3.)

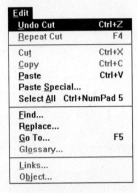

- The Undo command undoes the most recent operation; the actual wording of this command reflects the operation you performed last.

- The Repeat command repeats the action of the last operation or command. If an operation can't be repeated, the command appears on the menu as Can't Repeat.

- The Cut, Copy, and Paste commands are used to delete, copy, or move selections of text. Paste Special lets you establish a link between a Word document and a file in another Windows program, such as an Excel spreadsheet, or copy a Windows object (such as a graphic) into a document.

- The Select All command selects the entire document.

- The Find and Replace commands are used to search for specific text, or to find and replace specific text.

- The Go To command lets you move quickly to a specific location in a document.

- The Glossary command is used to insert or define items in a glossary (Chapter 13).

- The Links command is used to view all links you have in a document. Links between Word and other programs are covered in Chapter 11.

- The Object command opens the selected object for editing, using the program you used originally to create the object. For example, if the object is a graphic drawn in Microsoft Draw, choosing Object starts Microsoft Draw.

The View Menu

The View menu commands are used to control how Word appears on your screen.

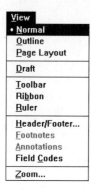

Tip. To speed up Word during text entry, choose View Draft. This displays characters in a standard font with standard spacing; screen movements are thus faster than when characters are displayed using selected fonts and styles.

- The first four commands, Normal, Outline, Page, and Draft, let you enable and disable an outline display style, a draft style (where characters appear with a standard display font and spacing), and a page style (where page endings and beginnings resemble the actual printed pages). Outline display is explained in Chapter 8; normal, draft, and page layout styles are covered in Chapter 2.

- The Toolbar, Ribbon, and Ruler commands let you enable or disable the display of the Toolbar, ribbon, and ruler. If you are not using these features, you can turn them off and have more room on the screen to view your documents.

- The Header/Footer command (Chapter 5) lets you place headers and footers in a document.

- The Footnotes (Chapter 5) and Annotations (Chapter 3) commands allow the viewing of footnotes or editorial annotations in an individual window beneath the text. If no footnotes or annotations have been entered, these commands appear dimmed on the menu.

- The Field Codes command lets you specify how *fields* are displayed. Fields are the entry spaces for certain text and graphics; this topic is covered in Chapter 9. The Preferences command lets you control whether nonprinting characters (such as tabs, spaces, and paragraph markers) are visible in a document.

- The Zoom command is used to change the magnification used by the editing view. You can choose normal (100%), 75%, 50%, 200%, or you can enter a custom value for magnification.

The Insert Menu

The Insert menu is used to insert various items into a document.

- Use the Break command to insert page breaks, column breaks, or section breaks. These topics are detailed in Chapter 5.

- Use the Page Numbers command to insert page numbering into a document (Chapter 5).

- Use the Footnote command to insert footnotes into a document (Chapter 5).

- The Bookmark command (Chapter 3) inserts a *bookmark*, or placemarker, at a specific location in a document; later, you can use the Edit GoTo command to find that bookmark.

- The Annotation command (Chapter 3) is used to place editorial annotations in your text. (You can view these annotations in a separate window by using the View Annotations command.)

- The Date and Time command is used to insert the current date or time (according to the PC's clock) into the document (Chapter 5).

- The Field command is used to insert a field into a document. Fields are special codes that provide information, such as the author's name or the current date. Fields are covered in Chapter 9.

- The Symbol command is used to insert symbols into a document, such as the copyright symbol, or the Greek letter π. When you choose this command, a dialog box appears, and you can select the desired symbol. See Chapter 2 for more details on this topic.

- The Index Entry, Index, and Table of Contents commands are used for building indexes and tables of contents. See Chapter 10.

- Use the File command to insert a file at the insertion pointer location. The file can be in Word format, or it can be in the format of another word processor.

- Use the Frame command to insert an empty frame in a document, or to insert a frame around the selected text or graphic. For more on frames, see Chapter 11.

- Use the Picture and Object commands to insert pictures or other objects into a document (Chapter 11).

The Format Menu

The Format menu is used to apply various types of formatting throughout a document. Document formatting is a major skill (and a significant part of your work) in Word, and various chapters of this book explore these menu commands extensively. Most aspects of character and paragraph formatting are covered in Chapter 4; Chapter 5 tells you how to format entire sections and documents. The use of the Style command to work with Word styles for specific documents is explained in Chapter 12. The Frame and Picture commands are detailed in Chapter 11.

The Tools Menu

The Tools menu provides important tools for working with your documents.

- The Spelling command is used to check spelling in a document. The Grammar command checks the grammer in a document, and the Thesaurus lets you look up synonyms for a selected word. The Hyphenation command hyphenates one or all words in all or part of a document. Spell-checking, grammar-checking and hyphenation are explained in Chapter 3.

- The Bullets and Numbering command is used to apply or to change paragraph numbering, or to add bullets to selected paragraphs. The Revision Marks command lets you apply marks to indicate revised areas of text in an existing document. The Compare Versions command lets you compare one version of a document with another. You'll find these topics discussed in Chapter 3.

- The Create Envelope command creates an envelope that will print along with the current document.

- The Sorting command (Chapter 7) lets you rearrange selected text.

- The Calculate command is used to perform calculations on numbers.

- Repaginate Now (Chapter 5) forces immediate repagination of the document, causing the appropriate page breaks to occur after any significant revisions.

- The Record command (Chapter 14) lets you record a series of keystrokes as a macro.

- The Macro command provides various options that apply to *macros,* which are series of stored keystrokes that can be played back when you press a single key or key-combination.

■ The Options command (Chapter 15) is used to change various settings in Word, such as whether documents are saved automatically at regular intervals, and whether document measurements are shown in inches or centimeters.

The Table Menu

The Table menu provides various options that apply to Word tables, such as inserting tables at the insertion pointer, adding or deleting columns in existing tables, changing the row height and/or column widths used by tables, and converting existing text to table form. All of the options within the Table menu are explained in Chapter 7.

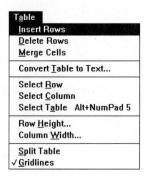

The Window Menu

The Window menu (Chapter 3) provides just two commands, New Window and Arrange All.

Use New Window to display a new window for editing the current document. Arrange All lets you rearrange all windows that are currently open. At the bottom of the Window menu you'll see the names of all currently open document windows; you can switch to any window by choosing the document by name.

Using the Help Menu

The Help menu lets you access Word's extensive help system.

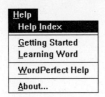

Word's comprehensive system of on-line help provides an excellent way to get a quick answer to many questions as they arise. The Help Index command on the Help menu displays the Help Index (Figure 1.5). You can also display the Index by pressing F1 within a document.

On the Help Index menu is a set of help topics. Use the Search option to display a text box for a keyword search. Here you can enter the search term and choose OK, and the list box will display a list of topics related to your keyword. Choose a topic from this list to see a window explaining that topic. To close a help window when you're done with it, press Alt+F4, or select the Close command from the Help Window control menu.

Also on the Help menu, the Getting Started and Learning Word commands can be used to start different parts of the built-in tutorial. Getting Started begins with the basics, and Learning Word covers the more advanced topics. The WordPerfect Help command lets you choose a WordPerfect topic or WordPerfect keyboard combination, and find the equivalent Word command or key-combination. The About command provides information about your version of Microsoft Word.

Word's help is *context-sensitive*, which means you get help that is related to what you are doing at that instant. For example, if you are in a document, pressing F1 displays the Help Index. But if you have a menu option highlighted or a dialog box open, pressing F1 displays help about that particular menu or dialog box.

The Insertion Pointer and the Mouse Pointer

If you are completely new to Word for Windows, you'll want to note the difference between the *insertion pointer* (previously known as the cursor) and the various shapes of the mouse pointer. As shown in Figure 1.6, the insertion pointer tells you where your typed input will appear. You can reposition the insertion pointer within a document by moving it with the keyboard's arrow keys, or by clicking the mouse at the desired location.

Figure 1.5

Word's Help Index

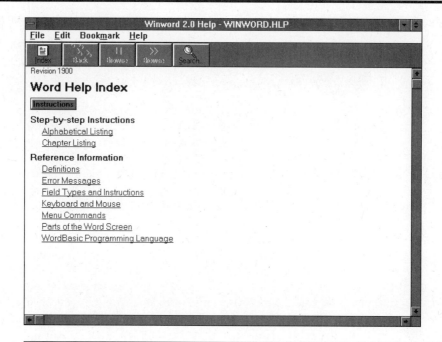

The *I beam* pointer is just one of many shapes the mouse pointer takes on when you are working in Word. (If you don't have a mouse, you won't see this element.) As long as you are in the text area of a document (and away from the outer edges of the window), you'll see the mouse pointer as an I beam. When you move the mouse pointer to any location in the document and click, the insertion pointer jumps to that location, and you can proceed to type in text.

When you move toward the edges of the window, the I beam changes shape. Usually, it becomes the normal mouse pointer (an arrow pointing up and to the left). If you move the mouse pointer to the left edge of the document window, however, the pointer retains its arrow shape, but points to the right. This means you are in the *selection bar* area of a document. Here you can click once to select a line of text adjacent to the pointer, or click twice to select an adjacent paragraph. At all four outermost edges of a window, the mouse pointer assumes the double-arrow shape that is common to all window moving and sizing operations. As with other programs under Windows, when the mouse pointer assumes the double-arrow shape, you can move and resize document windows by clicking and dragging.

Figure 1.6

The insertion pointer and the I beam mouse pointer

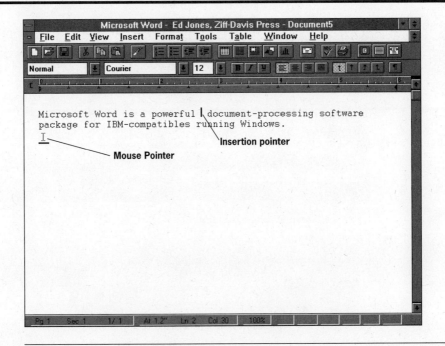

Selecting Text

Like most Windows applications, Word is an object-oriented program—you select objects and then indicate what you want to do with those objects by choosing a command. You will probably most often work with blocks of text as objects. Word provides a variety of ways to select text, and it'll be worth your time to get familiar with these techniques.

Selecting with the Keyboard

Tip. To select an entire document, press Ctrl-5, using the 5 key on the numeric keypad. This is useful for applying formatting throughout the document.

To select a block of text with the keyboard, use the arrow keys to place the insertion pointer at the start of the desired text, hold down the Shift key, and move the pointer to the end of the desired text. As you move the pointer, the selected text is highlighted, as shown in Figure 1.7. To quickly select large amounts of text, press the PgDn key while holding down the Shift key.

Another shortcut for selecting text is using the arrow keys with the Extend Selection (F8) key. Once you press F8, you can easily select text with the arrow keys; you do not need to hold down the Shift key. Also, you can select increasingly larger segments of text by repeatedly pressing F8. It works like this: Place the cursor at the beginning of the text you want to select. Press F8 once to enter the Extend Selection mode. Press F8 again, and a word is selected. Press it once more to select the entire sentence, and once yet again to select the entire paragraph. Each time you press F8, you select the next larger unit of text. To reverse the effects of F8, use the Shrink Selection (Shift+F8) key; you can thus shrink the selected text in the same word, sentence, and paragraph units.

Tip. You can cancel the effects of the first F8 by pressing Esc.

Figure 1.7
Selected text appears highlighted on your screen

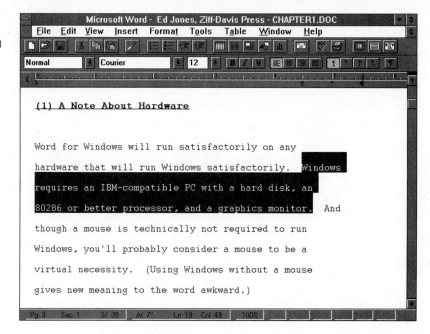

Selecting with the Mouse

If you find yourself selecting large amounts of text often, and you don't yet have a mouse, consider getting one—the mouse makes text selection a very simple matter.

With a mouse, you have a variety of ways to select text.

- The most basic of these is the "point, click-and-drag" method: You click at the start of the passage of text to place the insertion pointer there, and while holding down the left mouse button, you drag the pointer to the end of the passage. When you drag past the bottom of the screen, the document will scroll to reveal additional text.

- Using the mouse along with the Shift key, you click to place the pointer, move the pointer to the end of the desired selection, and hold down the Shift key while clicking with the mouse.

- With Ctrl, you can use the mouse to select words, sentences, paragraphs, or the entire document. Place the insertion pointer within the word or sentence you wish to select; click twice to select the word, or hold Ctrl down and click once to select the sentence. To select a line, paragraph, or a document, first move the mouse pointer to the selection bar area (the area at the left edge of the screen where the pointer changes to an arrow pointing up and to the right). Then click once to select the line adjacent to the pointer, or twice to select the adjacent paragraph. To select the entire document, hold Ctrl down and click once.

- Another method of selecting text is with the mouse and the Extend Selection (F8) key. Click to place the insertion pointer, press Extend Selection (F8), move the mouse pointer to the end of the desired selection, and click the mouse. Finally, press Esc to cancel the Extend Selection mode.

Quitting Word

To exit from Word, choose Exit from the File menu, or press Alt+F4. If you have made any changes to your document, Word displays a dialog box warning you that your latest revisions have not been saved. Click on Yes (or type **Y**) to indicate you want to save your changes. The edited document will be saved, and you will exit from Word. Chapter 2 contains more about saving files.

Note that when you quit Word, the WIN.INI file in your Windows directory is updated. Word reads this file at the next start-up, so that Word's overall appearance and configuration will be the same as when you last left it.

In Chapter 2, you'll learn more about the basics of Word, including how to create, edit, save, and manage documents.

2

Creating a Document

THIS CHAPTER EXAMINES THE TECHNIQUES OF BASIC TEXT ENTRY, SAVING documents, and opening documents. You will create a sample document that you will use in various exercises in this chapter and Chapter 3.

Starting Documents

Word gives you two ways to start documents: either with a blank document screen, or by using a *template*. You will probably use both methods in your work.

About Templates

You'll find a full description of templates later in this book (Chapter 12). For now, you'll want to remember that templates, or document models, help you streamline the creation of documents that you produce on a regular basis. As an example, if most of the documents you create are memos, you can use a template to begin all of your memos. When you create a document based on a template, the template controls the appearance of the document.

Many documents are made up of standard parts; for example, an interoffice memo often contains a company name and address heading; To, From, Date, and Subject headings; and closing information such as a routing list of persons receiving the memo. On a template designed for documents like your interoffice memos, you can let the template fill in certain *boilerplate* (standard) text for you. Templates can also be designed to prompt you for the specific information (such as the recipient's name) needed each time that template is used. The information you enter is automatically inserted into the proper place in the document, based on the template.

Creating a New Document Without a Template

You can create new documents from a blank document screen in either of two ways. You can start Word in the usual manner (described in Chapter 1), and begin working when the blank document appears automatically. Or, from within Word, you can choose New from the File Menu. If you don't use a template when creating a document, the document screen that appears resembles a blank sheet of paper, and formatting takes on a standard appearance, with margins and text style controlled by the default template, called NORMAL.DOT.

Entering Text

You insert text into a document by typing it, or by pasting it in from the Clipboard, a topic that is covered later in this chapter. (The Clipboard can also be used for the insertion of graphics.)

To enter text in Word, you type just as you would on a typewriter—with one difference. You don't have to press the Enter key at the end of each line as you would press the carriage return key on a typewriter. When you approach the end of a line, simply keep on typing; Word automatically starts a new line whenever it needs to in order to fit your text onto the page. This process is known as *word wrap*. When you do want to end a line and start a new one, you can press Enter or Shift-Enter. The difference between these two methods of starting a new line is explained in a later section, "About Paragraphs."

As you type, you may want to remove text when you make a mistake or change your mind. You can remove text by positioning the insertion pointer and then pressing either the Backspace or Del key. Practice with these two keys until you know how each one works.

There are other ways to add and erase text with Word commands, which you'll learn about as you work through this book.

Word usually operates in Insert mode, meaning that any characters to the right of the insertion pointer are pushed to the right by new characters that you enter. You can switch from Insert mode to Overtype mode by pressing the Ins toggle key. In Overtype mode, each character you type replaces the existing character at the insertion pointer. You can tell when Word is in Overtype mode by looking at the right end of the status bar, where you'll see the indicator OVR.

Try typing the text shown below. As you do, practice the text insertion and deletion techniques you've just read about until you are comfortable with how they work. Or you can load an existing document that you have already stored in Word by selecting the File Open command from the Word menu bar and entering the file name in the Open File Name dialog box that appears. See the end of this chapter for more on opening files.

Note. To open an existing document, select File Open (Alt+F+O), and enter the file name in the Open File Name dialog box.

```
Chess


Chess is a very old game of strategy in which players try
to capture, or checkmate, their opponent's King. Players
alternate turns, making one move at a time. Each player
has 16 playing pieces.

The Pawn usually moves first. It can be moved forward, one
square at a time, except for its first move (when it can
go one or two squares), or when it is capturing, at which
time it advances diagonally one square. The Rook can move
in a straight line forward, backward, or to either side.
The Bishop moves and captures diagonally. The Queen can
move in a straight line any number of spaces, or
diagonally any number of spaces. The King can move in any
direction, but only one space at a time.
```

About Paragraphs

As you type in Word, you can use two methods for designating separate units of text. You can create separate paragraphs by pressing the Enter key at the end of each paragraph, which creates an invisible *paragraph marker* (¶) in the text. Or you can use invisible *newline characters* (↓) at the desired intervals by pressing Shift+Enter. In Word, a paragraph is any amount of text (and graphics) from one paragraph marker to the next. Thus, a paragraph can be a single group of sentences, many groups of sentences, or entire pages of a document. What Word defines as a paragraph is determined by where you press the Enter key. This is important, because what encompasses a selection for formatting (as you'll learn later) is determined by where your paragraph starts and ends.

In most word processing programs, you typically press Enter to signal the end of one paragraph and the start of the next. In Word, you may not want to do this, because Word then defines these paragraphs as separate units of text. This may add to your work during the formatting process (detailed in Chapters 3 and 4), because you have to apply the format features by selecting paragraphs—either multiple paragraphs or separate paragraphs. On the other hand, if you use the newline character (Shift+Enter) rather than the Enter key at the end of paragraphs, Word considers what is above and below the newline character to be the same unit of text. You can later apply formatting to that entire unit of text as a single operation.

As an example, compare Figures 2.1 and 2.2. In Figure 2.1, the sample paragraphs have been separated with an Enter keypress; hence, double-clicking in the selection bar causes only the first paragraph of text to be selected; each section of text counts as an individual paragraph. In Figure 2.2, the sections of text have been separated with a newline character; this time double-clicking in the selection bar causes both sections of text to be highlighted, because Word considers all the text to be a single paragraph.

NOTE. *To enter text and keep it all in a single Word paragraph unit, use a newline character (press Shift+Enter) whenever you want to insert a blank line between text paragraphs.*

Creating a Document Based on a Template

Word lets you create documents based on templates, which are previously stored document models that contain any combination of boilerplate text, formatting, and customized styles for your paragraphs. You can think of a template as a framework on which your document will be based. Every time you create an ordinary document, you are using a template, because Word automatically uses a default template called NORMAL.DOT unless you select another specific template. Word comes with some sample templates for various tasks, but you will likely also want to create your own. The complete instructions for doing this are in Chapter 12.

Figure 2.1

When paragraphs are separated with an Enter keypress, Word sees two separate paragraphs.

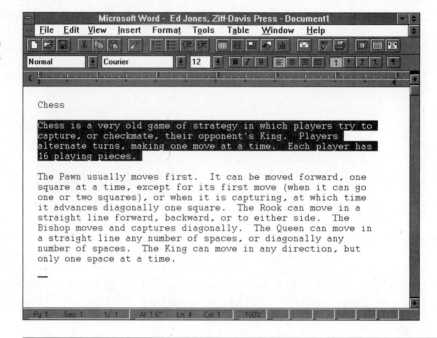

To create a new document based on a template, you use the File New (Alt+F+N) command and select a template from the File New dialog box's list of templates. Depending on the template you choose, you may be prompted for additional information; the information you supply will be inserted into your document.

You may want to try one of the useful sample templates supplied with Word, to get an idea of how they work; to do so, perform the following steps:

Note. Word lets you open several documents at a time, in multiple document windows.

1. Select File New (Alt+F+N) to create a new document file. (It does not matter if you have a document open or not when you invoke the File New command; don't worry about losing the "Chess" paragraph you just typed.)

2. Select the MEMO1 template from the Use Template list box and then choose OK. Word then displays a dialog box telling you to add names to a distribution list that will follow. (If someone has already added names to the distribution list, you won't see this dialog box. If you don't see this dialog box but instead see an Address Memo dialog box, proceed to Step 5.)

Figure 2.2

When paragraphs are separated with a newline character, Word sees all the text as a single paragraph.

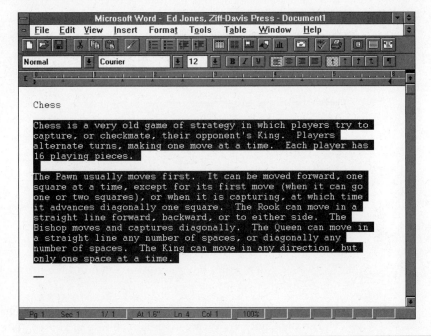

3. Choose OK again, and Word displays the dialog box titled Distribution List Manager. Here you can add the names of persons who will receive the memo.

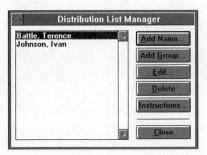

4. Choose Add Name (Alt+A). In the dialog box that appears, enter a name and then choose OK. When the Distribution List Manager dialog box reappears, choose Add Name again, enter another name, and choose OK. (This is necessary because you will need at least two names in the Distribution List later.) Finally, choose Close from the Distribution List

Manager dialog box. (If the list was empty, you'll have to choose OK from an additional dialog box.)

5. The Address Memo dialog box now appears, showing the names that are in the Distribution List. Highlight one of the names, choose Select (Alt+S) and then Done (Alt+D).

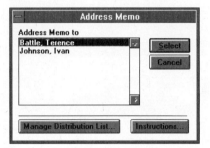

6. Word asks you to enter a name for the sender of the memo. Enter your name, and then choose OK.

7. Word displays a dialog box asking for the subject of the memo. Type **Upcoming Company Picnic**, and then choose OK.

8. Word asks who you want to receive copies of the memo, and displays the names you entered in the Distribution List. Highlight the remaining name (the one you didn't use as the addressee of the memo); then choose Select (Alt+S) and then Done (Alt+D).

9. You next see a dialog box indicating that you are ready to begin typing the body of the memo. Choose OK. The insertion pointer then appears in the new document, with the subject, author, and recipient names already placed in the appropriate locations (see Figure 2.3).

This exercise gives you an idea of the power of Word's templates. You will probably want to design your own templates to suit your needs. Since the templates are Word documents, you can create and modify them just as you do other Word documents. Chapter 12 covers the topic of templates in more detail; look there to see how you can tailor Word's MEMO.DOT template for your own specific use.

Inserting from the Clipboard

The Clipboard is an area of memory that is a standard feature of Windows (see your Windows documentation for additional information). You can paste both text and graphics from the Clipboard into a document. The Edit

Figure 2.3
A memo based on the MEMO.DOT template

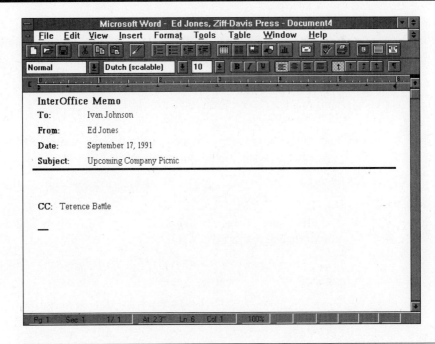

Tip. To see what is in the Clipboard at any time, press Alt+Spacebar, type **U**, and choose OK from the dialog box that appears. You can use this procedure in any Windows application.

Note. Windows Paintbrush, provided with Windows, lets you design and save graphic images. To learn more about Paintbrush, refer to your Windows documentation.

Paste command pastes whatever's in the Clipboard into the current document at the insertion pointer. (Of course, the Clipboard must contain something before you can insert it into your document.)

Text can be inserted into the Clipboard by selecting the desired text, and choosing either the Edit Copy (Alt+E+C) or Edit Cut (Alt+E+T) command, or the Copy and Cut icons of the Toolbar. If you then move the insertion pointer to the desired location in the document for the text and choose the Edit Paste command (Alt+E+P) or the Paste icon of the Toolbar, the text stored in the Clipboard appears in the document at the insertion pointer. The inserted text does not replace anything; existing text in your document is moved and realigned to make room for what came from the Clipboard.

If you want to paste graphics, first get into your drawing or graphics program (such as Windows Paintbrush) that contains the image you want to transfer. Use the selection tool within the drawing or graphics program to select the image; then invoke Edit Copy (Alt+E+C) to copy the selection into the Clipboard. Exit from the drawing or graphics program, and get into your document. With the insertion pointer at the desired location, select the Edit Paste command (Alt+E+P). The graphic will appear at the insertion pointer.

NOTE. *If you are running Word and your graphics (or any other Windows) program simultaneously, you can easily switch between the graphics program* *and Word by bringing up the Windows Task Switcher with Ctrl+Esc, and choosing an application from the Task List.*

If you want to try putting a Paintbrush graphic into your document, follow these steps:

In Chapter 3 you'll learn more about displaying several files at once on your screen, in multiple windows.

1. If you still have the MEMO.DOC file on your screen, close it with File Close (Alt+F+C). (If you want to save it, answer Yes to the prompt that appears.)

2. The "Chess" document is again visible on your screen. Place the insertion pointer on the blank line between the two paragraphs of text.

3. Press Ctrl-Esc to bring up the Windows Task Switcher, and choose Program Manager from the Task List.

4. Open the Accessories window if it is not already open, and double-click on Paintbrush to start the Windows Paintbrush program.

5. Choose File Open (Alt+F+O). The File Open dialog box for Paintbrush appears.

6. Select the file named CHESS.BMP from the list of illustrations supplied with Paintbrush, and then click OK.

7. Once the image appears, click on the selection tool icon (it's the one directly below the Edit choice in the Paintbrush menu).

8. Click and drag within the image to select a rectangular portion of it— perhaps one of the chess pieces. As you do so, a dotted line appears around your selection (see Figure 2.4). This is the selection that will be pasted into your Word document at the insertion pointer location.

9. Choose the Edit Copy command (Alt+E+C) from the Paintbrush menu. This puts the image in the Clipboard.

10. Press Ctrl+Esc to bring up the Task Switcher, and choose Word from the Task List.

11. With the insertion pointer positioned in the document where you want the art to be inserted, choose Edit Paste from the Word menu (Alt+E+P) or click the Paste icon in the Toolbar. The result, shown in Figure 2.5, is the Word document containing the graphic from Paintbrush along with the text. (If you do not see the picture but instead see an empty box, choose Tools Options (Alt+O+O), choose View in the Category list, and turn off Picture Placeholders in the dialog box that appears.)

Figure 2.4

A Paintbrush graphic image with a portion selected for pasting to another file

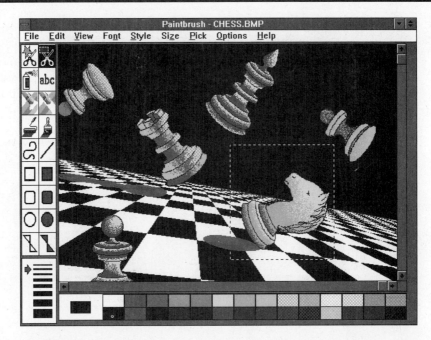

Figure 2.5

A Word document with a graphic image added

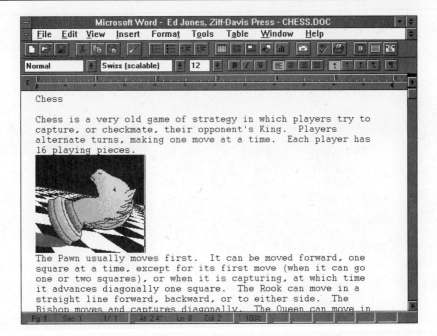

Inserting Symbols

In addition to normal text, you can also place special symbols in a Word document. Such symbols include familiar ones such as copyright and trademark symbols, and less common ones such as letters of the Greek alphabet.

To insert a symbol, place the insertion pointer at the desired place in the document, and choose Insert Symbol (Alt+I+S). The Symbol dialog box will appear.

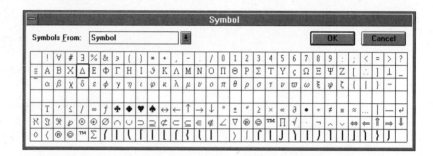

The Symbol dialog box contains a table of available symbols, along with OK and Cancel buttons, and a list box that lets you choose additional symbols. Use the mouse or the Tab key to navigate between the table of symbols, the list box, and the OK or Cancel buttons. In the list box, you can press the down-arrow button to select from other available tables of symbols; the available tables include Symbols (the default symbols shown in the illustration), Normal Text (the ANSI character set used by Word), and MS Line Draw (a set of line-drawing characters).

Within the table of symbols, use the mouse or the arrow keys to highlight the desired symbol; then choose OK to place the desired symbol at the cursor location. Note that whether the symbols can be printed or not depends on the capabilities of your printer.

WARNING! *Once a symbol is placed, Word will not let you delete the symbol by backspacing over it; if you try to backspace past a symbol, Word beeps. To delete an unwanted symbol, select the symbol as you would select any text, and press Del.*

The Different Views of Word

Word lets you view a document as you edit it, in one of three overall views: *normal, outline,* and *page layout.* With the normal and outline views, you can turn on or off the draft mode of Word. In effect, this gives you five different views of a Word document: normal, normal draft, outline, outline draft, and page layout. You can switch between the three overall views by using the View Normal (Alt+V+N), View Outline (Alt+V+O), and View Page Layout (Alt+V+P) commands. When it is turned on, a bullet appears beside the command in the View Menu. The Draft command is a toggle, and a check mark appears beside this command when it is turned on. (Since you cannot use the draft mode with page layout, if you are in page layout view and you choose Draft from the View menu, Word automatically switches from page layout back to normal view.)

When draft mode is turned off, you can see most formatting on the screen; for example, boldfaced characters appear in boldface, and italic characters appear in italic. When draft mode is turned on, you do not see most formatting on the screen; the various fonts look the same, and graphics images appear as empty boxes. Word's screen display operates faster when draft mode is turned on than when it is not, so when you are editing complex documents containing many graphics or several different fonts, you may want to switch to draft mode to speed up the action on the display. To turn draft on or off, choose the View Draft command (Alt+V+D).

Note. If Word's response to your commands appears sluggish on your display hardware, use draft mode for your editing.

The display in page layout view more closely resembles the document as it will look when printed, but page layout view is also the slowest view mode of all. When in page layout view, Word also displays any headers, footers, and footnotes (see Chapter 5) in the document. If you are using multicolumn text (also explained in Chapter 5), page layout view shows it on screen in multiple columns. To turn page layout view on or off, choose the View Page Layout command (Alt+V+P).

Outline view is designed specifically for the creation and editing of outlines in Word. You'll learn about outline view in Chapter 8.

An Introduction to Printing

Tip. Mouse users can get one copy of the current document by clicking on the Print icon in the Toolbar.

You will want to print most of the documents you create. In this chapter you'll see only how to print one copy of a simple document. Later, in Chapter 6, you will explore all the options of the Print dialog box, and learn how to use the Print Preview feature to get an advance look at how your printed document will appear.

To print a document, choose File Print (Alt+F+P). You'll see the Print dialog box shown here:

Tip. Remember to use the Print key (Ctrl+Shift+F12) if you want to print using all the default print settings. When you see the Print dialog box, just choose OK to start printing.

Tip. Whenever you have problems printing, make sure you can print from other Windows applications before you suspect a problem with Word. Try printing from the Windows Notepad. See your Windows documentation for details.

Assuming that the printer name at the top of the dialog box matches the printer connected to your PC, and your printer is connected and turned on, you are ready to print. The default settings in the Print dialog box specify one copy of the document, and that all pages in the document will be printed. You can, of course, change these defaults. You can alter the number of copies (in the Copies text box), and the first and last pages to be printed (in the From and To text boxes). For a complete explanation of all the options in this dialog box, refer to Chapter 6.

With the desired print options selected, choose OK to begin printing your document. If you have difficulty printing, or if the printer name in the dialog box doesn't match the machine that's connected to your PC, you may have to adjust how Windows is set up on your system (see "If You Have Trouble Printing" in Chapter 6). If you can't print from any Windows application (like Cardfile or Notepad), you won't be able to print from Word, either. Make sure the correct printer driver and printer port are chosen in the Print Setup dialog box; you can access this dialog box by choosing Setup in the Print dialog box, or from Word's File menu, or from the Windows Control Panel (see Chapter 6). Setup needs to be done only once.

Printing More Than Documents

In the Print dialog box, Word gives you the option of printing more than just documents. Using the Print list box, you can choose to print

- Style sheets
- Glossaries
- Annotations from a document
- Summary information for a document

Later chapters will provide more information on the use of these document enhancements.

To print something other than a document, choose File Print. When the Print dialog box appears, click on or tab to the Print drop-down list box; there you will see the additional choices. Select the desired item to print, adjust other elements of the dialog box as needed, and choose OK to begin printing.

Printing Part of a Document

Keep in mind that you can quickly print specific pages of a document by entering beginning and ending page numbers in the Print dialog box. Just enter the number of the first page to print in the From text box (Alt+F), and the last page to print in the To text box (Alt+T).

To print a selected passage from a document, first highlight the selection, using the selection techniques detailed in Chapter 1. Then choose File Print. In the dialog box, choose Selection (Alt+E). When you click on OK or press Enter, only the selected text will be printed.

Saving Documents

Saving document files is a basic but important operation with any word processor, and Word provides a variety of save options. You can save a file under a new name, or under an existing name. You can save files in Word's own file format, or in the formats of other popular word processors. And you can save all open files at once, with a single command.

Using File Save

Tip. You can also save the current file by pressing F12 and choosing OK, by pressing Shift+F12, or by clicking on the Save Icon in the Toolbar.

To save the currently open file, choose the File Save command (Alt+F+S). If the file has been saved previously, Word saves the new version of it without prompting you for any information. The document remains on the screen; if you want to leave Word, you must then use the File Exit command (Alt+F+X) or its hotkey, Alt+F4.

TIP. *If you want to save a document and immediately exit from Word, the Alt+F4 (Exit) hotkey is useful. When you press Alt+F4 to exit, Word automatically prompts you to save any changes made to the open document. To save your edited file, choose Yes in answer to the "Save Changes?" prompt, and supply a file name, if asked. You are then returned to the Windows Program Manager.*

When you use File Save to store a document that has never been saved, Word displays a dialog box (Figure 2.6) asking for the name of the file. Also in the Save As dialog box are two list boxes. The File Name list box contains all files that are in the current directory. The Directories list box contains all subdirectories (if any) under the current directory. You can type a name into the File Name text box, or you can choose an existing name from the list box to overwrite an existing file with the current document. You can tab to or click in the Directories list box to navigate to a different directory. And you can use the Drives drop-down list box (Alt+V) to select a different disk drive for saving the file. The Save File as Type list box at the bottom of the dialog box can be used to save files in other file formats, as discussed in the next section. (The File Sharing button lets you lock a file for annotations; this topic will be discussed in Chapter 3.)

In the File Name text box, enter a name for your new file, using the DOS file-naming conventions (eight characters or less, and no spaces). Word normally assigns an extension of .DOC to all files saved in Word's normal file format; to save your file with this .DOC extension, you need not include it when entering your file name. Or you may elect to assign your own file name extension by typing the period and an extension after the file name; however, you will then have to enter this specific extension any time you open the file with the File Open command.

Note. You'll have an opportunity to create a document summary when you save a file for the first time. See Chapter 4.

If you have created the sample "Chess" document for the exercises in this chapter, save it now by performing the following steps:

1. Choose File Save (Alt+F+S). Because you have never saved this file, the Save As dialog box will appear (see Figure 2.6).

2. In the File Name text box, enter **CHESS** as a name for the file.

3. Choose OK, and Word displays the Summary Info screen. You'll learn about this in Chapter 4. For now, click on OK or press Enter to skip this screen. Word now saves the document, under the name CHESS.DOC, in the current directory.

Figure 2.6

Save As dialog box

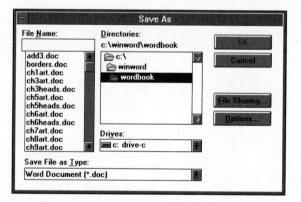

When deciding on a file name, remember that you can type the full DOS path name (see your DOS manual for details about paths) in the File Name text box when you want to store the file in another directory, or even on another drive. Word also provides an easy way to save files to other directories, or to a floppy disk, with the File Save As command (explained next).

Using File Save As

The File Save As command (Alt+F+A) lets you save files to other directories, or to a floppy disk. You can also use this command to save a file in the format of another word processor, or as ASCII text.

When you choose File Save As, you see the same dialog box as for File Save (Figure 2.6). If the document has been saved before, its name appears in the Save File Name box. To save the file under a different name, you can type a new name, and it will replace the existing name. Or, if the document has never been saved, this box is blank, and you can type in the file name of your choice.

To save a file to a different path (drive and directory), tab to or click in the Directories list box, and select the desired directory. To choose a different drive, press Alt+V or click in the Drives list box, and choose the desired drive from the list of available drives that appears. If you choose a different drive, the Directories list box lists the directories on that drive. Within this list box, you can navigate up and down within subdirectories. To move to a parent directory, select the parent directory by name. (Note that parent directories are also indicated by means of open file folder icons.) To move to a specific subdirectory, select its name. Word automatically adds the path name for the selected drive and directory to any file name you type in the Save File Name box.

Saving a File in Another Format

You may need to save a Word document in a different format, so you can use it in another word processor. You can do this using the File Save As command. Choose File Save As, and press Alt+T to open the Save File as Type list box. The Save As dialog box will show the Save File As Type list box, as illustrated in Figure 2.7.

Figure 2.7

Additional options are visible in the Save As dialog box when you select the Save File As Type list box.

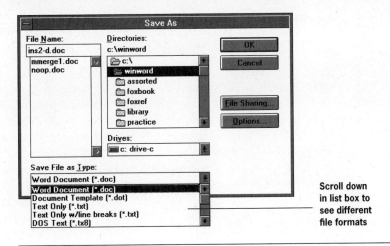

Scroll down in list box to see different file formats

To choose a file format other than the standard Microsoft Word format, scroll through the box until you find the format you want. The Text Only and Text with Line Breaks choices can be used to save a document as ASCII text. Keep in mind that the other formats available depend on which file formats were specified during the installation process. If you need a popular file format and you don't see it in the list box, it was not added at installation. See Appendix A for instructions on adding options to Word once it has been installed.

Other File Save Options

Additional options will appear in another dialog box when you choose Options (Alt+O) from the Save As dialog box as shown in Figure 2.8.

Figure 2.8

The Save As Options dialog box

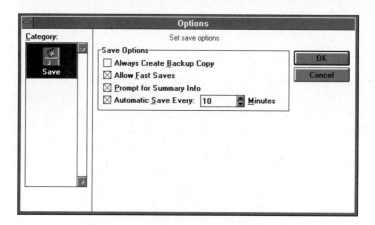

The options include Always Create Backup Copy, Allow Fast Saves, Prompt for Summary Info, and Automatic Save. Turn on the Always Create Backup Copy option if you want Word to automatically make a backup file every time you do a save. This backup file will be assigned the same name as the original, but with an extension of .BAK. Turn on the Prompt for Summary Info option if you want to see the summary information screen each time you save a new file. The Automatic Save and Allow Fast Save options are explained just below.

Using File Save All

The File Save All command is used to save all open documents. Chapter 3 will cover in detail the topic of multiple windows in Word; for now, note that you can have more than one document open at the same time, in several

Note. In addition to saving all open documents, the File Save All command will also save any open global macros (Chapter 14), templates (Chapter 12), and glossaries (Chapter 13).

Tip. Turning on Autosave may save you from a large loss of data in the event of a power failure.

windows on your screen. When you are working with multiple documents, you can quickly save the edits made in all the open documents using the File Save All command. Choose File Save All (Alt+F+E), and Word proceeds to display a dialog box for each document that has been changed since the last save, asking if the document should be saved. You can choose Yes to save each document, one by one. If any of the open documents have not been saved previously, Word will prompt you for a file name.

Changing the Autosave Interval

You can tell Word to automatically, at selected intervals, save changes to your work with the Autosave feature. Choose File Save As (Alt+F+A), and choose Options (Alt+O). Turn on the Automatic Save option (Alt+S) and enter the desired time interval in the Minutes text box (Alt+M). The default if you don't enter an interval is every ten minutes.

Fast Save vs. Full Save

Some of Word's behavior when you are saving files depends on how much editing work you've done since the last save. When you select File Save (Alt+F+S), Word saves files using one of two methods—*fast save* or *full save*. Normally, Word performs a fast save, in which your edits are appended to the end of the existing file. In a full save, Word saves the entire document, including unchanged parts, as if you were saving it for the first time. The first time you save a document, Word performs a full save. From then on, Word usually performs a fast save whenever you save updates to the document. If you make massive changes to a document, however, Word may perform a full save automatically.

You will see no visible difference between full saves and fast saves, other than in the speed of the operation. (Full saves take somewhat longer to perform than fast saves; this difference varies greatly with the speed of your hardware.) However, if you use the File Find File command (Chapter 4) to look for the file name of a document containing specific text, Word may not be able to locate the file name if the document was last saved with a fast save. If you use Find File often, you may want to turn off the fast save feature, forcing Word to do a full save each time the document is saved.

To turn off fast save, choose File Save As (Alt+F+A), click on Options (Alt+O), and turn off the Allow Fast Save check box by clicking on it or pressing Alt+F.

Opening Existing Files

When you need to open and edit your documents, you use the File Open command (Alt+F+O). File Open shows you a dialog box that is somewhat similar to the one for File Save, as shown in Figure 2.9.

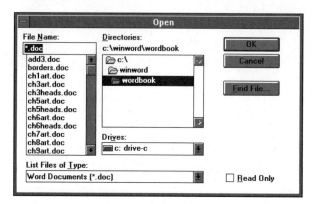

If you know the name of the file you want and it is in the current directory, you can type the name in the File Name text box. You can also select the file by name from the File Name list box. When you need to open a file in a different directory (or on a different drive), you can choose that directory from the Directories list box or choose the desired drive from the Drives list box. Once you have typed a file name or selected one from the list box, click the OK button to open the file.

In the File Open dialog box, there is also a check box labeled Read Only, and a button labeled Find File. The Read Only check box, when enabled, causes any file that is opened to be opened in a *read-only* mode. In this mode, changes to the file cannot be saved to the same file name; you can only save your edits if you save them under a different file name. The Find File button is used to locate a file based on an entry you make in the document summary, or based on a search for text within the document. Chapter 4 explains this option.

Now that you've entered and saved a document, Chapter 3 will show you how to refine it.

C H A P T E R

3

Refining Text

CREATING A DOCUMENT IS JUST THE BEGINNING FOR MUCH OF YOUR work in Word. Most of your documents will need to be refined by *formatting* techniques; anytime you work with text, formatting is a priority. In this chapter you will begin to learn about refining your Word documents. Chapters 4 and 5 will then introduce you to the complete range of Word's powerful formatting options.

The Vital Three: Margins, Tabs, and Line Spacing

The three most elementary aspects of formatting, found on even the most basic typewriters, are *margins*, *tabs*, and *line spacing*. This section shows you how to apply these formatting elements to all or part of a document. In Word, you use the Format Page Setup command (Alt+T+U) to control the margins, and you use the Format Tabs command (Alt+T+T) to set the default tab stops. Use the Format Paragraph command (Alt+T+P), or the line spacing speed-keys, to change the line spacing.

Keep in mind that these methods are not the only ways to change parameters affecting margins, tabs, and line spacing in Word. For example, though this chapter explains how to change the default tabs that automatically appear at specific locations, there are ways to set specific tabs at other locations, and that topic is covered in Chapter 4, where you'll find a more extensive discussion of many of Word's formatting capabilities.

Setting Margins

To set basic document margins, use the Page Setup (Alt+T+U) command, which shows you the dialog box shown in Figure 3.1. Click the Margins button (Alt+M) to access the Top, Bottom, Left, and Right options that let you change all four margins for the entire document. If these options are not visible in the dialog box, press Alt+M (Margins) to display them. (You can also give individual paragraphs margins of their own; see Chapter 4 for details.) The other options in this dialog box are discussed in Chapters 4 and 5.

Figure 3.2 illustrates the distances represented by the page margins. Top controls the distance between the top of the page and the top of the first line, and Bottom sets the distance between the bottom of the page and the bottom of the last line on the page. Left designates the difference between the left edge of the page and the left edge of the text; right designates the difference between the right edge of the page and the right edge of the text. The Left and Right dimensions are also affected by the settings for the Gutter and Facing Pages margins. These options, described in Chapter 5, are useful when printing documents that are to be bound into book form.

Word's default top and bottom margins are 1 inch, and the left and right margins are 1¼ inches. The default left and right margins result in fairly wide borders on a document page, so these may be among the first settings you decide to change.

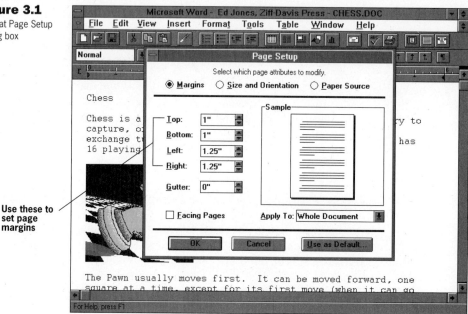

Figure 3.1

Format Page Setup dialog box

Use these to set page margins

Tip. If you make changes with Format Page Setup and then click the Use As Default button, the changes you have made are applied to the template currently in use. If you didn't pick a template when you started the document, the changes are applied to the default template (NORMAL.DOT).

The Page Setup dialog box also contains settings for Page Width and Page Height. To access these settings, click the Size and Orientation button (Alt+S). The defaults for these are 8 ½ inches wide and 11 inches high (U.S. letter-size paper). If you are using a different size paper, such as 8 ½-by-14-inch U.S. legal-size, you will want to change these settings accordingly. See Chapter 5 for complete information about page formatting.

Inches or Centimeters?

The various option boxes in Word that accept your typed-in settings for dimensions will accommodate dimensions in either inches (") or centimeters (cm). As an example, if you prefer the metric system, you might enter **4cm** for the Left and Right margins, and the result would be a 4-centimeter margin on both sides. However, though Word accepts your entry typed with cm for centimeters, it converts this to inches. If you later open the Format Document dialog box, you will see that Word has stored a value of 1.58 inches for the right margin. When you enter only a number for a dimension, without specifying inches or centimeters, Word records the value as inches.

Figure 3.2

Distances represented by page margin settings

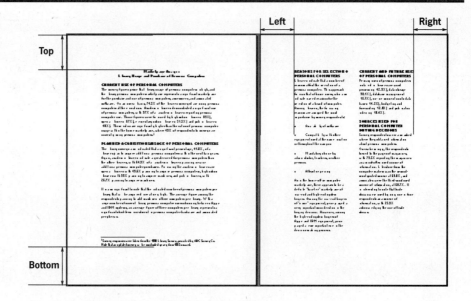

Setting Default Tabs

You use the Format Tabs command to set the default tab stops for a document. Choose Format Tabs (Alt+T+T), and you will see the Default Tab Stops option in the Tabs dialog box, illustrated here:

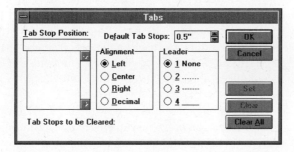

Note. Use the View Ruler command to turn on the ruler.

By default, Word sets tabs every half-inch (0.5"), visible on the ruler when the ruler is turned on. The tab stops resemble upside-down *T*s. In Figure 3.3, the Default Tab Stop option has been set to 1.0", causing tab stops to appear at one-inch intervals. You can set default tabs at any desired interval, in inches or centimeters.

You can also set individual tabs in a document, as you'll learn in Chapter 4.

Figure 3.3

Effects of setting the Default Tab Stops option

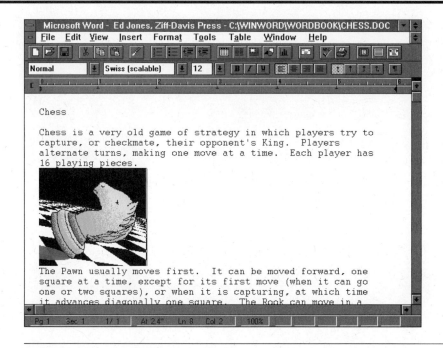

Setting Line Spacing

Tip. A quick way to change the line spacing for an entire existing document is to select all text by Choosing Edit Select All, or pressing Ctrl+5 using the 5 key on the numeric keypad. Then press the desired line spacing speed-key, or select Format Paragraph and enter the desired spacing in the Line Spacing box.

To change the vertical line spacing for a specific paragraph of text, select the desired paragraph, and then choose the line spacing setting. You can choose single-, line-and-a-half-, or double-spacing by using the speed-keys (Ctrl+1 for single, Ctrl+5 for line-and-a-half, Ctrl+2 for double). Or you can use the Format Paragraph command (Alt+T+P) and enter a spacing setting in the Line Spacing box. If you do this before entering any text, you establish the line spacing for all paragraphs, and it remains in effect until you choose a new one.

The Format Paragraph dialog box is shown in Figure 3.4. In the Spacing area's Line Spacing At option box, you can enter your desired line spacing value. Most options for the Format Paragraph command are covered in Chapter 4, and those for the Format Page Setup command are covered in Chapter 5.

A value of 1li for line spacing indicates single-spacing. You can enter 2li for double-spacing, or 3li for triple-spacing. You can also enter fractional values; for example, 1.5li provides line-and-a-half-spacing. If you omit the li designation from your entry, Word assumes you are specifying lines. You can also use inches (in) or centimeters (cm) to designate line spacing. In Figure 3.5, the first paragraph has been set to 1.5li, and the second paragraph remains single-spaced. In Figure 3.6, the first paragraph is double-spaced.

Figure 3.4

Format Paragraph
dialog box

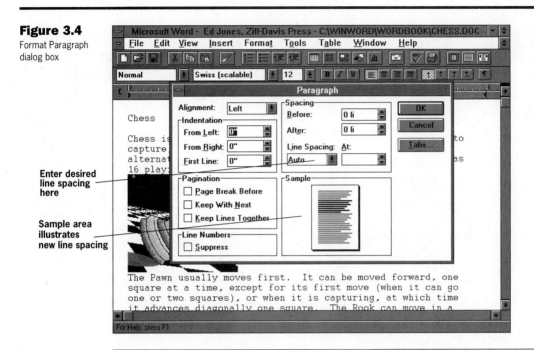

Enter desired
line spacing
here

Sample area
illustrates
new line spacing

An important point to remember about line spacing is that the default setting, if you do not change it, is not a numerical value; it is Auto. Auto line spacing causes Word to automatically adjust line spacing as needed to fit the size of the characters (font point size) that you use.

CAUTION! *If you override the default Auto and enter some other line spacing value, and then make major changes to the font's point size, you may find the results are unacceptable, and you will need to readjust the line spacing to compensate.*

An Exercise in Formatting

Now that you've learned the basics about setting the margins, tab stops, and line spacing in a document, here is an exercise that lets you practice all three operations. If the sample CHESS document is not already open on your screen, use the File Open command (Alt+F+O) to open it now, and perform the following steps:

1. Select the chess-piece graphic using your preferred selection method, and press Del to delete it.

Figure 3.5

Example of line-and-a-half-spacing

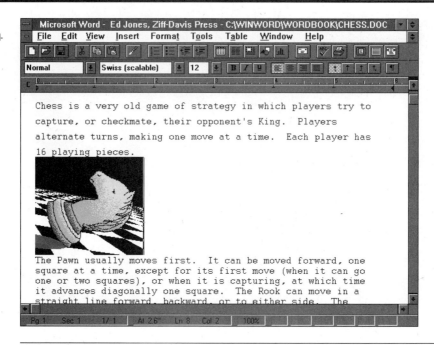

Note. The numbers of this table would likely have a better appearance if they were centered below the headings, but this is not necessary for this exercise. In Chapter 7, you'll learn how to control the appearance of entries in a table by using Word's table feature.

2. Move the insertion pointer to the blank line between the two paragraphs, and press Enter once to mark a new paragraph.

3. Select Format Tabs (Alt+T+T). Tab over to or click in the Default Tab Stops text box, enter **1** in this box (for tabs every 1 inch), and choose OK.

4. On the next two lines of the document, enter the following simple table, using your new tab stops. Start at the left margin, and press Tab after you type each word or value. *Exception:* After the last number, 1, under Queens, press Shift+Enter.

```
Pawns     Knights    Bishops    Rooks    Kings    Queens
8         2          2          2        1        1
```

Pressing Enter at the end of the second line adds a blank line between the table and the second paragraph of the document.

5. Now add 1-inch margins to both sides of the document. Select Format Page Setup (Alt+T+U). Tab over to or click in the Left text box, and enter **1"**. Then tab over to or click in the Right text box, and enter **1"**. Finally, choose OK or press Shift +Enter.

Figure 3.6

Example of double-spacing

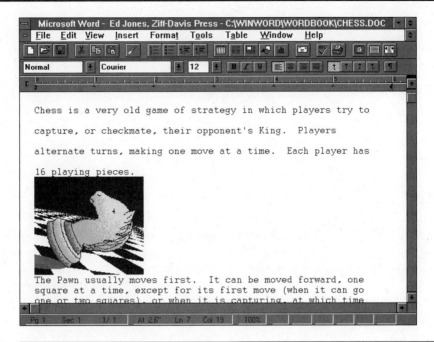

6. Place the insertion pointer anywhere in the first paragraph, and select Format Paragraph (Alt+T+P). Tab over to or click in the Spacing/Line Spacing text box, choose 1.5 Lines from the list box, and choose OK or press Enter. Move the insertion pointer to the last paragraph, and repeat this step.

Note that because you started a new paragraph for the new table, it is not affected by the new line spacing setting in Step 6, and remains single-spaced. Remember, too, that once you change the line spacing, it remains set that way for all new text you type until you change it again.

7. Don't save the edited document under its existing name. Instead, select Save As (Alt+F+A), and enter **CHESS2** for a document name. Choose OK to execute the save, and then select File Close (Alt+F+C) to put away the document. You'll use CHESS2 later, for an exercise in the use of multiple documents.

Moving and Copying Text

Text can be *moved* or *copied* within a Word document or among multiple documents. You can move and copy text using the Clipboard. Or you can use the Move (F2) and Copy (Shift+F2) keys independent of the Clipboard. Both methods provide the same result, but they operate slightly differently. You may recall from Chapter 2 (or from the use of other Windows applications) that any information you delete with the Edit Cut command (Alt+E+T) or copy into memory with the Edit Copy command (Alt+E+C) is placed in the Windows Clipboard. In Word, you can use the Clipboard to move or copy text between documents.

Note. Edit Cut deletes the current selection and puts it in the Clipboard. Edit Copy copies the current selection into the Clipboard, leaving the original intact. Edit Paste copies the Clipboard contents to the current insertion pointer location.

Moving Text with the Clipboard

To move text from one location to another, select the text to be moved (using the selection methods detailed in Chapter 1). Choose the Edit Cut command (or use Shift+Del). The selected text is deleted from its current location and placed in the Clipboard. Move the insertion pointer to the new location for the text, and choose Edit Paste (Alt+E+P) or use the Shift+Ins hotkey. The previously cut text reappears at the insertion pointer location. *Remember*—the Clipboard always contains the last selection you cut or copied. When you choose Edit Cut or Edit Copy, whatever you cut or copy overwrites the current contents of the Clipboard.

Try this operation in your practice document. Select the first sentence in the second paragraph, and choose Edit Cut (as shown in Figure 3.7). Then paste the text at the end of the paragraph, as shown in Figure 3.8. Position the insertion pointer in the new location, and select Edit Paste (Alt+E+P).

NOTE. *At any time, you can see what is in the Windows Clipboard by selecting Run from the main control menu and then choosing Clipboard. Press Alt+Spacebar+U, choose OK from the dialog box that appears, and the Clipboard will be visible.*

Tip. Mouse users can use the Cut, Copy, and Paste icons on the Toolbar in place of the Edit Cut, Edit Copy, and Edit Paste commands.

Copying Text with the Clipboard

Copying text from the Clipboard is much like moving text; the only difference is that you use the Edit Copy command, rather than the Edit Cut command, in conjunction with Edit Paste. To copy text from one location to another, select the text to be copied (using the selection methods detailed in Chapter 1). Choose the Edit Copy command (or press Ctrl+Ins) to copy the selected text from its current location into the Clipboard. Move the insertion pointer to the desired location for the copied text, and choose Edit Paste (Shift+Ins). The text in the Clipboard will appear at the insertion pointer location.

Figure 3.7

Selected sentence
to be cut from
paragraph with Edit
Cut (Alt+E+T)

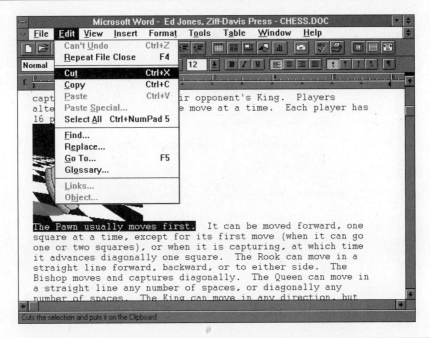

Moving and Copying Text Without the Clipboard

Word also provides a way to move or copy text without using the Windows
Clipboard. This method is helpful when you have something stored in the
Clipboard that you don't want to lose (remember, moving new data into the
Clipboard overwrites its current contents). In this case, to move text, you use
the Move (F2) key; to copy text, use the Copy (Shift+F2) key. Try it in your
practice document, to relocate the sentence you just moved back to the start
of the second paragraph.

1. As in most Word operations, you must first select the desired text.

2. Press F2 for Move or Shift+F2 for Copy. As shown in Figure 3.9, a message appears in the lower-left corner of the window asking you where
   the text is to be moved or copied.

3. Move the insertion pointer to the new location for the text, and press
   Enter; the selected text will be moved (or copied) to that location.

Figure 3.8

Selected sentence
moved to end of
paragraph with Edit
Paste (Alt+E+P)

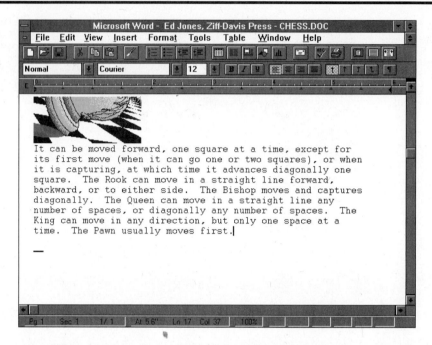

Figure 3.8

Selected sentence
moved to end of
paragraph with Edit
Paste (Alt+E+P)

Figure 3.9

Moving text with
the Move key (F2)

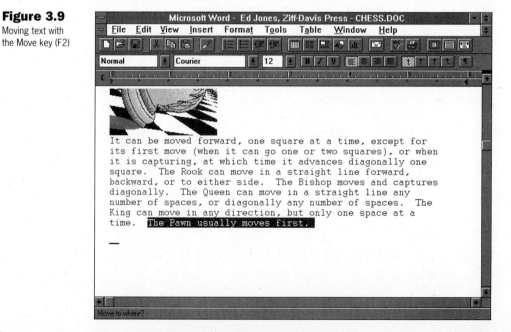

Using the Search and Replace Features

Like all full-featured word processors, Word offers a *search-and-replace* capability, through the Edit Find (Alt+E+F) and Edit Replace (Alt+E+E) commands. These commands in Word may offer more search power than you are accustomed to, because you can look for more than just raw text. With Word, you can also search for specific formatting, as well as for special characters such as paragraph markers, newline characters, and tabs.

Finding Text

Use the Edit Find command to search for text, formatting, or a combination of both. Choose Edit Find (Alt+E+F), and you see this dialog box:

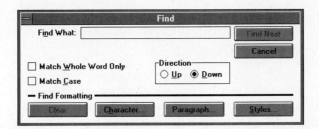

To look for ordinary text, for example, enter the desired word or phrase in the Find What text box. Choose OK or press Enter, and Word will find the first occurrence of that word or phrase. You can continue to search for repeated occurrences of the same text by choosing Find Next (Alt+F).

The other items in the Find dialog box are easy to understand and use.

- The Direction choice determines whether Word searches up (from the insertion pointer to the start of the document) or down (from the insertion pointer to the end of the document).

- The Match Whole Word Only check box lets you search for only whole words that match the search text. For example, if you search for the word *move* in your practice document, and the Match Whole Word Only box is not checked, Word will find *moves* and *moved,* as well as *move.* With Match Whole Word Only checked, only *move* will be found.

- The Match Case option tells Word whether you want the search to be case sensitive. Check this box, and Word will search for a match that uses exactly the same upper- and lowercase as the letters you entered.

- The Find Formatting buttons are discussed later in this chapter, under "Looking for Formatting."

You can begin your search anywhere within the document. Word begins at the current insertion pointer location, and from there you can direct Word to search up or down. If Word reaches one end of the document without finding any occurrences of the search term, you'll see a dialog box like this one:

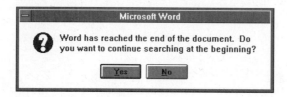

If you want Word to continue its search from the start or end of the document, choose Yes; the search will then continue until Word again reaches the insertion pointer. (If you begin a search from the beginning or end character of the document, you will never see this inquiry, because Word will be able to examine the entire document.)

TIP. *Yet another way to use the Clipboard is for storing a search string. Suppose you want to find an entire sentence or column of numbers. Select and copy that search string to the Clipboard, and then bring up the Find dialog box. To move the search string into the Find What box, just press Shift+Ins, and choose OK or press Enter to begin the search.*

Looking for Special Characters

You can also search for invisible special characters, such as paragraph markers, newline markers, or tabs. You specify characters like these in the Search For box by typing a special combination of the carat (^) followed by another character. Table 3.1 shows the key combinations that can be used in a search for special characters.

In the illustration below, the entry in the Find What dialog box tells Word to search for a paragraph marker, followed by the words *The Rook*. As demonstrated by this example, you can combine the special characters with text to further refine your searches.

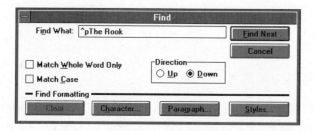

Table 1.1   **Special Entries to Find Special Characters**

Find What Box Entry	Character Searched For
^w	White space
^t	Tab
^p	Paragraph marker
^n	Newline marker
^d	Section marker or hard page break
^s	Nonbreaking (hard) space
^-	Optional hyphen
^~	Nonbreaking (hard) hyphen
^^	Caret character
^?	Question mark character

Looking for Formatting

To find formatting within a document, use one of the the Find Formatting buttons in the dialog box If you choose Character (Alt+H), you will see the Find Character dialog box, shown here:

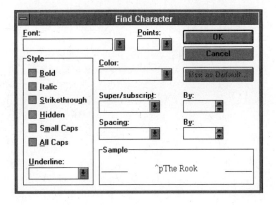

If you choose Paragraphs (Alt+G), you will see the Find Paragraph dialog box here:

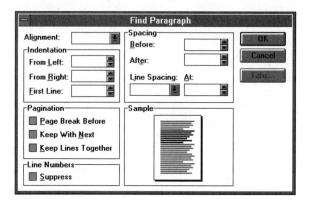

If you choose Styles (Alt+S), you will see the Find Styles dialog box here:

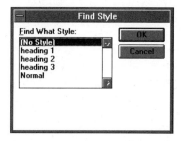

To look for the desired formatting, simply choose the formatting you want to find by selecting the appropriate options in the dialog box. (The various options of character and paragraph formatting are explained in Chapter 4, and styles are explained in Chapter 12.) You need only select as many of the options in the dialog box as are necessary to find the desired text. Clicking any check box selects that format for the search, and clicking again turns it off.

The Character, Paragraph, and Styles buttons of the Find dialog box are powerful options, because they can be used alone or in combination with a search string that you enter in the Find What text box. For example, if you select Edit Find, enter *Bakersville* in the Find What box, then select Character and turn on the Bold and Italic options, Word will find the word *Bakersville* only when it has bold and italic formatting applied.

Once you have selected the desired formatting from the appropriate dialog box (Character, Paragraph, or Style), choose OK to close the dialog box; then choose Find Next from the Find dialog box to initiate the search.

Replacing Text

When you search for text, formatting, special characters, or a combination of all three in order to *replace* that text, you can use the find techniques just described in the previous sections. Suppose you want to replace every occurrence of the word *version* with the word *level* throughout a document and make *level* appear in italic. Or perhaps a certain word has been underlined throughout a document, and you want to remove the underlining from every occurrence of the word. To replace text, you use the Edit Replace (Alt+E+E) command, which displays a dialog box similar to that for Edit Find:

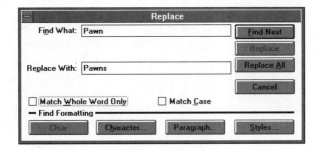

Enter the search term as usual in the Find What box, including any of the key combinations described in Table 3.1 to include special characters in the search. In the Replace With box, enter the text to replace the search term when it is found. As with the Find dialog box, you can click a Character, Paragraph, or Styles button to look for formatting, or to replace text with formatted text.

NOTE. *When the insertion pointer is in the Replace/Find What text box, selecting the Character, Paragraphs, or Styles buttons tells Word that the formatting you indicate in the subsequent dialog boxes should be included in the text that is* searched for. *When the insertion pointer in in the Replace/Replace With text box, selecting the Character, Paragraph, or Styles buttons tells Word that the indicated formatting should be included in the* replacement text.

The Match Whole Word Only and Match Case options work as explained earlier. Word places no restrictions on your replacements. You can replace text with blank spaces, or you can replace codes with formatting.

As an example, suppose you do the following: Select Edit Replace, click the Character button and turn on the Bold Option, and choose OK. Press Tab to move to the Replace With box, select Character again and turn on the Italic option, choose OK, and then choose Replace All. The result is that Word replaces all bold text with italic text.

Now that you've read about Word's find-and-replace features and how they work, you might want to try out the Edit Find and Edit Replace commands, using your practice document or any other file. Try looking for special characters and formatting, as well as text. Be sure to practice refining your search criteria using the Match Whole Word Only and Match Case options.

Spelling Correction

Word's spelling correction utility is a handy tool for finding misspelled words in your documents. The Spelling utility offers multiple dictionaries; you can create your own custom dictionaries, and you can have different dictionaries for special uses, such as medical or legal terminology. The main dictionary is supplied with the program and cannot be changed. One supplemental dictionary, called CUSTOM.DIC, is the default supplemental dictionary. New words that you add to the spelling checker are added to STDUSER.DIC, unless you specify the use of a different supplemental dictionary. You'll learn how to set up and use other dictionaries later, in "Choosing Supplemental Dictionaries."

Note. To select text, click and drag with the mouse, or use the Shift key in combination with the arrow keys. See Chapter 1 for details on selecting text.

The Tools Spelling command (Alt+O+S) lets you check a single word, a selected portion of a document, or the entire document. When you select a word or a passage of text, Word checks only the selection. Otherwise, Word assumes that you want to check the entire document.

One way to check a single word is to first highlight the word you want to check, and then select Tools Spelling (Alt+O+S). The word you highlighted is checked, and Word displays the Spelling dialog box shown in Figure 3.10 (explained below). To check the spelling of all words in a selected passage of text, first make the selection (or if you want to check the entire document, be sure no selection exists). Then, choose Tools Spelling (Alt+O+S).If the insertion pointer is at the start of the document, Word checks the whole document. If the insertion pointer is somewhere within the document, Word starts from there, checks to the end, and then asks if you want to continue checking from the start of the document.

Once you start the spell-check, Word proceeds to check the word you designated or all words in the selected passage against the dictionaries. For each suspected misspelling that it finds, the Spelling dialog box (Figure 3.10) appears. Let's take a closer look at the buttons and boxes in Figure 3.10.

- In the Not in Dictionary box, you see the misspelled words as they are found.

- The Suggestions list box offers a list of alternative spellings for the misspelled word. If one of these suggestions is the desired spelling, highlight it in the list box. Then you can select either the Change button (Alt+C), or the Change All (Alt+H) button to correct all occurrences misspelled in the same manner.

Figure 3.10

Dialog box for
Spelling utility

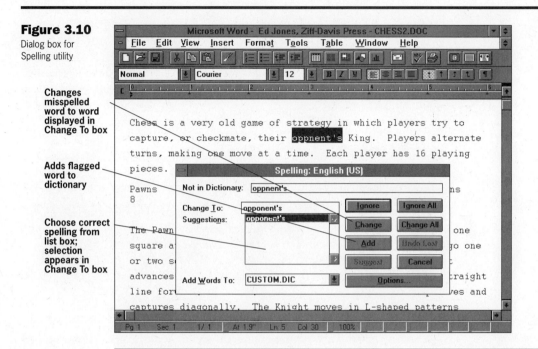

■ The Ignore (Alt+I) button lets you leave the word unchanged, and Ignore All (Alt+G) tells word to ignore all successive words spelled in the same manner.

■ The Cancel button cancels the entire spell-checking operation.

■ The Add button (Alt+A) lets you add the word to the selected supplemental dictionary (CUSTOM.DIC by default).

■ The Undo Last button lets you undo the last correction made by the Spelling utility.

Also on the Spelling dialog box is an Options button, which displays another dialog box; if you want to take a look at this dialog box, look ahead to Figure 3.11. The Options dialog box contains these features:

■ There are two Ignore check boxes. Use Ignore Words with Numbers to tell Word not to include words containing numbers in the spell-check. Use Ignore Words in UPPERCASE to tell Word to skip words composed of all uppercase letters. (Such words are often abbreviations or acronyms, and if you use them often in your documents, you probably don't want Word to identify them as misspellings.)

- The Always Suggest check box is turned on by default—this is what tells Word to list words in the Suggestions list box of the Spelling dialog box, from which you can choose replacements for misspelled words. (Although this is a helpful feature, it slows down the spell-checking process somewhat.) If you decide to turn off Always Suggest, you will have to use the Suggest button in the Spelling dialog box to produce replacement words in the Suggestions list box.

- You'll learn about the Custom Dictionaries list box and the Category icon list box in the section that follows.

Later in this chapter after you read about Word's Thesaurus, you'll find an exercise that lets you practice with both the Spelling and Thesaurus utilities.

TIP. *You can use the Spell key (F7) to spell-check one word or start the checking of a selected portion of a document. Pressing F7 is equivalent to choosing the Tools Spelling command. If no text is selected and you press F7, Word checks the word at the insertion pointer, and Word then asks if you want to continue checking the rest of the document.*

Choosing Supplemental Dictionaries

Tip. You can have as many as three custom dictionaries in use at one time. To stop using a custom dictionary, click on it in the list box.

Note. You'll learn more about the Category list box in Chapter 15.

As mentioned, Word always uses the main dictionary and at least one supplemental dictionary (CUSTOM.DIC). The supplemental dictionary is where words are normally added when you choose the Add button in the Spelling dialog box. You can add words to other dictionaries, as well, by changing the designated supplemental dictionary. You might want to use various supplemental dictionaries for specific purposes. For example, one supplemental dictionary might be for medical terms, another for legal terms, and so on.

To change supplemental dictionaries, select Tools Options (Alt+O+O), click on Spelling in the Category list, or press Alt+C and highlight Spelling. The dialog box that appears is shown in Figure 3.11. In the Custom Dictionaries list box, select a dictionary name, or choose Add (Alt+A) and type in a new name. When entering names for dictionaries, you can use any name of eight characters or less. Word automatically assigns an extension of .DIC to the name. If you choose Add and enter a new name and then choose OK, Word creates a new dictionary and adds it to the Custom Dictionaries list box. Any words added to the dictionary with the Add button during a spell-check are stored in the supplemental dictionary you designate.

When checking large documents, you can accelerate the spell-checking operation somewhat by reducing the overhead needed by Windows for other operations. Close any other documents that are open under Word, and close any other Windows applications that you are not using. Turn on draft mode with the View Draft (Alt+V+D) command, and turn off the ribbon

(Alt+V+B), ruler (Alt+V+R), and status bar (use the Tool Options command) on your Windows desktop. It may also help to minimize MS-DOS Executive (under Windows 2.x) or Program Manager (under Windows 3.0 and above); see your Windows documentation for details.

Figure 3.11

Tools Option Spelling dialog box with dictionary options

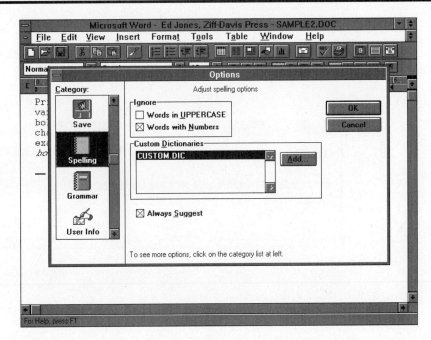

Using the Thesaurus

Note. Remember, you can double-click anywhere within a word to select it.

Word's Thesaurus utility lets you find synonyms for specific words in your documents. A thesaurus can be useful in avoiding repetition and clarifying text. To find a synonym for a word, first select it. Then select Tools Thesaurus (Alt+O+T), or use its hotkey combination, Shift+F7. The dialog box shown in Figure 3.12 appears.

In the Synonyms list box, you'll see a display of any synonyms found for the selected word in Word's built-in thesaurus. Also in the Thesaurus dialog box is a Meanings list box, containing one or more brief definitions for the selected word. Select another meaning, and the list of available synonyms changes correspondingly. You can use the Tab key or the mouse to move between the Synonyms and the Meanings list boxes.

To replace the selected word with a synonym from the Synonyms box, simply choose the desired synonym and click on the Replace button (or press Alt+R). The Cancel button cancels the Thesaurus. The Look Up button displays a list of synonyms for the word shown in the Replace With box.

Figure 3.12
Utilities Thesaurus
dialog box

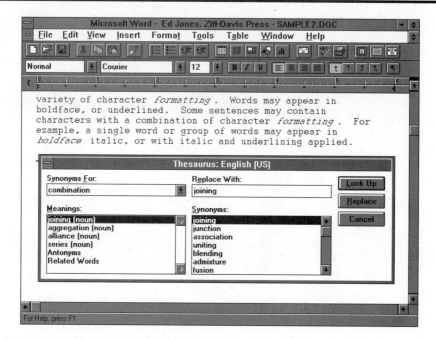

An Exercise Using the Spelling and Thesaurus Utilities

To practice with the Spelling and Thesaurus utilities, open the CHESS document if it is not already open, and perform the following steps:

1. Create an intentional misspelling in one of the words in the first paragraph. Then move the insertion pointer to any position ahead of the misspelled word.

2. Select Tools Spelling (Alt+O+S). The misspelled word will appear in the Spelling dialog box.

3. Type in the correct spelling or choose the correct spelling from the Suggestions list box, and then choose Change (Alt+C). Word corrects the word and then continues to check the rest of the document; correct any other misspelled words that Word may find.

4. When the spell-check is complete, move the insertion pointer to the word *alternate* in the first paragraph.

5. Select Tools Thesaurus (Alt+O+T).

6. When the Thesaurus dialog box appears, notice that the Meanings list box shows five definitions for the word; one is a noun, two are verbs, and two are adjectives. In this case, the word *alternate* is being used as a verb, so tab over to or click in the Meanings list box, and select *interchange*. Six synonyms appear in the Synonyms list box.

7. Tab to or click the Synonyms list box, and highlight the word *exchange*.

8. Click on Replace (or press Alt+R) to replace *alternate* with *exchange*.

9. Select File Save (Alt+F+S) to save the modified document.

Using the Grammar Checker

To check your documents for proper grammar and style, Word provides the Tools Grammar command. When you choose Tools Grammar, Word checks the text you have selected (or the entire document) for grammatical errors. If Word finds an error, it will often suggest ways to correct the sentence containing the error. You can make changes based on Word's suggestions, or on your own preferences, or you can bypass the error altogether (it may be OK as is).

When you use Tools Grammar, Word simultaneously checks your spelling, so you may see the Spelling dialog box (explained earlier) overlay the Grammar dialog box during a grammar-check.

To check grammar in a document, first select a passage of text, or make sure no selection exists if you want to check the entire document starting at the insertion pointer. Then invoke the Tools Grammar command (Alt+O+G). If Word finds an error, it will display the following Grammar dialog box:

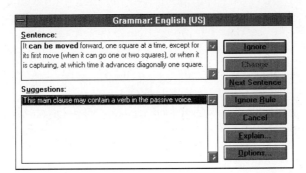

The Sentence list box contains the sentence flagged as incorrect by the grammar checker, with any words related to the cause of the problem in boldface. The Suggestions list box contains any suggestions Word has for correcting the problem.

If the specific words of a replacement sentence appear in the Suggestions box, you can double-click that suggestion, or highlight it and select the Change button; Word then inserts this text into the document. Sometimes Word cannot supply a specific correction, but can only give an overall definition of the problem. In such cases, the Change button remains dimmed. At any time during the grammar-checking operation, you can enter your own corrections in the document. To get into the document window, click it or press Ctrl+Tab. The Change button becomes a Start button, which you can click to restart the grammar-check after you edit the document. You can also choose Cancel from the dialog box to end the grammar-check, and make manual changes in the document, as needed.

The Next Sentence button tells Word to ignore the suspected problem and proceed to the next sentence. The Ignore Rule button tells Word to skip the current error, plus all additional errors that are based on the same rule of grammar. The Explain button produces a dialog box containing an explanation of the grammar rule used by Word to identify the error.

Note. Chapter 15 tells you how to customize grammar-checking so that Word applies only the grammar and style rules you specify.

The Options button displays another dialog box that lets you change the rules used by Word's grammar checker. (You can also display this screen by choosing Tools Options and opening the Grammar category.) Select from one of three buttons: Strictly, For Business Writing, and For Casual Writing. The button you mark determines how Word applies grammar and style rules to your document. With Strictly, all available rules are enforced. The For Business Writing choice tells Word to apply rules appropriate for business correspondence. The For Casual Writing level of checking enforces the fewest rules, as acceptable in informal correspondence.

When Word reaches the end of your selection (or the end of the document), it asks if you want to continue the grammar-check at the start of the document. Choose Yes to continue checking grammar; Word continues to check grammar until it reaches the point where the grammar-checking operation began.

In the Tools Options Grammar category is an option called Show Readability Statistics After Proofing. If this check box is turned on, Word displays a statistics box once the grammar-check is complete, as shown below. The Readability statistics box provides information about the overall readability of your document, according to the set of grammar rules you have chosen. Choose OK from this box to return to your document.

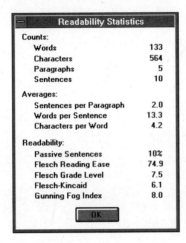

Using the Hyphenation Utility

Word provides different ways to handle *hyphenation*—the process of adding hyphens to reduce the ragged appearance of a document's right margin. Hyphenation makes more effective use of page space by enabling more words to fit on a page. And hyphenation also improves the appearance of justified text by reducing the amount of space needed between the justified words. In Word, you can add hyphens manually, semiautomatically, or automatically. Manual hyphenation means entering hyphens by pressing the hyphen key or key combination for each hyphen you want. With semiautomatic hyphenation, Word adds hyphens and you confirm them. With fully automatic hyphenation, Word adds all hyphens automatically, making its best guess as to where hyphenation should occur.

Manual Hyphenation

If you choose to hyphenate manually, you can use one of three types of hyphens: regular, optional, and nonbreaking (hard).

- Regular hyphens—inserted with the hyphen (-) key—are used in situations where you always want a hyphen to appear; compound words (such as *high-tech*) fall into this category.

- Optional hyphens appear only when the word must be divided at the end of the line. You can insert optional hyphens manually by positioning the insertion pointer, and pressing the Ctrl+Hyphen key combination. Word also inserts this type of hyphen when you select semiautomatic or automatic hyphenation.

- Nonbreaking, or hard, hyphens are used when you do not want words connected by a hyphen to be separated at the end of a line. Hyphenated terms that must appear hyphenated, such as negative numbers, hyphenated surnames, or words normally spelled with hyphens (like *re-create*) all make use of nonbreaking hyphens. To insert a nonbreaking hyphen, position the insertion pointer and then press Ctrl+Shift+Hyphen.

TIP. *If you use all of the various kinds of hyphens, you can tell them apart visually by choosing Tools Options (Alt+O+O), choosing View in the category list, and turning on Optional Hyphens in the dialog box. Regular hyphens look like regular hyphens (-); optional hyphens have a downward tail at the end (¬); and nonbreaking hyphens are longer than regular hyphens (—).*

Automatic and Semiautomatic Hyphenation

To let Word hyphenate your documents, select Tools Hyphenation (Alt+O+H). In the dialog box that appears (Figure 3.13), you'll use the Confirm check box to determine whether hyphenation is semiautomatic or automatic. When the Confirm box is checked, hyphenation is semiautomatic; at each word that is a candidate for hyphenation, Word stops and displays a suggested hyphenation point, and you can change the suggested location with the ← and → keys. When the Confirm box is not marked, hyphenation is fully automatic, and Word inserts hyphens without asking.

When you choose semiautomatic hyphenation (the Confirm check box is marked), Word displays the dialog box in Figure 3.14 each time it finds a candidate for hyphenation. If you agree with Word's suggestion for the word division, choose Yes. Word then proceeds to the next word that can be hyphenated. Choose No, and Word proceeds to the next word without hyphenating the current word. When you do want to divide the word but at a different location, use the ← or → keys to move the hyphen as needed, and then select Yes. Be careful—if you move the hyphen past the right margin, Word will ignore your suggestion and place the entire word at the beginning of the next line.

The other options in the Hyphenate dialog box control Word's hyphenation decisions.

- The Hyphenate CAPS option tells Word it's OK to hyphenate words that are expressed in all capital letters.

Figure 3.13

Tools Hyphenation
command dialog
box

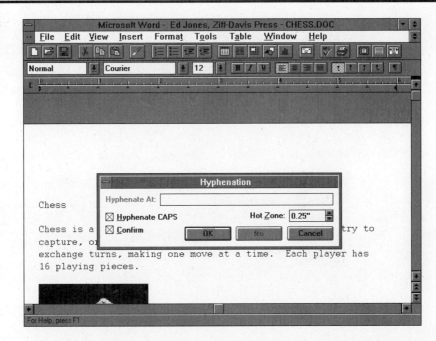

- In the Hot Zone entry box, you can enter a decimal number indicating the size of the *hot zone*. The Hot Zone measurement indicates how far into the text from the right margin Word should go to determine a location for the hyphen. With a larger Hot Zone value, fewer hyphens will appear in the text, but the right edge will be more jagged. With a smaller value, the right edge will be smoother, but more hyphens will appear in the text. The default of one-quarter inch (0.25") is a good compromise. As with all measurements, Word assumes you want inches (in), but you can also enter centimeters (cm).

Using Annotations

You can easily create and edit *annotations* in your Word documents. Annotations are a form of notes regarding your document; these notes can be created by you or by others who are revising or processing the document. Those of you who do programming might think of annotations as comments; they are not normally visible in the document, but can easily be seen by using the View Annotations (Alt+V+A) command. Annotations are very useful when multiple Word users work with a single document. Because each annotation

Figure 3.14

Hyphenation
Confirmation dialog
box

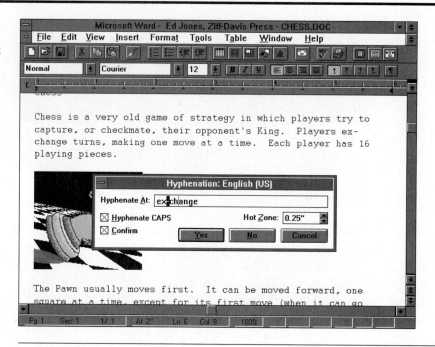

includes the initials of its creator, the writer of a document can more effi-
ciently decipher the annotations and follow up as necessary with the annota-
tors for help in incorporating changes. Even when you are working on a
document alone, you may find annotations to yourself to be useful reminders.

To create an annotation, place the insertion pointer at the desired point
for the annotation, and select the Insert Annotation (Alt+I+A) command.
Word then splits the current window, and inserts your initials within a
bracket at the annotation point, as shown in the bottom portion of the screen
in Figure 3.15. Next to your initials, Word provides a sequential annotation
number.

The insertion pointer is automatically placed in the annotations *pane,*
which is the lower half of the split window. You can proceed to type in your
comments; there is no limit to the length of an annotation. To switch between
the annotation pane and the document, press F6, or click in the pane you want
to use. Figure 3.16 shows a document with two annotations added.

To view a document's annotations, use the View Annotations command
at any time. The command is a toggle, so choosing it repeatedly will turn the
annotations pane on or off. Or you can turn the annotations off by dragging
the split bar within the right scroll bar to the bottom of the window.

Note. Word obtains
your initials (and
your name, when
needed) from
settings recorded
during installation.
You can change the
name and/or initials
at any time, with the
User Info category
of the Tools Options
command
(Alt+O+O).

Figure 3.15
Adding an
annotation to a
document

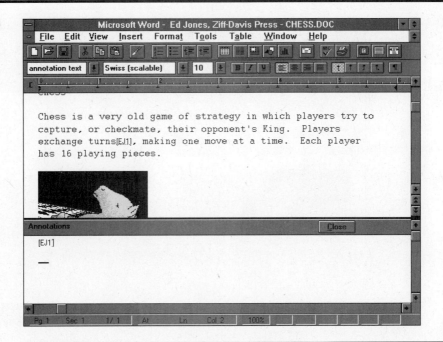

To edit the text of an existing annotation, open the annotation pane if necessary; then edit the annotation text as you would any other Word text. Deleting an annotation is a simple matter; just go to that annotation's marker in the document, select it, and press Del. And you can print all the annotations in a document by choosing the File Print command, selecting the Options button, and turning on the Annotations check box.

TIP. *You can use the cut-and-paste techniques outlined earlier in this chapter to move text from the annotations pane into the document. This can be particularly helpful when other users are adding comments to your documents, and you want to edit and incorporate them into the document.*

Finding Annotations

In a large document, you can quickly get to a specific annotation with the Edit Go To (Alt+E+G) command (or with the F5 hotkey). Select Edit Go To or press F5, and enter **A** (for annotation) followed by the annotation number. For example, to go to the second annotation in the document, press F5, and enter **A2** in response to the prompt. If you enter A without a number, Word jumps to the next annotation mark.

Figure 3.16

A document with
two annotations

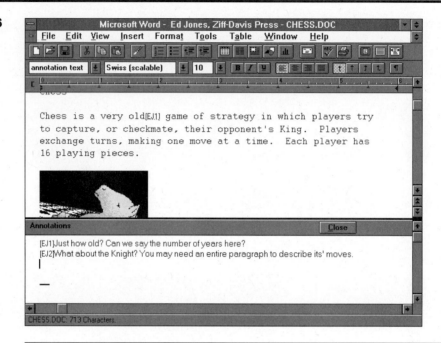

Tip. You can see the
annotation markers
in the document if
you turn on Word's
Hidden Text option.
Choose Tools
Options (Alt+O+O),
choose View in the
Category list box,
turn on Hidden Text
(Alt+I), and choose
OK (or you can click
on the Hidden
Characters button in
the Toolbar).

When you use the Edit Go To command to find an annotation, you may not know its number; in this case, you can move forward through the annotations until you find the one you want. Do this by entering **A+n** in response to the "Go to" prompt, where *n* represents the number of annotations from the position of the insertion pointer. For example, entering A+4 moves you forward to the fourth annotation after the insertion pointer.

Locking a Document for Annotations Only

When multiple workers are commenting on a document, you may find it helpful to lock the document for annotations only. This prevents anyone but the author from changing the document itself; others can only add or edit annotations. You can thus safely pass the file around for comments without endangering the data it contains.

To lock a file for annotations, save the file with File Save As (Alt+F+A) and choose File Sharing (Alt+F) from the dialog box. In the dialog box that next appears, turn on Lock File for Annotations and enter a password if one is desired. Then execute the save by choosing OK twice. If you leave the Password box blank, anyone can then turn off Lock for Annotations. If you do fill in a password, you must re-enter that password before you can turn off Lock for Annotations.

Adding Bullets and Paragraph Numbers

You can automatically number the paragraphs in a document, or you can add bullets at the start of each paragraph, with the Tools Bullets and Numbering command. Legal documents, for example, usually contain numbered paragraphs. The Tools Bullets and Numbering command can also be used to number headings within outlines, a topic that's discussed in Chapter 8. Documents that use numbered paragraphs are easy to revise. As you add, delete, or move paragraphs within existing text, Word maintains the correct numbering automatically.

To add bullets or paragraph numbers, follow this procedure:

1. Open the document, and select the paragraphs to which you want to apply the numbering or bullets. (If no selection is made, the bullet or numbering will be applied to the paragraph containing the insertion pointer.)

2. Select Tools Bullets and Numbering (Alt+O+B).

3. If you want to add bullets at the start of each paragraph, click Bullets (or press Alt+B). If you want to add sequential numbers or letters at the start of each paragraph, click Numbered List (or press Alt+L). If you want to number the paragraphs in outline style, click Outline (or press Alt+O).

4. Next, a dialog box appears that displays options for the format you chose (Bullets, Numbered List, or Outline). Select the desired options. The different dialog boxes and their various options are explained in the paragraphs that follow.

5. Once you have selected your options in the dialog box, choose OK or press Enter. Numbers or bullets will then appear beside the selected paragraph.

Working with the Bullets and Numbering Dialog Boxes

After you select one of the Tools Bullets and Numbering options, you see one of three dialog boxes (Bullets, Numbered List, or Outline). Each of the dialog boxes contains a Sample area, which shows a visual representation of your selected numbered or bulleted format when applied to the text. Each box also contains a Remove button, which you can use to remove bullets or numbering from your document at any time.

If you choose Bullets, the Bullets and Numbering dialog box resembles this one:

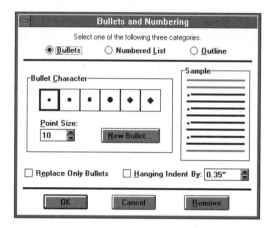

You can choose the desired bullet character by clicking on it, or by pressing Alt+C and then using the arrow keys to highlight the desired character. Use the Point Size box (Alt+P) to change the bullet's point size. If you click on New Bullet (or press Alt+N), Word's Symbol table appears, and you can select a different symbol for use as the bullet. The Replace Only Bullets check box lets you change the bullets for paragraphs that already have them. The Hanging Indent option, when turned on, formats selected paragraphs so that the bullet forms a hanging indent (that is, the rest of the paragraph is indented to the right of the bullet location). If you turn on Hanging Indent, you can then enter the value in the By text box as the measurement of the hanging indent.

Here is the dialog box for the Numbered List option of Tools Bullets and Numbering:

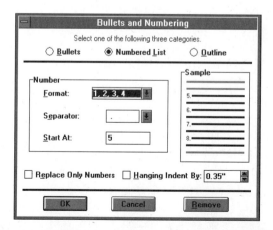

Three options appear in the Number area of the dialog box: Format, Separator, and Start At. The Format list box lets you select: a format for the numbering—standard sequential arabic (1,2,3,4), large roman numerals (I,II,III,IV), small roman numerals (i,ii,iii,iv), uppercase letters (A,B,C,D), and lowercase letters (a,b,c,d). Also in this Number area is a list box for the separator character that appears with the numbers. By default this is a period, but you can enter another character or choose one from the list box. The Start At box is used to designate a starting number (or letter) for the numbering. The Replace Only Numbers and Hanging Indent work as described for the Bullets dialog box.

If you select the Outline option on Tools Bullets and Numbering, you'll see this dialog box:

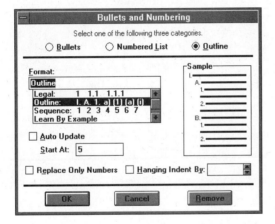

In the Format list box, you can choose the style of outline numbering desired. Your choices are Legal, the common legal format; Outline, which follows the Chicago Manual of Style format for outlining; Sequence, similar to legal but with arabic numbers and periods; Outline All, similar to Outline but with numbers included at all levels; and Learn By Example, where Word patterns its numbering format after a Word style you create for the first heading in the selection. The Auto Update option lets you apply outline numbering by inserting fields instead of actual numbers into the document. Word updates these fields automatically, so if you move outline headings around, the numbers are still in the proper order (see Chapter 8). The Start At, Replace Only Numbers, and Hanging Indent options work as described for the Numbered List dialog box.

Using Toolbar to Add Bullets or Numbering

Mouse users can also use the Numbered List or Bulleted List icons on the Toolbar to add numbering or bullets to a document's paragraphs. Simply select the desired paragraphs and then click on the appropriate button. If you do not make a text selection first, Word adds the bullet or the number to the current paragraph. This method can be especially handy when you want to add bullets or numbers to paragraphs as you type them; simply click on the appropriate icon at the start of the paragraph, and then continue typing.

When you use the Toolbar's Bulleted List icon, the bullet character Word uses is the bullet you last selected in the Bullets and Numbering dialog box. When you use the Numbered List icon, Word checks to see if the previous paragraph is numbered. If it is, Word uses the same style of numbering. If the previous paragraph is not numbered, Word uses the numbering format you last selected in the Bullets and Numbering dialog box.

Bookmarks

Word lets you use *bookmarks* in your electronic documents just as you would use a conventional bookmark to flag a place to which you want to return at a later time. As an example, if you were creating a report with ten parts, you might place bookmarks at the start of each part. You could later quickly find the beginning of each part by searching for the appropriate bookmark. As placemarkers, bookmarks offer an advantage over page numbers, because page numbers will change as you add or delete text. Bookmarks, on the other hand, will not change when the document is edited unless you move them.

NOTE. *Bookmarks can refer to one location in a Word document or to a selected passage of text. If you use a bookmark to identify a text selection, when you later search for that bookmark, the text it marks will be selected. This saves time when you routinely copy a selected passage of text to other locations in a document.*

Note. The hotkey for the Insert Bookmark command is Ctrl+Shift+F5. With this key, a prompt appears in the Status Bar.

To insert a bookmark, first place the insertion pointer at the desired location (to mark a location), or select some text that you want the bookmark to identify. Then select Insert Bookmark (Alt+I+M). The Bookmark Name dialog box appears, as shown here:

Enter a name for the bookmark in the Bookmark Name text box. You can enter up to 20 characters; the first character must be a letter, and spaces are not allowed. After entering a name for the bookmark, choose OK or press Enter. The list box below the text box contains the names of any existing bookmarks in the document. To delete a bookmark, use Tab or the mouse to select the bookmark by name in the list box, and then choose the Delete button.

You can later jump to a bookmark with the Edit Go To command (Alt+E+G), or with the F5 hotkey. Choose Edit Go To; in the dialog box that appears, type the name of the bookmark, and choose OK. Or press F5, and in response to the prompt in the status bar, enter the name of the bookmark. Press Enter, and the insertion pointer moves to the bookmark. If you selected text when you inserted the bookmark, the same text will be selected.

Using the Revision Marks Utility

Often, it is helpful to be able to identify changes that have been made in a document. *Revision marks* in Word come in three varieties: underlining or other emphasis added to inserted text, a strikethrough character added to deleted text, and a revision bar next to changed lines. Revision marking is a common practice in the legal profession and in some areas of government, where changes made to a document must be visually apparent to concerned parties before the document is finalized. Here is how Word's Revision Marks utility applies revision marks to a document:

Note. Added or changed text includes words affected by the Spelling and Thesaurus utilities, as well as page breaks, footnotes, and annotations you enter with the Insert command.

- Word places a vertical bar, called a revision bar, beside each changed line. You can designate on which side the bar appears, or you can omit it entirely.

- When you add or change text, Word identifies that text with underlining. You can change this to double-underlining, boldface, italic, or no markings.

- When you delete text, the text remains in the document, but it appears as *strikethrough* characters. The illustration below shows a paragraph containing a revision bar, added text, and deleted text, with Word's Revision Marks feature turned on:

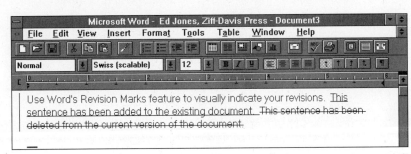

With Revision Marks turned on, you can visually keep track of your changes as you work through a document. When the document is ready to be finalized, you can take a last look at your edits before you accept the revisions, using the Accept Revisions button within the Mark Revisions dialog box. Once you accept the changes, Word removes the revision marks and the deleted text from the document. (Up to this point, you have the option of undoing the revisions.)

Adding Revision Marks

To add revision marks to a document as you edit it, select Tools Revision Marks (Alt+O+K). This Revisions Marks dialog box will appear:

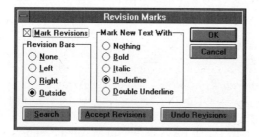

Turn on the Mark Revisions option (Alt+M) to add the revision marks to your document.

The Revision Bars buttons in the dialog box determine how your revision marks are printed in the document. (Note that in Word's normal galley view, the revision marks are always displayed in the left margin or to the left of a column, regardless of where you choose to print them.) You can choose None to repress printing of revision bars; Left to print bars in the left margin; Right to print bars in the right margin; or Outside to print bars in the outside margin (when creating a document that is to be printed double-sided in book form).

The Mark New Text With buttons determine how your inserted text is marked in the display and in the printed document. You can choose Nothing, Bold, Italic, Underline (the default), or Double Underline. Note that you cannot change the style used for deleted text; it always appears in strikethrough characters.

At the bottom of the dialog box are the Search, Accept Revisions, and Undo Revisions command buttons. You can use these buttons to search for revision marks in a document, to accept all revisions, or to undo revisions. (These features are explained in the next couple of sections.)

NOTE. *Once revision marking is enabled, the indicator MRK appears in the status bar to remind you that Revision Marks is running. As long as the feature is enabled, you cannot enter Overtype mode; also, pressing the Backspace* *key to erase existing text will create strikethrough characters instead of deleting the characters.*

You can later turn off the revision marks feature by again selecting Tools Revision Marks (Alt+O+K) and turning off the Mark Revisions button (Alt+M) in the dialog box. Any revisions you've already made will retain their markings, but further revisions will not be marked.

Accepting or Undoing Revisions

Note. Accepting revisions does not automatically turn off Revision Marking. If you want to accept revisions and turn off Revision Marking, choose the Accept Revisions button, and turn off the Mark Revisions button in the dialog box.

You can accept or undo the revisions you've made, for an entire document or for a selected passage. If a selection exists in a document, and you tell Word to accept or undo revisions, it does so only for the selection. If no selection exists, Word accepts or undoes the revisions in the entire document.

To accept revisions, permanently incorporating them into your document, select Tools Mark Revisions (Alt+O+K), and click Accept Revisions (Alt+A) in the dialog box. Any text marked as new text is permanently inserted, and text marked as deleted (in strikethrough characters) is permanently deleted. Also, Word removes the revision bars from the document.

To undo the revisions in a document, click Undo Revisions (Alt+V) in the Mark Revisions dialog box. Any text marked as new text is deleted, text marked as deleted is maintained in the document as normal text, and revision bars are removed.

Searching for Revisions

You can use the Search button (Alt+S) in the Mark Revisions dialog box to search for marked revisions in a document. Word starts from the location of the insertion pointer or at the start of any selected text, finding and highlighting the first text containing revision marks. The Mark Revisions dialog box is then redisplayed. You can choose Cancel to put away the dialog box and edit the text as desired, or Search (Alt+S) again to find the next revision mark.

An Exercise Using Revision Marks

Note. While you use Revision Marks, you cannot use Overtype mode, and Backspace creates strikethrough characters if you try to backspace over existing text.

To see how revision marks can be used to indicate changes within a document, open the CHESS2 document if it is not already open, and try the following exercise:

1. Select Tools Revision Marks (Alt+O+K). In the dialog box, turn on Mark Revisions (Alt+M).

2. In the Mark New Text With box, choose Italic (Alt+I) as the way of marking new and changed text, and then choose OK or press Enter. Notice that MRK appears in the status bar.

3. In the first sentence of the second paragraph, delete the word *usually*. Replace it with the word *generally*.

4. Move the insertion pointer to the start of the last sentence in the second paragraph, and insert the following sentence:

   `The Knight moves in L-shaped patterns measuring two board spaces by one board space.`

   When these revisions have been made, your document resembles the one shown in Figure 3.17.

Figure 3.17

Sample document containing insertion and deletion revision marks

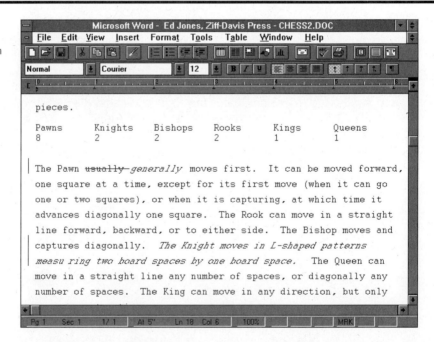

5. Select Tools Revision Marks (Alt+O+K) again, turn off Mark Revisions (Alt+M) and choose Accept Revisions (Alt+A) in the dialog box. Choose Yes (Alt+Y) from the confirmation box that asks if you want to accept all revisions.

6. Click on Close (or press Enter) to put away the Revision Marks dialog box. Notice that the revisions have been incorporated into your document.

7. Save this edited version of the document with File Save (Alt+F+S).

Using the Compare Versions Utility

In addition to the revision marks feature, Word also lets you consider revisions you have made to a document by comparing one version of a document with another, using the Compare Versions utility. This utility compares the current document with an earlier version that is stored on disk. Once Word makes the comparison, revision bars are added in the current document beside text that differs from the older document, and inserted text is underlined. If you have enabled Mark Revisions for the Revision Marks utility, Compare Versions will mark the new and revised text in your current document using the same method of revision marking you have selected for Revision Marks. Word cannot, however, indicate deleted text that may have been present in the earlier version.

To compare an existing document to a previous one, perform the following steps:

1. Open the current version of the document that you want to compare to an earlier version.

2. Select Tools Compare Versions (Alt+O+V), and you'll see this dialog box:

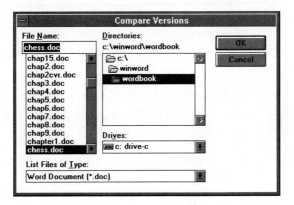

3. In the File Name text box, enter the name of the document to which you want to compare the active document. Or choose a file name from the list box. (You may need to switch to another directory to find your file, by selecting it from the Directories list box.)

4. Choose OK to execute the comparison. Revision marks are added to the active document where the differences exist.

5. To remove the revision marks and incorporate the changes into the current document, select Tools Revision Marks (Alt+O+K), choose Accept Revisions (Alt+A), and then choose Yes.

File Names for Different Versions

When you use the Compare Versions utility, Word compares the current document (the rewrite) with another document stored on disk (the original); the current document need not be saved to disk before running the utility. Thus it is possible to open a document, make changes to it, and then run Compare Versions, using a previously stored document that has the same name. Or you can save the rewrite with a different name and then run Compare Versions.

CAUTION! *If you have enabled the Automatic Save feature through the Save category of the Tools Options command, Word may automatically try to save your revised document while you are working on it with Compare Versions, and overwrite your original file with the revised file before you are ready for this to happen. To avoid this, early in the revision process be sure to save your revised document under a name different from the original.*

Working with Documents in Multiple Windows

Until now, exercises throughout this book have been done using a document in a single window. Whenever a document is opened in Word, it resides in a window. Since as many as nine windows can be open at once, you can really make the most of Word's capabilities by working in multiple windows.

If you are drafting a lengthy proposal and you need to refer to something at the start of the document while you are editing near the end it, you can split one window into two panes to simultaneously view the different parts of the proposal. And cutting and pasting data from one document to another is an easy task once you have both documents open in different windows. You are also likely to find multiple windows quite helpful when you are performing significant editing of documents that are dependent on one another. For example, using two windows is another way, in addition to the Revision Marks and Compare Versions utilities, to compare two copies of the same document.

Editing Documents in Multiple Windows

Word automatically opens windows as you open documents. To demonstrate this, open the CHESS2 document created earlier, if it is not already open. Then open the CHESS document. Next, choose Window Arrange All (Alt+W+A). This command neatly arranges all open windows in an equally-spaced *tiled* layout on the workspace; as a result, your screen will resemble the one shown in Figure 3.18. In a moment, you'll use these windows in an exercise. For now, try opening more documents if you have them to see what happens in the Word workspace.

Figure 3.18

Multiple open windows in a tiled layout in the workspace

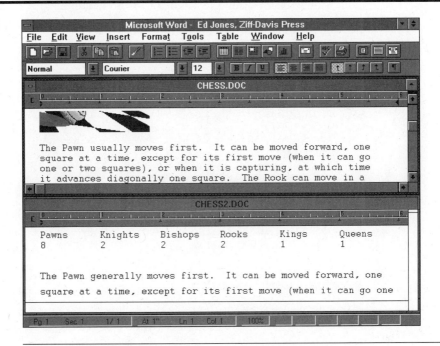

Though you can have as many as nine open windows on the workspace, only one window is the *active* window (the window where any editing you perform takes place). You can see which is the active window by its highlighted title bar, and the presence of the scroll bars (scroll bars are not shown in inactive windows). Also, only the active window contains a Control menu button. You can make any window the active window by clicking anywhere in the window with the mouse or by pressing Ctrl+F6 (Next Window) to move between windows. Another method of moving between windows is to choose the desired window by name from the Window menu; whenever you have multiple windows open, you can open the Window menu (Alt+W), and choose from the numbered list of windows.

With multiple windows open, you can copy or move data between the documents, using the same easy techniques explained earlier in this chapter for moving and copying text. Note that it is not absolutely necessary to have two windows open to copy and move text between them, because you can always cut or copy from one document into the Clipboard, close that document, open another, and paste the text from the Clipboard into the other

Tip. You can use the window moving and sizing techniques common to all Windows applications (detailed in Chapter 1) to move or resize your windows as desired. To have horizontal scroll bars in your windows, select this feature in the View category of the Tools Options dialog box.

document. The advantage to using multiple windows is simply that you can see everything you are doing at all times.

Try the following simple copy-and-paste operation that duplicates the table from CHESS2 into the original CHESS document.

Note. If Word starts up with a document open in a full-sized window, you will need to reduce it from full-screen before you can move or resize the window. Do this by choosing Arrange All from the Window menu or by pressing Ctrl+F5.

1. Press Ctrl+F6 until CHESS2 is the active document.

2. Move the insertion pointer to the blank line above the table. Hold Shift down, and press the ↓ key three times to select the table and the blank line above it.

3. Select Edit Copy (Alt+E+C) to copy the table to the Clipboard.

4. Press Ctrl+F6 to make CHESS the active document.

5. Place the insertion pointer in the blank line between the two paragraphs.

6. Select Edit Paste (Alt+E+P) to paste the table into the document.

7. Close both CHESS documents now without saving the changes; select File Close (Alt+F+C), and choose No (Alt+N) in response to any "Save changes?" prompts that appear.

Splitting a Document

If you want to see one portion of a document while editing another, you can split the window into two panes. Do this by selecting the Split option on the active document's Control menu or by dragging the *split bar*. (The split bar is the horizontal black bar located just above the up arrow in the vertical scroll bar.) Use the mouse to click and drag the split bar down the scroll bar to the point where you want the window divided. Or with the keyboard, press Alt+Hyphen and choose Split from the menu that appears. Then use the ↑ or ↓ keys to position the dotted line at the desired split point, and press Enter. With either approach, the window is split horizontally, and separate vertical scroll bars appear for each pane, as shown in Figure 3.19.

To move between the panes of the window, click in the desired pane with the mouse, or press F6 (Next Pane) and Shift+F6 (Previous Pane). You can use Word's normal navigation and editing techniques to move independently within either pane. For example, you could display the introduction to a report in the top pane, while editing a specific part of the report in the lower pane. To close the split and have one window again, use the mouse or keyboard methods outlined earlier to drag the split bar to the top or the bottom of the screen.

The techniques outlined in this chapter and in Chapter 2 will be sufficient for your basic text entry and editing needs. However, Word has much to offer in the way of more complex formatting; the two chapters that follow will cover these features in detail.

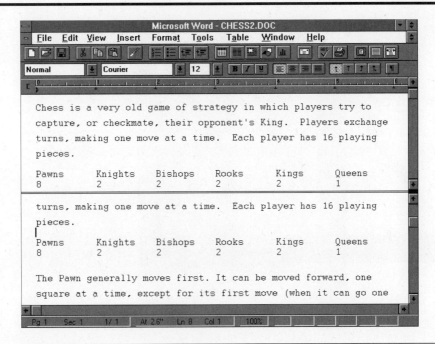

CHAPTER

4

Formatting with Word

AS YOU CREATE AND REFINE YOUR TEXT, YOU WILL NEED TO CONTROL the appearance of the document, and you can do this with formatting. In Chapter 3, you were introduced to some of the basic ways of formatting your text. Here in Chapter 4 you will learn how formatting can apply to characters and to paragraphs in a Word document. Chapter 5 will then continue the discussion of formatting, applying it to whole pages of a document and occasionally to multiple sections.

Before applying the powers of Word's formatting options to a document, you should first understand how Word defines and interprets your format settings. If your last word processor was Microsoft Word for DOS, you already have an idea of how formatting is applied in Word; Word for Windows does a few things differently. If you are accustomed to any word processor other than Word for DOS, you will likely find formatting in Word to be substantially different.

The Levels of Formatting in Word

Word provides formatting options for four different types of text: characters, paragraphs, sections, and documents. Later in this chapter you'll see Word's Format menu, which offers many of the features that control Word's formatting.

The smallest unit of formatting is *character formatting;* any formatting that you apply affects all of the characters within a selected area of text, or all of the characters that you type after you select the formatting. For instance, when you select a sentence and then click on the Bold button in the ribbon to transform the sentence into boldfaced text, you are applying character formatting to every character in the sentence. Character formatting is often used to make a word or group of words in your document stand out.

The next size up in the formatting arena is *paragraph formatting,* where the formatting that you apply controls the appearance of the text from one paragraph marker to the next. In Chapter 2 you learned that a paragraph marker occurs whenever you press the Enter key. If you press Enter once, type seven lines of text, and then press Enter again, those seven lines of text constitute one paragraph. Once you select a paragraph, you can designate the formatting for that entire paragraph; for instance, you can change its alignment or its line spacing.

Because paragraphs are made up of characters, you may be confused about the difference between these two levels of formatting. It may help to remember that paragraph formatting generally controls the appearance of lines, because typically it is a group of lines that make up a paragraph. Paragraph formatting controls the alignment of lines, the spacing between lines, the indentation of the lines within the paragraph, and any borders that appear around the paragraph.

Next, there is *page formatting*. With page formatting, you control the appearance of every page in the entire document, including such settings as page size, default tab stops, and margins. (A brief introduction to some of these settings was provided in Chapter 3.)

Optionally, you can apply another level of formatting, *section formatting,* to entire sections of a document. (A document can be made up of a single section, or you can divide a document into multiple sections.) When you format a section of a document, you change certain formatting aspects for the pages within that section. For example, you might want to change the number of columns in a portion of the document, or change the look of the headers and footers for a portion of the document. Once you divide a document into sections, you can use many formatting commands to format each section individually.

Here in Chapter 4 you will learn the ways in which you can control formatting for specific characters or paragraphs of a document. Then Chapter 5 will examine formatting for entire documents, and for optional sections of documents.

A Note About Choosing Your Formatting Parameters

Though Word divides formatting into the aforementioned levels, these formatting definitions govern Word's behavior, but need not control your formatting choices. Where you start and end a particular type of formatting depends entirely on you and your wishes for the document's appearance. For example, suppose you want to display all the text of two paragraphs in italic. Because you are formatting characters, you can use a character formatting parameter for the italic attribute, even though in this case you are working with paragraphs. This book explains the levels of formatting in Word for Windows terms because that is how Word provides access to them within its menus. You can, however, choose to apply formatting using any combination of methods that suits your needs.

A Word About Styles

Like most programs under Windows, Word gives you more than one way to accomplish the same task. Character, paragraph, and page formatting are known as *direct formatting* options. Another way to control formatting is with *styles*. When you use styles, you apply a group of formatting settings to an entire document. As an example, if a certain style defines indented paragraphs, and you apply that style to a document, that document's paragraphs will be indented. Chapter 12 explores the use of styles.

The How and When of Formatting

Word provides a great deal of flexibility, offering many options for performing your formatting tasks. You can apply formatting as you are creating a document, changing the appearance of text as you go along. Or you can enter all of the raw text using a single format, and then later change the formatting in selected areas of the document. Or you can use both methods in combination.

If you choose to format as you go along, remember that many aspects of formatting (particularly for characters and paragraphs) can be turned on and off as you work. For example, if you are in the middle of a paragraph and you decide to turn on underlining, everything that you type from that point on will be underlined until you turn underlining off. This is true whether you apply the formatting with commands, with Ctrl+key combinations (*speedkeys*), or with buttons in the Toolbar and ribbon.

If you want to enter the text of a document first and then apply formatting to specific areas later, you will use the "select and act" technique that you have already learned to use in Word. That is, you first select the affected text, and then execute an action (by choosing a formatting command or button) that applies to the selection.

Your Windows Formatting Toolbox

Word gives you several ways to format your documents: with the icons in the ribbon and Toolbar; through the dialog boxes of the Format command; and with various Ctrl+key combinations, or speed-keys. These different methods make up your formatting "toolbox."

One significant advantage Word offers is that the formatting commands are all in the same place: on the Format Menu. Numerous commands in this menu, when chosen, display dialog boxes that let you control the types of formatting named earlier—character, paragraph, section layout, page setup, and columns.

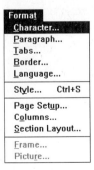

Here in Chapter 4 you'll learn about the Format Character and Format Paragraph commands. The Format Tabs command, used to set and clear tabs, is also explained in this chapter, as is Format Border, which lets you apply borders and shading to selected paragraphs.

Several other format options are found on the Format menu:

- Format Language is used to change language attributes for selected characters (Chapter 15).

- Format Style lets you define and apply styles to a document (Chapter 12).

- You'll work with the Page Setup and Section Layout options in Chapter 5.

- Format Columns is used to change column formats (Chapter 5).

- Format Frame, to change the properties for a frame, and Format Picture, to change the appearance of a picture frame, are both covered in Chapter 11.

Applying Character Formatting

Note. You will not see all of your formatting on the screen if you are using draft view. Choose View Draft (Alt+V+D) to turn draft view off or on.

The first level of Word formatting is character formatting. Character formatting governs how your characters look on the screen and in print. When you apply character formatting, you are changing the format for each character. Character formatting is the most common type of text formatting; a glance at any newspaper illustrates this. Headlines appear in boldfaced characters in large fonts; secondary headlines may employ bold italic type; leading words in some stories or in photo captions may also be in boldface, in yet another font. The role of character formatting is to emphasize text—for example:

you can produce boldfaced characters
<u>or underlined characters</u>
<u>or</u> characters <u>with</u> word <u>underlining</u>
or italic characters
and <u>**character formatting**</u> *<u>can be</u>* **applied** *<u>in combinations.</u>*

You can also add color formatting to the characters of your document. Whether you can view and/or print the colors you select will depend on your display and printer hardware.

Character formatting is divided into six areas, all of which are controlled by options in the dialog box for the Format Character command, or the Word ribbon, or the speed-keys.

- *Fonts*　These are sets of characters in a specific shape or style.

- *Point Size*   This governs the height and width of the characters. (A point is a unit of typesetting measurement; one point is $\frac{1}{72}$ of an inch.) Though point size is measured in height, characters will proportionally increase in width as they increase in height.

- *Color*   Word offers eight possible colors (blue, black, cyan, green, magenta, red, yellow, and white). An Auto choice is also provided; if selected, the color used will be the same as the color designated in the Preferences Screen Colors dialog box of the Windows Control Panel.

- *Emphasis*   These are appearance attributes such as boldface, underlining, small capitals, and so forth.

- *Hidden*   This causes characters to be hidden (not visible) unless the Hidden Text option in the View Preferences dialog box is turned on.

- *Position*   This refers to the vertical position of the characters—normal, raised (superscript), or lowered (subscript).

- *Character Spacing*   This controls the amount of space that appears between characters. Word allows a default amount of space between characters, but you can expand or condense this allowance.

Choosing Your Weapon

Since Word provides different ways to implement the same types of formatting (the Format Character command, the ribbon, and the various speed-keys), you may wonder which method is best. There is no "correct" method; use whichever techniques you are comfortable with. Mouse users will find the ribbon a powerful tool; the speed-keys are likely to appeal to mouse and keyboard users alike because they save time. Another advantage of the speed-keys is that Microsoft has made them mnemonic, associating the letter of the key with the result. For example, Ctrl+B applies boldface, Ctrl+I applies italic, Ctrl+F changes fonts, and so on. When you need to apply a number of formats to the same text, the Format Character command may be best, because you can select multiple options from the dialog box. For performing character formatting as you type, the speed-keys also work well; you can press a key-combination to turn on the desired formatting, type some text, and press the same keys again to turn the formatting off.

The Format Character Command

Using the Format Character (Alt+T+C) command is one way to accomplish character formatting. The options that control all the character formatting features are available on the dialog box for this command, as shown in Figure 4.1.

Figure 4.1

Format Character
dialog box

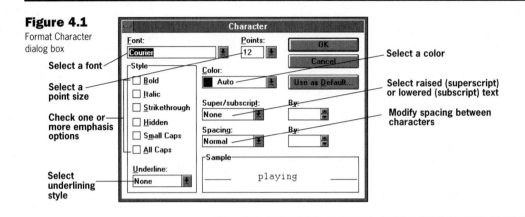

As you work with this dialog box, consider the following:

- If you are not using a mouse, remember to use the Alt key plus the under-lined letter to quickly move to an option.

- The Font, Points, Color, Underline, Super/Subscript, and Spacing options are offered in combination list boxes, so you can easily choose the desired selection from the drop-down list box, or (in the case of Fonts or Points) type in the one you want. If you choose to type in the selection, remember that it must be an appropriate one; for example, entering Courier into the Fonts box works only if your printer installed under Windows supports the Courier font.

- Before using the Color list box, remember that you must have a color mon-itor in order to display the colors, and a color printer to print the colors.

- You can select one or more of the various emphasis options.

To try some character formatting, you can enter the following text:

Note. If you are
using a laser printer
that accepts font
cartridges, you can
use the additional
fonts with Word. To
select a different
font cartridge,
choose File Print
Setup (Alt+F+R),
and then Setup
(Alt+S). Choose the
desired font
cartridge from the
Cartridge list box.

```
Printed newspapers, periodicals, and books often contain a
variety of character formatting. Words may appear in
boldface, or underlined. Some sentences may contain
characters with a combination of character formatting. For
example, a single word or group of words may appear in
boldface italic, or with italic and underlining applied.
```

Save the text with the name SAMPLE2. As with other formatting in Word, you will select some text, and then apply the appropriate formatting choices.

Follow these steps:

1. Using standard selection methods, select the word *boldface* in the second sentence.

2. Select the Format Character (Alt+T+C) command. In the Style box, turn on the Bold option (Alt+B), and choose OK.

3. In the same sentence, select the word *underlined*, and choose Format Character (Alt+T+C). From the Underline list box (Alt+U), choose Single, and choose OK.

4. Select the entire last sentence, and choose Format Character (Alt+T+C). In the Style box, turn on Bold, and choose Single from the Underline list box. Then choose OK. Figure 4.2 shows the results of all these formatting options applied to the sample text.

5. Leave the SAMPLE2 document open on your screen for more practicing.

Figure 4.2

Sample text with formatting applied

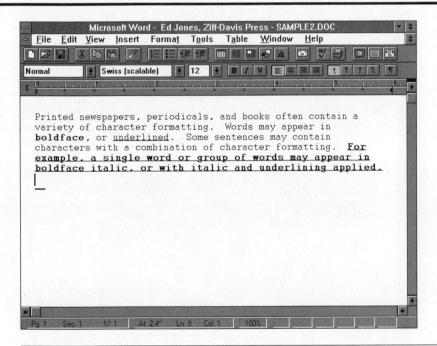

TIP. *Step 4 in the foregoing exercise demonstrates one advantage of using the Format Character command: You can apply more than one format*

simultaneously. However, if all you need is a single element of character formatting, using the ribbon or the speed-keys is often faster.

Character Formatting with the Ribbon

When the ribbon (Figure 4.3) is visible, you can use it to apply some aspects of character formatting, such as bold, italic, and underlining, or font choices and point sizes. If the ribbon is not visible, you can turn it on with the View Ribbon command. When you aren't working with the ribbon, turn it off to gain space on the document screen.

Figure 4.3

Character formatting made easy with the ribbon

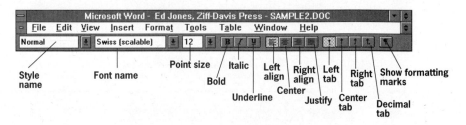

The ribbon makes it easy for mouse users to apply formatting to a text selection, or to turn on/off various aspects of formatting during text entry. To apply formatting with the ribbon, simply click on the button for the desired option. If you select some text first, and then click on the option in the ribbon, that formatting feature is applied to the text selection. With no text selected, clicking on a ribbon option turns it on (or off) for all further text entry.

Let's try this. If you have a mouse, first click on the Bold and Underline buttons, to turn off the formatting that was turned on in the previous exercise. Then click on the Italic button, and add the following sentence to the end of the SAMPLE2 text:

```
Headings are often formatted in italic, to make them stand
out.
```

Note that as you type, every character appears in italic formatting. Notice, also, that while Italic is enabled, the Italic button on the ribbon appears depressed, as shown in Figure 4.4. The ribbon always thus indicates whatever character formatting applies at the location of the insertion pointer. During text entry, the ribbon buttons act as toggles, so you can turn off Italic after you have typed the sentence by again clicking on the Italic button.

If you want to, select a sentence or two, or even the whole paragraph, and turn on another formatting feature using a ribbon button. The formatting will be applied to all the selected text.

Figure 4.4

Using the ribbon to apply italic format

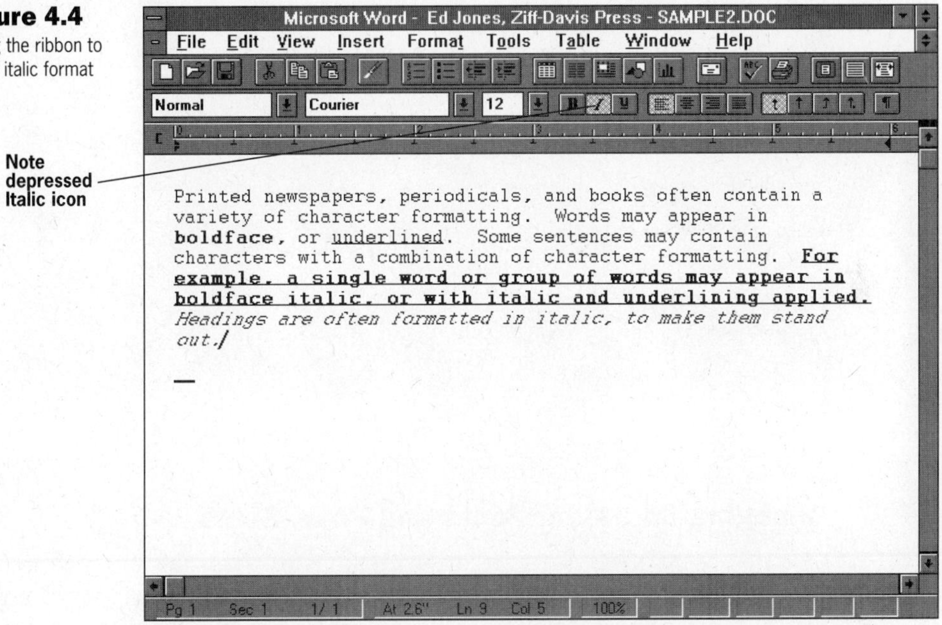

Note depressed Italic icon

Character Formatting with Speed-Keys

You can also use certain Ctrl+key combinations (speed-keys) to apply character formatting to selected text, or to turn formatting on/off during text entry. For example, the Ctrl+B combination controls the Bold format feature. As with the other formatting methods, pressing Ctrl+B when text is selected applies boldface to the entire selection. If no selection exists, pressing Ctrl+B toggles boldface on/off as you type. The speed-keys used with character formatting are listed in Table 4.1.

TIP. *You can turn off all character formatting for a selection by pressing Ctrl+Spacebar. This is especially useful when you've used several speed-keys to turn on various formatting features for a selection, and you want to turn them all off.*

Table 4.1	**Character Formatting Speed-Keys**

Formatting	Key-Combination
Bold	Ctrl+B
Italic	Ctrl+I
Small Caps	Ctrl+K
Hidden	Ctrl+H
Underline	Ctrl+U
Word underline	Ctrl+W
Double underline	Ctrl+D
Change font style	Ctrl+F
Change point size	Ctrl+P
Superscript	Ctrl+Plus
Subscript	Ctrl+Equal
None	Ctrl+Spacebar

Changing Character Fonts and Point Sizes

One significant advantage of using Word for Windows is the ability to see and utilize various fonts within your document. The font used as the default varies, depending on the printer you are using under Windows; you may wish to change this default with the Define option of the Format Style command. The fonts available to you will depend on the type of printer you are using, and on the fonts that were installed as part of your Windows installation. Here are examples of some fonts available under Windows:

Courier

Dutch

Modern

Roman

Swiss

In addition to choosing among fonts, you can also select various point sizes. Each point is $1/72$ of an inch, so in a ten-point type size, characters would be roughly $10/72$ of an inch high.

The following lines demonstrate various point sizes:

This is twelve-point Roman

This is fourteen-point Roman

This is sixteen-point Roman

This is eighteen-point Roman

This is twenty-point Roman

Tip. You can also use Ctrl+F2 (Grow Font) to increase the font size for a selection, or Ctrl+Shift+F2 (Shrink Font) to decrease the font size for a selection.

You can choose both fonts and point sizes with the ribbon, or with the Format Character command. For both of these formatting features, you select available options from a combination list box. With the mouse, you can select the Format Character command and work with these options in the dialog box; or you can click on the Font or the Points list box in the ribbon to display the available choices there. Keyboard users can select the Format Character command (Alt+T+C) and then choose from the Font and Points combination list boxes; or, in the ribbon, press Ctrl+F to choose fonts, and Ctrl+P to choose point sizes. (If necessary, make the ribbon visible with the View Ribbon command.)

TIP. *With varied fonts and point sizes, it is all too easy to get carried away. A document with too many different fonts and/or point sizes can take on a busy look and be visually distracting to the reader.*

Applying Superscript and Subscript

You can create raised (superscript) text and lowered (subscript) text with the Ctrl+Plus and Ctrl+Equal speed-keys, or with the Super/Subscript list box in the Format Character dialog box. Super- and subscript text appear frequently in scientific documents, and in mathematical formulas. Superscript numbers are often used for footnote references. Here are examples of these attributes:

This is superscripted text. And this is back to normal.
This is subscripted text. And this is back to normal.

Most formatting of this kind is done while typing the affected text, although (as with other formatting in Word) you can apply the formatting later by selecting the desired passage and choosing the superscript or subscript attribute, as follows:

■ For superscripted text, press Ctrl+Plus, or choose Format Character (Alt+T+C) and choose Superscript from the Super/Subscript list box.

■ For subscripted text, press Ctrl+Equal, or choose Format Character and choose Subscript from the Super/Subscript list box.

TIP. *One advantage of using the Format Character command to enable super/-subscript formatting is that you can also change the measurement used for the raised or lowered text; just enter a new numeric value in the By: text box. The default is 3 points above or below the normal text. If you are content with this default, you can quickly designate superscript with Ctrl+Plus, or subscript with Ctrl+Equal. Note that the "By" text box does not change the default.*

An Exercise with Character Formatting

Here is an exercise to practice changing fonts and point sizes and using subscript in the SAMPLE2.DOC file:

1. Select the entire paragraph in SAMPLE2. (A fast way to do this is to place the insertion pointer anywhere in the paragraph, press F8 to start Extended Selection mode, and press F8 three more times. Mouse users can move the pointer to the left of the paragraph, and double-click.)

2. Select Format Character (Alt+T+C).

3. From the Font list box, choose Courier (or another font if your installation of Windows does not have Courier).

4. In the Points list box, set the point size to 12, and then click on OK or press Enter.

5. Select the second sentence in the paragraph.

6. Press Ctrl+I to apply italic to the selection, and Ctrl+U to underline the selection.

7. Select *Printed newspapers* in the first sentence.

8. Press Ctrl+F to change the font. If the ribbon is turned on, the Font list box will be selected; use the arrow button and scroll to the Modern font, and press Enter. If the ribbon is not turned on, the prompt "Which font?" appears in the status bar. Type **Modern** and press Enter. (If Modern is not available with your printer, choose another font.)

9. Press Ctrl+P to change the point size for the font. If the ribbon is turned on, the Points list box will be selected; use the up or down arrows to highlight 14, and press Enter. If the ribbon is not turned on, the prompt "Which font size?" appears in the status bar. Type **14** and press Enter.

10. Place the insertion pointer just in front of the period in the first sentence.

11. Press Ctrl+Equal to begin typing subscripted text.

12. Type the following:

```
(or appear visually emphasized)
```

The document should now resemble Figure 4.5.

Figure 4.5
SAMPLE2
document with
various fonts and
point sizes

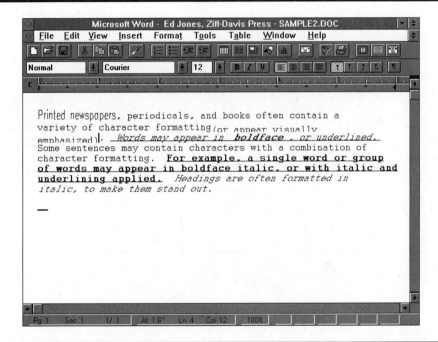

Copying Character Formatting

When you are using a particular set of character formatting often in a document (but not in the entire document), you can save time by copying the format from one place in the document to another. To copy a character format, first select the characters to be formatted. With the selection made, point at the characters that currently have the desired formatting, hold down Ctrl and Shift, and click the left mouse button. The formatting will be copied to the selected passage.

Applying Paragraph Formatting

Word lets you apply paragraph formatting to any area that Word considers to be a paragraph. Remember—Word defines a paragraph as any amount of text between two paragraph markers.

TIP. *You can tell where paragraphs begin and end in a document by choosing the Tools Options command, and turning on Paragraph Marks in the View category (or by clicking on the Paragraph button in the ribbon). The document will then display all its paragraph markers, as shown in Figure 4.6.*

Figure 4.6

Use Tools Options and turn on Paragraph Marks to show paragraph markers in a document

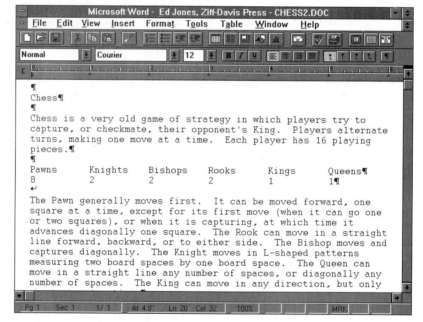

Remember—the use of newline characters (Shift+Enter) instead of paragraph markers (Enter) can make paragraph formatting easier, because Word does not consider a newline to be the start of a paragraph.

When you're deciding where paragraph formatting is necessary, it helps to remember that a paragraph is simply a collection of lines. Hence, any formatting change that you would want to apply to a collection of lines will usually be a type of paragraph formatting—such as controlling the length of lines, setting the alignment of lines at the left and right edges of the document, and determining the space between lines and between paragraphs. You can also designate the placement of tab stops, including how text is aligned at the tab stops.

If the ruler is not visible, you can turn it on with the View Ruler command (Alt+V+R). When you are not doing any paragraph formatting, you can gain viewing space by turning off the ruler again.

As with character formatting, you can apply paragraph formatting in different ways. You can use the Format Paragraph command, or speed-keys, or the the triangular indent markers on the Word ruler.

The ruler measurement line displays important information about the existing formatting for the current paragraph. The ruler line displays the left and first-line indents by means of the two small triangle-shaped markers at the left edge (these will be explained in more detail shortly). At the right edge, a single small triangle marker indicates the right indent. Default tab stops also appear along the ruler line. These can be changed with the Format Tabs command, as explained in Chapter 3.

Paragraph Indentation

Note. Mouse users can also indent and unindent paragraphs using icons in the Toolbar.

A common formatting element for paragraphs in a business document involves setting the indentation. When you are indenting paragraphs, it is important to remember that all paragraph indentation is relative to any page margins you may also have specified (see Chapter 5).

Word lets you indent entire paragraphs from the left or right edges of the document. You can also indent only the first line of a paragraph. For practice, do one or both of the following exercises. The first exercise shows you how to set left, right, and first-line indents using the Format Paragraph command; the second exercise is for mouse users who want to do these tasks using the ruler.

1. Place the insertion pointer anywhere within the first paragraph of the sample CHESS2 document. (If SAMPLE2 is still showing on your screen, close it now with File Close (Alt+F+C); you may also want to save the formatting changes you made in previous exercises.)

2. Select the Format Paragraph (Alt+T+P) command; the Format Paragraph dialog box appears (Figure 4.7).

3. You will use the Indentation area of the dialog box to control the paragraph indents. Enter **0.5"** in the From Left text box, and click on OK or press Enter. The result resembles that shown in Figure 4.8; the entire paragraph is indented a half-inch.

4. Select Format Paragraph again, and enter **0.5"** in the From Right box. Click on OK or press Enter, and the paragraph now appears indented by a half-inch on both sides, as shown in Figure 4.9.

5. To indent only the first line of this paragraph, choose Format Paragraph, and enter a value of **1"** in the First Line box. When you choose OK or press Enter, the first line of the paragraph is indented by one inch, as shown in Figure 4.10.

Figure 4.7

Format Paragraph
dialog box

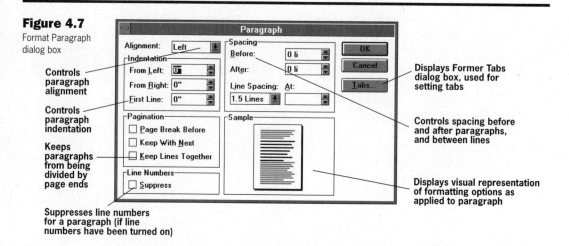

Controls
paragraph
alignment

Controls
paragraph
indentation

Keeps
paragraphs
from being
divided by
page ends

Suppresses line numbers
for a paragraph (if line
numbers have been turned on)

Displays Former Tabs
dialog box, used for
setting tabs

Controls spacing before
and after paragraphs,
and between lines

Displays visual representation
of formatting options as
applied to paragraph

Figure 4.8

A paragraph with a
left indent of 0.5"

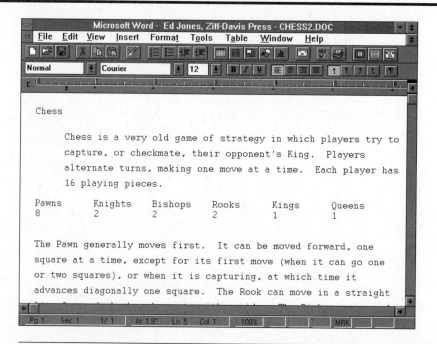

Figure 4.9

A paragraph indented 0.5" on both sides

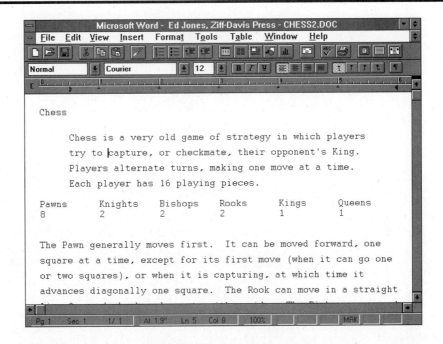

Figure 4.10

A paragraph with the first line indented

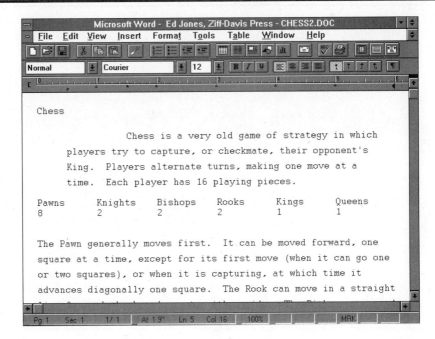

Mouse users can also use the ruler line to set the left, right, and first-line indent values. You may have noticed in the first exercise that when you set the indent values using the Format Paragraph command, the triangle-shaped indent markers on the ruler were repositioned accordingly. With the mouse, you can set paragraph indents by dragging the indent markers on the ruler.

1. With the mouse, drag the left indent marker (the lower of the two triangles) back to the zero on the ruler line, and watch how the left edge of the paragraph is thus realigned. The paragraph is no longer left-indented, although the first line remains indented by one inch.

2. Now drag the first-line indent marker back to the zero on the ruler.

3. Drag the right indent marker one-half inch to the right.

The paragraph now looks as it did before you changed any of the indents.

When you set indents by dragging the markers in the ruler, keep in mind that the indent measurement set by the first-line marker is always relative to that of the left indent marker. Thus, to use this method to indent an entire paragraph by a half-inch and the first line by another half-inch, you would first drag the left indent symbol to the right by a half-inch, and then drag the first-line marker to the right another half-inch *past* the left indent marker. To drag the left indent marker without dragging the first-line indent marker, press the Shift key while dragging.

Yet another method of indenting an entire paragraph is by using icons in the Toolbar. The Indent icon indents the current paragraph to the next tab stop. The Unindent icon moves the current paragraph to the left to the previous tab stop, or to the left margin.

Keyboard users, too, can set paragraph indents with the ruler. First press Ctrl+Shift+F10 to activate the ruler. Then use the ← and → keys to move the ruler cursor to the desired indent position. Type **L** to set a left indent, **R** to set a right indent, or **F** to set a first-line indent. Finally, press Enter to apply the settings and exit the ruler.

Working with Hanging Indents

Some documents need *hanging indents* (also called *outdents*), where successive lines of a paragraph are indented more than the first line. Hanging indents are useful for creating numbered and bulleted lists. One way to establish a hanging indent is to use the Format Paragraph command, and specify a negative value in the First Line box. In our example, place the cursor in the first paragraph, select Format Paragraph (Alt+T+P), and enter **1.0"** for the From Left indent, and **–0.5"** for the First Line indent, then press Enter. The result, shown in Figure 4.11, is a paragraph with a hanging indent.

Before proceeding to the next section, choose the Edit Undo Formatting command (Alt+E+U) to restore the sample paragraph to its original form.

Figure 4.11

A paragraph with one-inch hanging indent

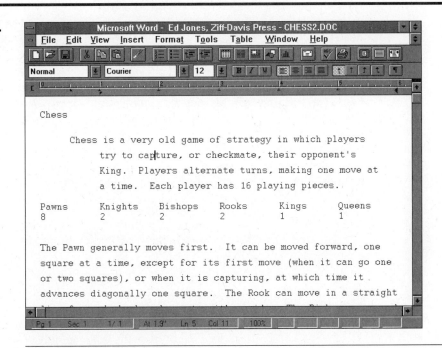

Setting Indents with Speed-Keys

As in most Word formatting, you can also use speed-keys to set paragraph indents. For example, place the insertion pointer anywhere in a paragraph and press Ctrl+N, and you increase the left indent (move it forward) to the next tab stop. The tab stops used to set indents can be either default tab stops or custom tabs, as explained in "Applying Tabs" later in this chapter.

Here are the speed-keys for setting paragraph indents:

Speed-Key	Function
Ctrl+N	Increases left indent and first-line indent to next tab stop.
Ctrl+M	Decreases left indent and first-line indent to prior tab stop.
Ctrl+T	Increases left indent to next tab stop; keeps first-line indent at its existing position. This increases a hanging indent.
Ctrl+G	Decreases left indent to prior tab stop; keeps first-line indent at its existing position. This decreases a hanging indent.

Paragraph Alignment

Paragraphs in Word can be aligned in four ways: flush left, flush right, centered, or justified (aligned on both sides). Until now, all text you've typed in the exercises has been left-aligned, meaning the left edge of the paragraph is even and the right edge is ragged. There may be times, however, when you need justified text, where both edges of the paragraph are aligned. (Justification is commonly used for text in books and magazines, where a flush-right margin presents a neater appearance.) Word justifies your text by adding extra space between words where necessary, to make the right end of the lines even with the right margin of the paragraph. Or you may want centered paragraphs. In rare instances, you may even need to right-align a paragraph; in such cases, the right side aligns flush, while the left edge of the paragraph remains ragged.

You can change the paragraph alignment setting by using the Alignment text box of the Format Paragraph dialog box, or by using the appropriate speed-keys. Let's create an example in which to try the possible paragraph alignments.

1. Open a new document and type the following lines, using newline characters (Shift+Enter) to end each line. This paragraph is left-aligned:

    ```
    WIN!
    A trip to the Bahamas!
    Just answer the following five questions correctly.
    ```

2. Place the cursor anywhere within the paragraph, select Format Paragraph (Alt+T+P), choose Right from the Alignment list box (Alt+G), and click on OK or press Enter. The paragraph is now aligned at the right margin, as shown in Figure 4.12. (Note that you can also right-align the paragraph by positioning the cursor and pressing Ctrl+R.)

Figure 4.12
A paragraph with right alignment

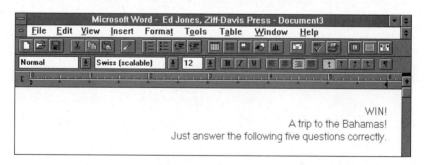

3. Again use the Format Paragraph command, and this time choose Centered. (Or use the Ctrl+E speed-key.) The paragraph is now centered, as shown in Figure 4.13.

Figure 4.13
A paragraph with
center alignment

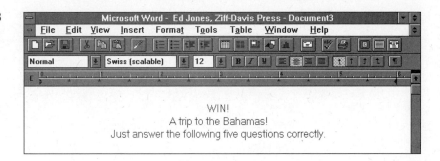

4. Close the document with File Close (Alt+F+C), and answer No (Alt+N) to the "Save Changes" inquiry (you will not need this document elsewhere).

5. To see an example of justification, use the CHESS2 document. If necessary, open the document, and place the insertion pointer anywhere in the last paragraph. Choose Format Paragraph (Alt+T+P), select Justified from the Alignment list box (Alt+G), and click on OK or press Enter. The result, shown in Figure 4.14, is a paragraph with flush-left and -right edges.

NOTE. *The appearance of justified paragraphs is often improved by hyphenation. To let Word hyphenate automatically, choose Tools Hyphenation (Alt+O+H), turn off Confirm, and then choose OK. See Chapter 3 for details about hyphenation.*

Setting Paragraph Alignment with Speed-Keys
You can also use the Ctrl key combined with the letters indicating paragraph alignment (L for left, R for right, E for center, and J for justified) to align paragraphs. As an example, place the insertion pointer anywhere within a CHESS document paragraph, and press Ctrl+E; that paragraph will be centered. Press Ctrl+L, and the paragraph returns to the flush-left alignment.

Line Spacing

In Chapter 3, you learned that line spacing affects the amount of space between lines of a paragraph. (In Word, you can also change the space between paragraphs; this technique is explained in the next section, "Paragraph Spacing.")

To change a paragraph's line spacing, place the insertion pointer anywhere within the affected paragraph, and then choose the desired line spacing. One way to do this is to choose standard single-, line-and-a-half-, or double-spacing. You can do this by using speed-keys: Ctrl+1 for single-spacing; Ctrl+2 for double-spacing; or Ctrl+5 for line-and-a-half spacing.

Figure 4.14

The second paragraph is justified

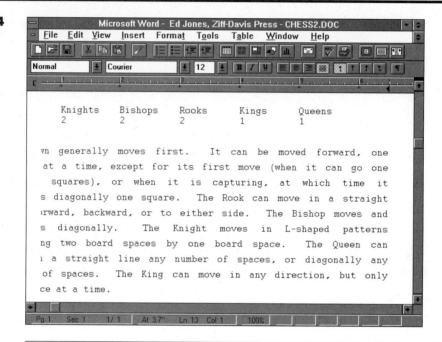

For added flexibility, Word lets you specify other line-spacing alternatives in addition to the three commonly used choices assigned to the speed-keys. If you choose the Format Paragraph command, in the Line Spacing list box you can choose the Exactly option, and in the At box enter any specific measurement value that Word understands—in inches (in), centimeters (cm), picas (pi), points (pt), or lines (li). Picas and points are units of typesetting measurement; 6 picas equal 1 inch, and 72 points equal 1 inch. If you enter a numeric value alone, Word assumes that you mean lines; this is the default.

Remember, also, that you can choose Auto from the Line Spacing list box to indicate automatic line spacing. With automatic line spacing, each line is as tall as the tallest character in that line. Word is set to automatic line spacing by default.

Paragraph Spacing

Word also lets you control the amount of space that appears before and after paragraphs. When you used the Format Paragraph command in earlier exercises, you may have noticed the Before and After text boxes in the Spacing area of the dialog box. (Take another look at Figure 4.7.) In these boxes, you can enter numeric values to add additional space before or after a paragraph. This space is added to any line spacing you specify. As with line spacing, you can enter any unit for paragraph spacing that Word understands—inches (in), centimeters (cm), picas (pi), points (pt), or lines (li). Word assumes lines as the default measurement unit.

The Ctrl+O and Ctrl+Zero key-combinations can also be used to set paragraph spacing. Press Ctrl+Zero to eliminate any added spacing between paragraphs; this sets the Before value for the selected paragraph to zero. Press Ctrl+O to set the Before value to one line (12 points).

Adding Borders and Shading to Paragraphs

The Format Border command can be used to apply borders, or shading, or both, to emphasize certain paragraphs in Word. You can use this same command to apply borders to graphics and tables (see Chapter 7 for details on applying borders to cells of a table). Borders are commonly used in newsletter layout, and you'll see examples of this in Chapter 11.

Applying Borders

Use the Format Border command (Alt+T+B) to place borders around a paragraph. When you choose Format Border, the Border Paragraphs dialog box appears. (If the insertion pointer is in a Word table or at a picture when you issue the command, the name of this dialog box changes to Border Cells or Border Picture; however, its operation is virtually identical.)

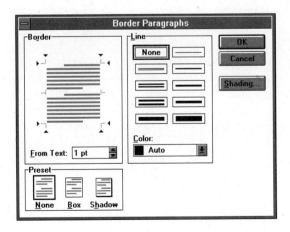

- The Border diagram in the upper-left of the dialog box displays a visual representation of the border options that you select. The From Text box can be used to specify the amount of space between the text and the border.

- In the Preset area, you can choose None (Alt+N) to have no border (useful for removing an existing border); Box (Alt+B) to have a box border drawn with a thin line; or Shadow (Alt+H) to have a shadow border.

- The Line (Alt+L) area offers line samples from which you can choose a line type for the border; as you choose a line type, a representation of it appears in the Border diagram. Word provides single- and double-line borders, in varying degrees of thickness.

- Use the Color (Alt+C) list box to choose a different color for the border. Remember that you must have a color monitor to display colors, and a color printer to print in color.

When you've chosen your border options, you can choose OK to apply them, or click the Shading button to design a shading pattern for the selected paragraphs.

TIP. *You can add a single-line border (rule) at the bottom of a paragraph, to separate a paragraph (such as a heading) from the text that follows it. To do this, select the paragraph and choose Format Border (Alt+T+B). With the mouse, click between the two bottom border indicators in the Border diagram. Choose a line thickness in the Line box, and then click OK. On the keyboard, press Alt+R to get into the Border diagram, and highlight the lower border indicators. Press Alt+L to choose a line thickness, and press Enter.*

Applying Shading

Another technique for emphasis is to apply shading in the background for paragraphs. Shading can be applied alone, or used along with borders to emphasize part of your document and make it stand out from other text.

To apply shading, select the Format Border command and choose the Shading button (Alt+S) to bring forth the Shading dialog box, shown here:

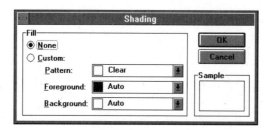

The Shading dialog box offers you a choice of shading patterns for the selected paragraphs. Choose Custom (Alt+C), and in the Pattern list box (Alt+P) scroll to or enter the desired pattern for the shading. As the illustration below shows, when you open this list box, Word displays a range of possible shadings, from Clear to Solid. Also available are various patterns based on small lines, such as DK Horizontal and DK Vertical, shown here:

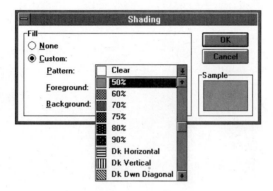

Once you have selected a pattern, you can also use the Foreground (Alt+F) and Background (Alt+B) boxes to add a foreground and background color for the shading. The default setting, Auto, uses the colors that are specified as default foreground and background colors in your Word Setup.

Choose OK twice, and all your chosen shading and border options will be applied to the selected paragraphs, or to the paragraph containing the insertion pointer if no selection exists.

TIP. *A centered paragraph stands out nicely if you make the heading a separate paragraph and add a shadow border to it.*

An Exercise with Borders and Shading

Try using borders and shading on the table in the CHESS2 document. Perform the following steps:

1. Use your favorite selection methods to select both lines of the table.

2. Press Ctrl+B to apply boldface to the table. (This isn't necessary, but is appropriate here because the shading you are about to apply tends to overpower letters in a normal font.)

3. Select Format Border (Alt+T+B).

4. In the Preset box, choose Shadow (Alt+H).

5. Choose the Shading button (Alt+S).

6. Open the Pattern list box (Alt+P), and choose 20%.

7. Choose OK twice to close both dialog boxes and apply the shading and the border to the table. Your document now resembles the example shown in Figure 4.15.

A Tip About Borders, Shading, and Typed Text

Borders and shading that you apply to a paragraph are stored by Word as part of the paragraph's formatting. Therefore, if you apply a border or shading to a paragraph and then continue typing, each new subsequent paragraph takes the same border or shading setting. If you don't want this to happen, move the insertion pointer outside the paragraph containing the border or shading, and then continue typing new paragraphs.

Keeping Paragraphs Together

There will be times when you want to prevent a paragraph from being divided at the end of a page, or two paragraphs from being separated by the end of a page. You can keep paragraphs together with the Pagination options of the Format Paragraph dialog box.

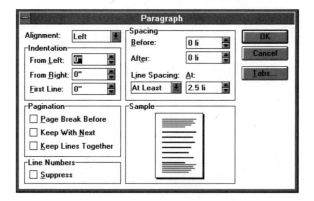

Select the affected paragraph first, and then choose Format Paragraph (Alt+T+P). The three Pagination options are Page Break Before, Keep With Next, and Keep Lines Together. If you mark the Keep Lines Together check box, the selected paragraph will not be divided over two pages; a paragraph that will not fit on one page will be printed at the start of the next page. Turn on the Keep With Next option, and you prevent a page break from occurring between the selected paragraph and the one that follows it. The Page Break Before option inserts a page break before the paragraph.

Figure 4.15
CHESS2 document, with border and shading added to the table

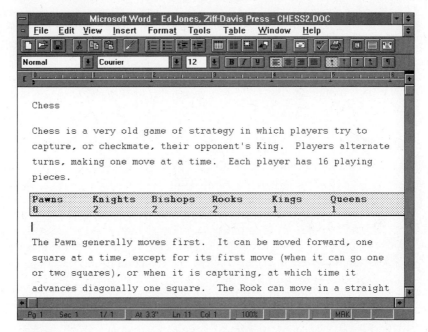

Tip. If you have created a table with a combination of tabs and newline characters, you can use the Keep Paragraph Together option of the Format Paragraph dialog box to keep the table from being divided by a page end.

NOTE. *If you have many long paragraphs in your document, it may not be possible for the Keep With Next and Keep Lines Together options to operate properly, in which case Word will ignore them. For example, if a single paragraph won't fit on a single page, Word ignores the Keep Lines Together option.*

Copying Paragraph Formatting

Mouse users can easily copy paragraph formatting from one paragraph to another. To copy a paragraph format, first select the paragraph to be formatted. Move the mouse pointer to the selection bar beside the paragraph containing the formatting you want to copy. Hold down the Ctrl and Shift keys, and click the left mouse button. The formatting will be copied to the selected paragraph.

Applying Tabs

Tabs (which were introduced in Chapter 3) are a typical method of organizing text in columns. For simple tables, and for a quick indentation of a single heading, tabs are a handy tool.

NOTE. *Although tabs are often used in the design of complex tables and for indenting the first line of a paragraph, you will want to remember that there are easier ways to do both in Word. To indent the first line of a paragraph, you can use the Indentation/First Line value in the Format Paragraph dialog box, or drag the first-line indent marker in the ruler, as described earlier. And complex tables are easily designed with Word's table feature, detailed in Chapter 7.*

As explained in Chapter 3, Word has default tab stops at every half-inch. You can use the Format Tabs command (Alt+T+T) to reset these default tabs, by changing the value for Default Tab Stops to any desired number of inches or centimeters.

Note. If you select a group of paragraphs having different tab settings, the ruler displays the tabs in effect for the first paragraph of the selection.

In addition to the default tab stops, Word lets you set custom tab stops for each paragraph. Custom tabs take precedence over default tabs; that is, whenever you set a custom tab, Word clears all default tabs that occur to the left of the custom tab. Custom tabs remain in effect until you change them; however, each paragraph in Word can have its own tab settings, so remember to use newline characters between lines of text whenever you want the same set of tabs to apply to all of the lines.

The default tab stops (or the custom ones you set) are visible as upside-down Ts along the ruler when it is turned on.

Types of Tabs

You can use the View Ruler command to turn on the ruler if it is not visible.

In Word, you can set four different types of tabs: left, center, right, and decimal. The type of tab indicates precisely where the text aligns with the tab stop. When you use a left or right tab, the left or right edge of the text aligns with the tab stop. With center tabs, the text automatically centers at the tab stop. And decimal tabs are used when you want to align the decimal point in numbers with the tab stop. Figure 4.16 illustrates all four types of tabs.

In the foregoing example, the first tab (set at the 1" position) is a center tab, so the text in the Department column appears centered at the tab stop. The second tab (set at the 2.5" position) is a left tab. This is the type of tab most commonly used in word processing applications, where the text is typed following the tab stop. The third tab, over the column labeled No. Emp., is a right tab. This type of tab is useful with whole numbers of varying lengths, because the right edge of the numbers will align with the tab stop. The last column (Budget) is a decimal tab. Here, even when the numbers vary in length, the tab causes the column to align correctly at the decimal point.

Figure 4.16

Types of tabs

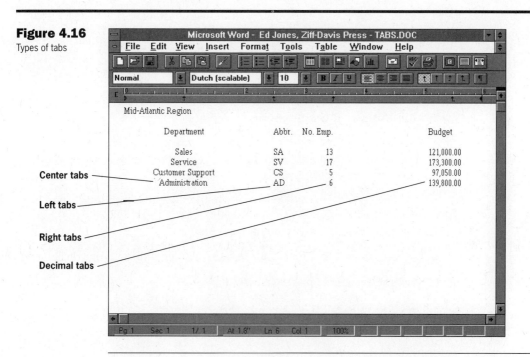

Also visible in Figure 4.16 are the appearances of the different tab types on the ruler. Left and right tabs appear as arrows pointing up and to the left or the right. A center tab appears as a simple upward-pointing arrow, and a decimal tab appears as an upward-pointing arrow beside a decimal point. The same symbols are used on the tab icons in the ribbon, as illustrated below.

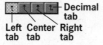

Setting Custom Tabs

There are three techniques for setting custom tabs: with the mouse and the ribbon icons, with the keyboard and the ruler cursor, or with the Format Tabs command. (The mouse-and-ribbon method is generally accepted to be the easiest way.)

With the Mouse and the Ribbon

Click on one of the tab icons in the ribbon to set a left, right, center, or decimal tab; then click just *under* the ruler line at the desired location for the tab.

For example, to set a center tab at the 2.5" point of the ruler, first click on the Center Tab icon in the ribbon, and then click just *under* the ruler line at the 2.5" marker.

WARNING! *If you click above or directly on the ruler line, the tab will not set. You must be pointing just* under *the ruler line.*

With the Ruler and the Keyboard

- Place the insertion pointer at the desired paragraph. Then activate the ruler mode by pressing Ctrl+Shift+F10. (You will see a block cursor appear within the ruler when you do this.)

- Press the ← and → arrow keys to move the ruler cursor to the desired location for the tab stop. You can also press Home and End to move the ruler cursor to the left or right indent marker.

- Type **1** for a left tab, **2** for a center tab, **3** for a right tab, or **4** for a decimal tab.

- Press the Ins key to insert the tab.

Repeat these steps to set additional tabs. When done, press Enter to deactivate the ruler cursor and apply the tabs to the paragraph.

With the Format Tabs Command

- Place the insertion pointer at the desired paragraph. Then select Format Tabs (Alt+T+T) to display the dialog box shown in Figure 4.17.

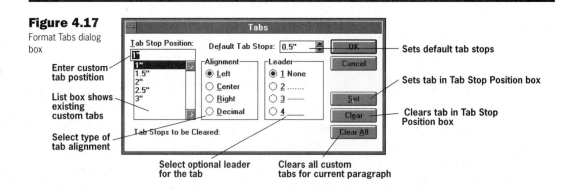

Figure 4.17
Format Tabs dialog box

- Enter the location for the tab in the Tab Stop Position (Alt+T) text box. Remember, Word assumes inches, but you can enter metric values by adding cm after the value; you can also enter points or picas.

- Specify the type of tab by choosing one of the buttons in the Alignment box.

- Choose the Set button (Alt+S) to set the tab.

To set additional tabs, go back to the Tab Stop Position and Alignment boxes and choose the location and alignment for each tab, choosing Set to establish each one. (The Leader option in the dialog box is for filling the tab space with leader characters, discussed in a later section.) When you have finished setting tabs, choose OK from the dialog box.

You may want to experiment to find which technique you prefer for setting different types of tabs, based on your hardware and the type of document you're working on. To start, duplicate the table shown in Figure 4.16. Using the various techniques, set a center tab at 1", a left tab at 2.5", a right tab at 3.5", and a decimal tab at 5.5". You can then type the table data as shown in the figure. Remember to use newline (Shift+Enter) between each line, so Word will recognize the entire table as a single paragraph. Try different tab alignments and positions for the columns. Save the document under the name TABS.DOC.

Moving and Clearing Tabs

After you've set tabs, you can move them and clear them with the same three methods: the ribbon icons and the mouse, the ruler and keyboard, or the Format Tabs command. Again, the mouse excels in these tasks. To move a tab with the mouse, simply click on the tab marker and drag it to the desired location. To clear a tab, drag the tab marker up or down off the ruler.

Without the mouse, using the ruler to move and clear tabs is a little more complicated. You cannot move a tab along the ruler without a mouse, but you can accomplish the same result by clearing the tab and then setting a new one in the desired location. To clear tabs, first turn on the ruler mode with Ctrl+Shift+F10. Move the ruler cursor to a tab stop, and press the Del key to clear it.

Using the Format Tabs command, you can move and clear tabs by working with the tab locations listed in the Format Tabs dialog box. Choose Format Tabs (Alt+T+T), and in the dialog box you'll see a scrollable list of the tab positions for all custom tabs. As an example, let's examine the tab positions in the TABS.DOC file you just created. Place the insertion pointer in the table of that document, and select the Format Tabs command. You'll see the dialog box shown in Figure 4.18. (If you've experimented with entering other custom tab settings in this file, your list of tab locations will be different.)

When you select a tab from the list box (using the mouse or the ↑ and ↓ keys), you can change its location by choosing Clear (Alt+E) and then typing in a different ruler location. Or you can select a different alignment (Alt+L for left, Alt+C for Center, Alt+R for Right, or Alt+D for decimal).

Then choose Set (Alt+S) to enter the tab marker. Repeat these steps to change another tab stop, or choose OK when you are done changing tabs. To clear a selected tab, choose the Clear button (Alt+E).

Figure 4.18

Format Tabs dialog box showing custom tabs from TABS document

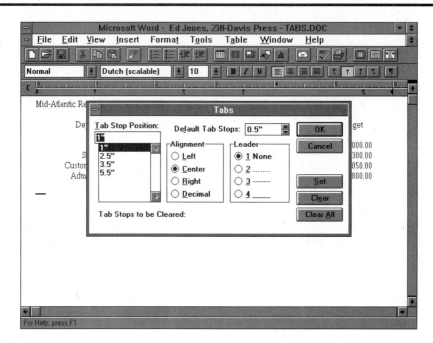

Clearing All Tabs

The fastest way to clear all custom tabs is to select Format Tabs (Alt+T+T), click on or select Clear All (Alt+A) from the dialog box, and then click on OK or press Enter. When you clear all custom tabs, the default tabs automatically take effect.

Using Leader Tabs

Some documents, such as tables of contents, can be enhanced by the use of *leader tabs*. With leader tabs, the blank space in front of the tab character itself is filled in with a series of characters (usually periods). Figure 4.19 shows a document that uses a leader tab set at the 4" position.

To define a leader tab, first set the tab using the Format Tabs command. When the dialog box appears, indicate the location and alignment for the tab, as explained earlier. Then choose the desired leader character (a period, hyphen, or underline). Select OK from the dialog box to set the tab, or choose Set and continue if you have more tabs to set.

Figure 4.19

Document with a
leader tab at 4"

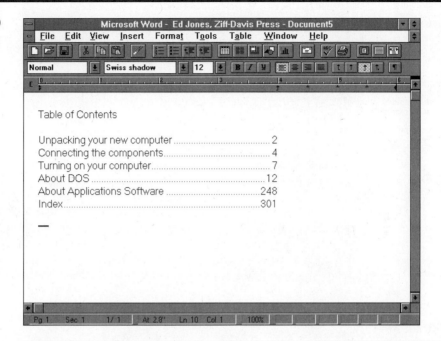

Editing Document Summaries

Though not part of document formatting per se, Word *document summaries* are an important aid to the document editing process. If you customarily press Enter to bypass the document summary screen every time you save a new document, you are missing out on a powerful and flexible tool for storing information about a document. This information is a helpful way to search for documents when you can't remember their file names. Document summaries are also useful for keeping track of author names associated with a document, and for storing comments and notes.

Tip. If you can't recall a file name, you can still find the file—by searching document summaries, using the File Find File command.

To view or edit the document summary for a file, open the document and select File Summary Info (Alt+F+I). The Summary Info dialog box appears, as shown in Figure 4.20.

The fields of this dialog box are self-explanatory; you can enter a document title, a subject, and any keywords that may help you identify the document later. The author's name is automatically inserted by Word, based on the name stored in the User Info category of the Tools Options dialog box, but you can change this author name here in the Summary Info dialog box. You can enter up to 255 characters in any of the fields.

Figure 4.20

Dialog box for editing document summary information

Enter information and comments about your document, to be used by the File Find File command

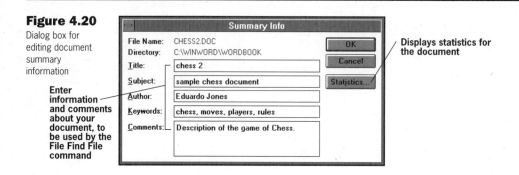

Displays statistics for the document

The Statistics button in the Summary Info dialog box is useful for obtaining productivity statistics and other facts regarding the document. Click this button, and you will see an information box like the one in Figure 4.21. The OK button returns you to the Summary Info dialog box, and the Update button lets you update the counts shown in the Statistics information box.

Figure 4.21

Statistics information box for the CHESS.DOC file

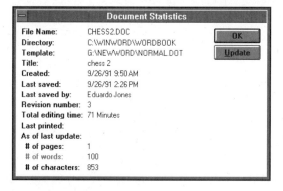

If you use the items in the Summary Info dialog box wisely for all your documents, you can later find documents based on those items—using the File Find File command. This is often helpful when you need to retrieve a document but you can't remember its file name. To look for a document based on document summary information, first select the File Find File command (Alt+F+F). From the dialog box that appears, choose Search to reveal the Search dialog box, as shown in Figure 4.22. Here you'll find text boxes for entering the title, subject, author, keywords, and other information on which to base your search. For example, if you typically fill in the Subject text box of the Summary Info dialog box, you can then enter your search criteria in the Subject field.

In the Path text box, enter the path names of any directories that you want to search through, separated correctly by commas or semicolons. Then fill in as much search criteria as possible to find the file. Choose Start Search or press Alt+S to begin the search. Word compiles a list of documents matching your search criteria and displays it in a drop-down list box; you can then select a document, and choose Open to open the file. For more details on the various options in the Find File and Search dialog boxes, refer to Chapter 16, "Finding and Managing Files."

Figure 4.22

Search dialog box

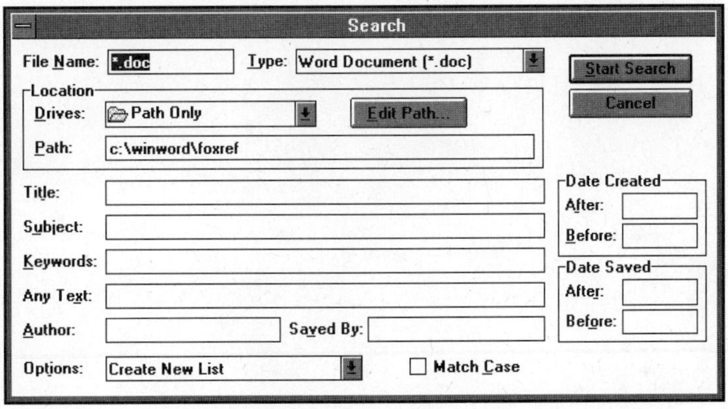

In the next chapter, you'll study how formatting can be applied to pages of a document, and to optional sections of a document.

Controlling the Page Layout

AS EXPLAINED IN THE PREVIOUS CHAPTER, WORD CAN FORMAT THE characters of your document, its paragraphs, and the entire document. Some other aspects of your documents, such as sections and columns, also affect Word's formatting of a document. Chapter 4 discussed formatting as it applies to characters and paragraphs of text. Here in Chapter 5 you'll continue your examination of formatting in Word, this time looking at the entire document, and at sections of documents.

Your document formatting tasks are accomplished using the Format Page Setup, Format Section Layout, and Format Columns commands, as well as some options from the Insert command menu.

Viewing Your Document Formatting

Many aspects of document formatting are not immediately visible on the screen. You can, however, get a preview of how they'll look on the printed page. One way is to turn on page layout view, described in Chapter 2. Choose the View Page Layout command (Alt+V+P), and you will enter page layout view. In this view, multiple columns appear side by side, and headers, footers, and footnotes appear in their proper locations. The View Page Layout command is a toggle, so you can turn page layout view on and off. Remember, Word is somewhat slower in page layout view than in its normal view. Figure 5.1 shows a portion of a sample document in page layout view.

Another technique you can use is Word's File Print Preview command (Alt+F+V). Described in Chapter 6, this command provides a visual representation of the printed page (see Figure 5.2).

Page Formatting

In Word, you use *page formatting* to control the appearance of *each page for the entire document*. Page formatting controls settings such as page size, orientation, and page margins. To change most aspects of page formatting, you use the Format Page Setup command (Alt+T+U). (Later you'll see how the Insert Footnote command also contributes to the page format.) When you choose Format Page Setup, you see one of three possible dialog boxes, depending on whether you select Margins, Size and Orientation, or Paper Source at the top of the dialog box. Look ahead to Figures 5.3, 5.6, and 5.7 to see these dialog boxes.

In all versions of the Page Setup dialog box, you will see a button called Use as Default, a list box called Apply To, and a Sample diagram. The Use as Default button lets you apply your page setup changes to Word's default settings. (If you are using a template other than the default NORMAL.DOT template, the changes are applied to the template you are using.) The options in the Apply To list box determine the portion of a document to which the choices you make will apply. Whole Document applies your changes to the entire document and This Point Forward applies your changes to the current page and all pages that follow. In a document with multiple sections, you are also given a choice called This Section; this setting applies the dialog box options to the current section of the document. The Sample diagram provides a visual representation of how your formatting changes will appear when applied to the printed page.

Figure 5.1

Sample document with two columns in page layout view

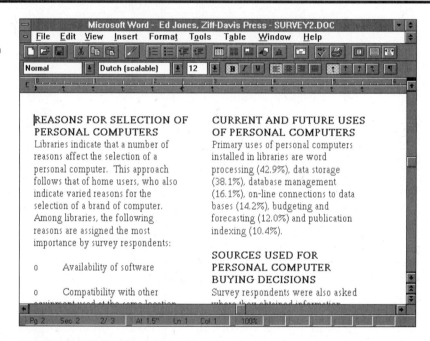

Setting Page Margins

The options that appear in the Page Setup dialog box when you select Margins are summarized here and shown in Figure 5.3.

- *Top and Bottom*: Enter a numeric value to determine the distance between the top of the page and the first printed line, or between the bottom of the page and the last printed line.

- *Left and Right*: Enter a numeric value to determine the distance between the left edge of the paper and the left edge of the printed lines, or between the right edge of the paper and the right edge of the printed lines. Remember that any indentations you give paragraphs will be added to this amount. Note that when you turn on the Facing Pages option (explained just below), the names of these options change to Inside and Outside.

Figure 5.2

A sample document in Print Preview mode

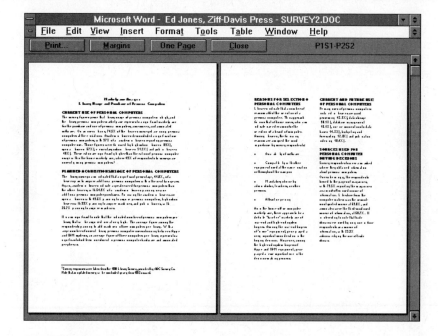

- *Gutter*: Enter a numeric value to determine the width of an optional *gutter*—the additional white space allowed for the binding of a document.

- *Facing Pages*: Turn on this feature to force inside and outside margins to alternate between odd and even pages (typically used when a double-sided document is to be bound in book form).

Page margins probably have a more significant effect on the page layout of a document than any other setting in Word. You use the page margins to adjust overall space on both sides of the printed text, as well as above and below the printed text.

In addition to the left, right, top, and bottom margins, Word also lets you specify a *gutter width*. This is a measurement of space that is added to the left side of odd-numbered pages, and to the right side of even-numbered pages. Gutter widths are typically added when you need to print a document that will be bound into book form; the added width provides room for the binding.

Figure 5.3

Format Page Setup
dialog box for
setting Margins

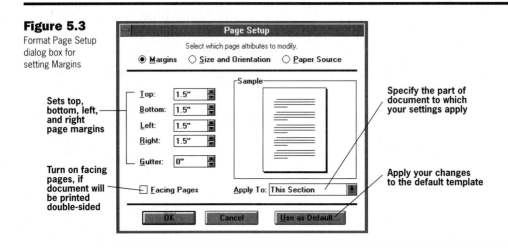

Sets top,
bottom, left,
and right
page margins

Turn on facing
pages, if
document will
be printed
double-sided

Specify the part of
document to which
your settings apply

Apply your changes
to the default template

Word also provides an option called Facing Pages that, when turned on, causes the inside and outside margins to alternate between odd and even pages. The Facing Pages feature is useful when you'll be printing a document on both sides of the paper and binding it into book form. In such cases you'll want the margin to always be wider on the inside, so you have to vary the margin placement on odd- and even-numbered pages.

All page margin settings are available when you choose Format Page Setup, and select Margins. In Figures 5.4 and 5.5, you can see the relationships between the various page margins, without and with the Facing Pages option enabled.

To set the page margins, select Format Page Setup (Alt+T+U), and if the margin settings are not visible in the dialog box, choose Margins (Alt+M). Tab to or click in the appropriate boxes for top, bottom, left, and right margins (or inside and outside if Facing Pages is turned on), and enter the desired values, in inches (the default). As with other measurements in Word, you can also enter the values using metric units, by typing cm for centimeters. And the top and bottom margins can be set in lines (li) if you wish.

If you have duplicated the sample document used in this chapter (or are using one of your own), try this next exercise. Many magazines require that article manuscripts be submitted with very wide margins (typically one-and-a-half inches) on each side of the document. With your sample document on screen, perform the following steps to apply this style of page formatting:

1. Choose Format Page Setup (Alt+T+U). If the page margin settings are not visible in the dialog box, press Alt+M.

2. Tab to or click in the Left entry box, and change the value to 1.5".

Figure 5.4
Relationship of
margin settings
when Facing Pages
is turned off

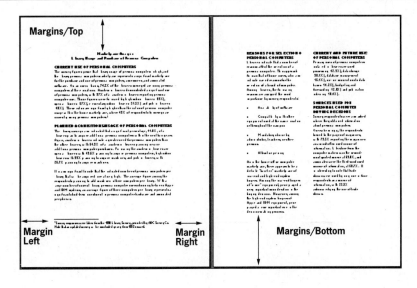

Figure 5.5
Relationship of
margin settings
when Facing Pages
is turned on

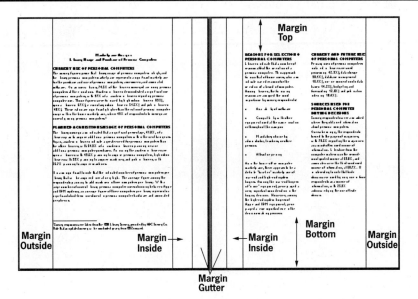

3. Tab to or click in the Right entry box, and change the value to 1.5".

4. Choose OK or press Enter.

One way to see the effect of the wider margins is to print the document. Also, keep in mind the File Print Preview and View Page commands. These can be very useful for getting an idea of what your document's margins will look like, before you print.

Setting Page Size and Orientation

The options that appear in the Page Setup dialog box when you select Size and Orientation are summarized here and shown in Figure 5.6.

- *Paper Size*: Select the desired paper size from this list box. The available choices are Letter, Legal, Executive, A4 and B5 (European), or Custom Size.

- *Width and Height*: When you use Custom Size as a paper size, enter the exact width and height for the custom paper in these text boxes.

- *Orientation*: In this list box, you can choose the printing orientation (Portrait or Landscape).

Various paper sizes can be accommodated in Word with the Width and Height settings available in the Page Setup dialog box for Size and Orientation. Word uses these settings to adjust the format of the page to the size of the paper you're using. The default page width is 8.5 inches and the default height is 11 inches; this matches standard American letter-size paper. Just choose Format Page Setup (Alt+T+U), and choose the Size and Orientation version of the dialog box (Alt+S). Next, enter the desired paper dimensions in the Width and Height text boxes.

If you're using international (metric-sized) paper, remember that you can enter measurements in Word's dialog boxes using centimeters, so it is a simple matter to enter dimensions for European paper sizes. For example, paper dimensions of 21cm wide and 29.7cm long correspond to European A4 letter-size paper.

From this same dialog box, you can also select Portrait or Landscape as the orientation for the paper. In Portrait (what most users consider "normal" orientation) text runs from left to right across the width of the page. Choose Landscape, and the orientation is rotated 90 degrees from normal, so text runs from left to right down the length of the page. The landscape format can be useful for very wide documents, such as budgets and tables of information.

Figure 5.6

Format Page Setup
dialog box for
setting Size and
Orientation

Sets paper
size

Choose
orientation

Specify the
part of
document to
which your
settings apply

Applies your
changes to the
default template

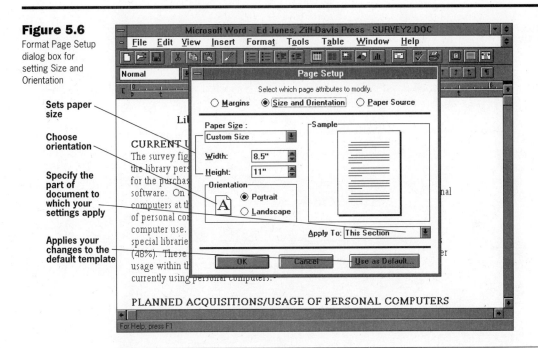

Setting the Paper Source

The options that appear in the Page Setup dialog box when you select
Paper Source are First Page and Other Page (see Figure 5.7). Use either of
these options to specify which bin of your printer will supply paper for the
first printed page and for the remaining pages of the document. (If your
printer does not support multiple-bin printing, you will not be able to
access these options.)

If your printer provides multiple feeding sources (bins or trays) of paper,
you can use the Paper Source option of the Page Setup dialog box to choose
a source for the first page, and for all other pages. This is useful with printers
that may have letterhead loaded in one bin, and normal paper in another
bin. Just select Format Page Setup (Alt+T+U), and click the button or press
Alt+P to bring up the Paper Source version of the dialog box. Choose the
appropriate bins from the First Page (Alt+F) and Other Pages (Alt+O) list
boxes, and choose OK.

Inserting Page Breaks

In a document of any complexity, there are likely to be places where you do
not want Word to insert an automatic page break. Perhaps you have a table

that should not be split between two pages, or you want to make sure a new page starts after a certain paragraph. You can control where new pages begin by adding *page breaks* to your documents. In Word, as in most word processors, there are two kinds of page breaks: soft and hard. A *soft page break* is one that Word inserts automatically, when typed text reaches the end of a page. A *hard page break* is manually inserted with the Insert Break command or its Ctrl+Enter hotkey.

Figure 5.7

Format Page Setup dialog box for setting Paper Source

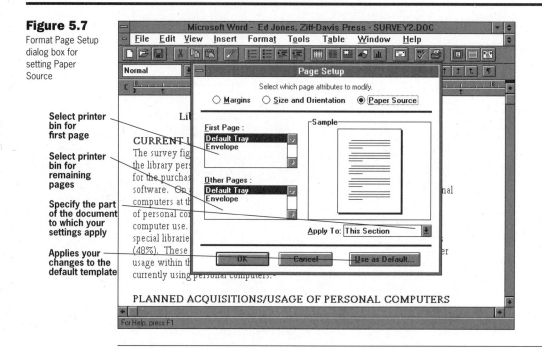

Select printer bin for first page

Select printer bin for remaining pages

Specify the part of the document to which your settings apply

Applies your changes to the default template

- To insert a hard page break, place the insertion pointer at the location for the desired page break. Press Ctrl+Enter to insert the page break, or you can select the Insert Break command. In the dialog box that appears, click the Page Break check box (or press Alt+P) and choose OK. The page break is visibly indicated on screen by a single dotted line.

- To delete an unwanted hard page break, use the Backspace or Del key, or select the page break line itself and choose Edit Cut (Alt+E+T) or click the Cut icon in the Toolbar.

The dotted lines for hard and soft page breaks look slightly different on the screen. Figure 5.8 contains both a soft page break (after the first paragraph) and a hard page break (after the second paragraph). In the hard page break line, you can see that the dots are spaced closer together.

Figure 5.8

Soft and hard page breaks within a document

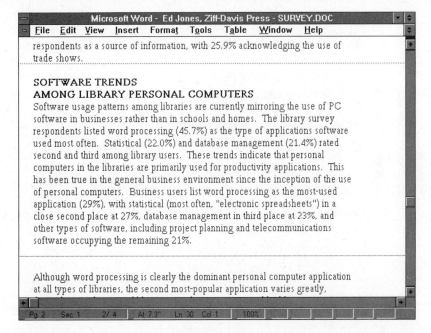

TIP. *In large documents, it may be wise to avoid using hard page breaks unless absolutely necessary, because they tend to cause problems when you edit the document. If you add, delete, or move significant amounts of text during editing, chances are that some of the existing hard page breaks will no longer be in the proper location, and you will then need to delete them and add others elsewhere. You can often avoid using hard page breaks altogether, by employing a combination of newline characters between lines, and the Keep Lines Together option of the Format Paragraph command. As explained in Chapter 4, when you turn on Keep Lines Together for a given paragraph, Word will not divide that paragraph by a page break.*

A Note About Widow Control and Page Breaks

In Word, *widow/orphan control* is turned on by default. Widow/orphan control prevents page breaks from occurring between the first two or the last two lines of a paragraph. This keeps the document from having "orphans" and "widows," where a line of a paragraph gets separated from the remainder of the paragraph and appears isolated on the previous or following page.

Word's widow/orphan control moves the page break forward a line, so that at least two lines of the paragraph will always print on the same page. Widow/orphan control is only effective for paragraphs that are at least four lines in length.

If, for some reason, you want to disable Word's widow/orphan control, you can do so from the Print category under the Tools Options command. Select Tools Options (Alt+O+O), then choose Print in the Category list box (Alt+C), turn off the Widow/orphan Control feature (Alt+W), and then choose OK or press Enter.

Note that Word's widow/orphan control does not prevent an entire paragraph from being interrupted by a page break. You can, however, use the Keep Lines Together option of the Format Paragraph dialog box to accomplish this task. See Chapter 4 for details.

Section Formatting

Think of sections in a document as "portions" that carry certain formatting characteristics of their own. At first, the concept of sections may be difficult to conceive, because so many DOS-based word processors apply formatting to characters, lines, or entire pages. But learning how sections operate in Word is worth the effort, because section formatting can add flexibility to how your document is formatted overall. If you have used Word for DOS, or powerful desktop publishing software such as Xerox's Ventura Publisher or Aldus's PageMaker, the concept of formatting in sections will be more familiar to you. Word for DOS uses "divisions," which are equivalent to sections under Word for Windows.

Typically, you'll use section formatting when you want to change the number of columns, or the style of page numbering for a section of the document. Changes that affect all pages of a document, such as page margins, are part of page formatting (as detailed earlier in this chapter).

Even in a very short document, you are still using sections, although you may not give them any thought. In a short document (like a one-page memo), the entire document generally consists of a single section, and so you can use Word's section formatting commands to control certain elements of its layout.

NOTE. *Users of earlier versions of Word for Windows will note a significant change in section formatting in Version 2.0. With Word for Windows Versions 1.0 and 1.1, the Format Section command provided most of the options needed for changing section formatting. In Word for Windows 2.0, however, many aspects of section formatting are now controlled by commands other than the Format Section Layout command. The paragraphs that follow will familiarize you with these commands and how to use them to accomplish section formatting.*

The Format Section Layout Command

You control some aspects of section formatting with the Format Section Layout (Alt+T+S) command, which offers the Section Layout dialog box shown in Figure 5.9. At the top of the dialog box, the words *Apply To Section* followed by a number indicate the current section number, and the options you choose will apply to that section. These format options are summarized in the following paragraphs.

Figure 5.9

Format Section
Layout dialog box

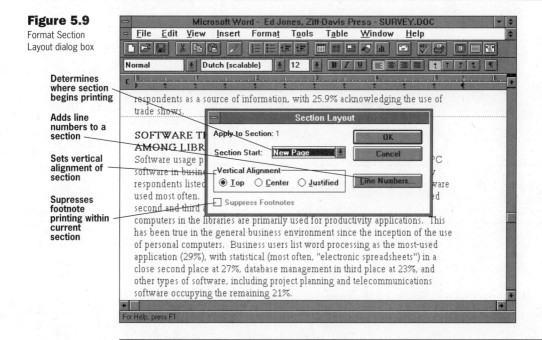

Section Start   Select an option in the list box to determine where the section should begin printing, in relation to the previous section. The choices are Continuous (immediately following the prior section, with no page break), New Page (at the top of a new page), New Column (at the top of a new column), Even Page (on the next even-numbered page), or Odd Page (on the next odd-numbered page).

Vertical Alignment/Top, Center, or Justify   You can align the top line of a page with the top page margin (the default), or center the lines of a page between the top and bottom page margins. Or, with Justified, you can increase space between paragraphs as necessary, so that the top line aligns with the top margin, and the bottom line aligns with the bottom margin.

Supress Footnotes   When turned on, this option supresses footnotes for the current section. For this check box to be available, you must select End of Section in the Footnote Options dialog box. (See the section "Adding Footnotes" at the end of this chapter for details.)

Line Numbers   Select this button to see another dialog box that lets you add line numbers to the section.

Starting Sections with Insert Break

The simple documents you have worked with in examples so far have all been single-section documents. In more complex documents, you'll need a way to define a new section whenever you need to change an aspect of section formatting. To start a new section, use the Insert Break (Alt+I+B) command. The Insert Break dialog box is shown in Figure 5.10.

Figure 5.10

Insert Break dialog box

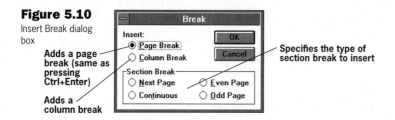

Adds a page break (same as pressing Ctrl+Enter)

Adds a column break

Specifies the type of section break to insert

In addition to starting a new section, the options in this dialog box also let you start a new column or insert a page break. Word usually inserts page breaks automatically as you go along, but when you need a page break before the normal end of a page, you can use the Page Break option, or its Ctrl+Enter hotkey equivalent, to insert one. (This subject is covered more thoroughly in "Inserting Page Breaks" earlier in this chapter.) Turning on Column Break causes a new column to begin in the text. You'll learn more about columns later. You can insert both types of breaks at the same location; for example, you might want to begin a new page and switch from a single column to double columns at the same point in a document.

When you use Insert Break to designate a section, you can choose one of four types of section breaks; Next Page, Odd Page, Even Page, or Continuous. Next Page means the new section will begin at the next page break; this can be a page break that Word inserts automatically, or a page break that you add. Odd Page and Even Page mean that the new section will begin on the next odd-numbered page or even-numbered page. Continuous means that the new section will begin immediately following the prior section.

Once you select the desired type of break and choose OK (or press Enter), a section break appears in the document. As Figure 5.11 shows, a section break is shown as two closely adjacent dotted lines.

Figure 5.11

The CHESS document with a section break inserted

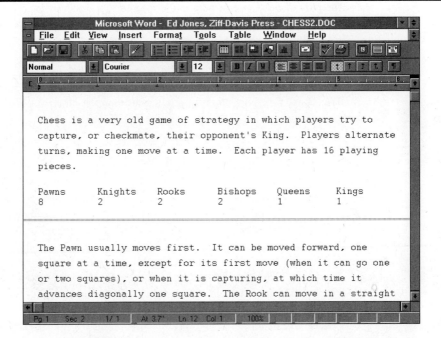

Formatting a Complex Document

To illustrate techniques of page and section formatting, this chapter will use the sample two-page document shown in Figure 5.12. If you want to follow the exercises throughout this chapter, you can enter and save the text in this document (excluding the footnote), or use an existing document of your own that is two or more full pages in length.

Starting a New Section

Suppose you want to switch to multicolumn text at a point in the sample document. First, follow these steps to start a new section. Later you will choose the new column format.

Figure 5.12

Example of a
complex document

Marketplace Analysis
Library Usage and Purchase of Personal Computers

CURRENT USE OF PERSONAL COMPUTERS

The survey figures prove that library usage of personal computers is high, and the library personal computer marketplace represents a significant marketplace for the purchase and use of personal computers, accessories, and associated software. On an overall basis, 74.5% of the libraries surveyed are using personal computers at their locations. Academic libraries demonstrated a significant use of personal computers, with 97% of all academic libraries reporting personal computer use. Those figures were followed by high school libraries (83%), special libraries (67%), elementary school libraries (51.5%) and public libraries (48%). These ratios are significantly higher than the ratios of personal computer usage within the home marketplace, where 43% of respondents to surveys are currently using personal computers.[1]

PLANNED ACQUISITIONS/USAGE OF PERSONAL COMPUTERS

The library surveys also indicated that a significant percentage, 41.8%, of all libraries plan to acquire additional personal computers within the next two years. Again, academic libraries indicate a greater need for personal computers than the other libraries, with 64.9% of all academic libraries planning new or additional personal computer purchases. Following the academic libraries are special libraries with 43.6% planning to acquire personal computers, high school libraries with 33% planning to acquire machines, and public libraries, with 26.7% planning to acquire machines.

It is also significant to note that the indicated number of personal computers per library that will be acquired is relatively high. The average figure among the respondents planning to add machines is three computers per library. With a large number of current library personal computer users choosing between Apple and IBM systems, an average figure of three computers per library represents a significant short-term investment in personal computer hardware and associated peripherals.

---

[1]Survey responses were taken from the 1990 Library Survey, provided by ABC Survey Co. Note that an updated survey will be conducted yearly from 1992 onward.

Figure 5.12
(continued)

REASONS FOR SELECTION OF PERSONAL COMPUTERS
Libraries indicate that a number of reasons affect the selection of a personal computer. This approach follows that of home users, who also indicate varied reasons for the selection of a brand of computer. Among libraries, the following reasons are assigned the most importance by survey respondents:

o   Availability of software

o   Compatibility with other equipment used at the same location or throughout the campus

o   Mandatory choice by administrator, teachers, or other persons.

o   Attractive pricing

As in the home–office computer marketplace, there appears to be a definite "two–tier" marketplace of low–end and high–end system buyers. Among the low–end buyers of "clone" equipment, price played a very important consideration in the buying decision. However, among the high-end system buyers of Apple and IBM equipment, price played a less–important role in the decision–making process.

CURRENT AND FUTURE USES OF PERSONAL COMPUTERS
Primary uses of personal computers installed in libraries are word processing (42.9%), data storage (38.1%), database management (16.1%), on–line connections to data bases (14.2%), budgeting and forecasting (12.0%) and publication indexing (10.4%).

SOURCES USED FOR PERSONAL COMPUTER BUYING DECISIONS
Survey respondents were also asked where they obtained information about personal computers. Overwhelmingly, the respondents turned to the pages of magazines, with 73.5% reporting the magazines as a most–often used source of information. Literature from the computer makers was the second–most quoted source at 63.0%, and associates were the third–most used source of information, at 60.7%. It is interesting to note that trade shows were used by only one in four respondents as a source of information, with 25.9% acknowledging the use of trade shows.

1. Place the insertion pointer near the bottom of the first page of your two-page document.

2. Select Insert Break (Alt+I+B) to start a new section.

3. In the dialog box that appears, turn on the Next Page button (Alt+N) in the Section Break area, and choose OK or press Enter.

As a result, the section break appears between the first and second pages of the document, replacing Word's automatic page-break line. When you use the Format Section Layout command, the options you select there will apply to the section of the document in which you position the insertion pointer. (This is not meant to imply that a section can contain only one page; you can have as many pages within a section as you wish.)

Now that you've inserted the section break, you can proceed to apply different formatting to each section, as in these next examples.

Creating Multicolumn Text

A common use for sections is when you need to change the number of columns in a document. Most business documents contain just one column, but multicolumn text appears in many reports and is common in newsletters. There are three ways you can add columns to a document: with the Format Columns command as discussed here, with the Columns icon in the Toolbar (which accomplishes the same result as the Format Columns command), or by adding columns as paragraphs of text within Word tables. If you use the Format Columns command or the Columns icon of the Toolbar, your columns must all be the same width. If you want to create columns of differing widths, use Word's table feature, as described in Chapter 7.

Columns created with the Format Columns command (or with the Columns icon) are formed (by Word) by evenly dividing up the space available based on your page layout. Word takes the available printing space (the paper width minus the page margins) and divides it by the number of columns you have requested. Note that there is a limit to how many columns you can have; each column must be at least as wide as the space between the default tab stops. If you attempt to create a section with columns that would be narrower than this space, Word displays an error message stating that your margins are too large.

To designate multicolumn text for a section, select Format Columns (Alt+T+O). In this dialog box, you enter the desired number of columns; you can also determine the space between columns, and whether a line appears between the columns. As an example, let's arrange the second section (page) of the sample document in two columns, separated by a half-inch of white space.

Tip. A quick way to view multicolumn text on your screen is to turn on page layout view with the View command (Alt+V+P). The lines between columns are visible only with Page Preview, however.

1. Place the insertion pointer anywhere within the second page of the document.

2. Select Format Columns (Alt+T+O).

3. Enter **2** in the Number of Columns text box.

4. Leave Space Between set at the default of 0.5 inches. This provides for a half-inch of white space between the columns.

5. Make sure that the Line Between option is turned on (if necessary, click in the check box or press Alt+L). This tells Word to draw a solid line between the columns.

6. Choose OK or press Enter.

When printed, the second section of your document will be in two columns, resembling Figure 5.13. (Take another look at Figure 5.2 to see this text on the screen in page view.)

Applying Line Numbering

Some documents (particularly those produced in attorneys' offices) utilize *line numbers*. You can add line numbers to a section by selecting Format Section Layout (Alt+T+S), and clicking the Line Numbers button. You'll then see another dialog box as shown here:

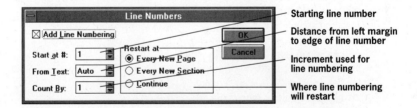

Note. Line numbers appear in your printed document, but not on screen, unless you use Print Preview. Select File Print Preview (Alt+F+V), and choose Cancel when done to return to your document.

You must turn on Add Line Numbering in this dialog box. Once you do so, the remaining options are enabled. The Start At option lets you specify the first line number. By default this is 1, but you might need to change this (for example, after a section that ended with line 52, you would want to start a new section's line numbering with 53. In the From Text box, you can enter a decimal value indicating the distance from the left margin to the right edge of the line numbers. If you leave this value set at the default of Auto, Word makes its own judgment for the best distance to use, based on the page margins. Use the Count By box to enter a value for the line numbers increment.

In the Restart At box, the Every New Page, Every New Section, and Continue buttons let you designate when the line numbering will begin.

Figure 5.13
The second section
of the sample
document with text
in two columns

REASONS FOR SELECTION OF PERSONAL COMPUTERS

Libraries indicate that a number of reasons affect the selection of a personal computer. This approach follows that of home users, who also indicate varied reasons for the selection of a brand of computer. Among libraries, the following reasons are assigned the most importance by survey respondents:

o   Availability of software

o   Compatibility with other equipment used at the same location or throughout the campus

o   Mandatory choice by administrator, teachers, or other persons.

o   Attractive pricing

As in the home–office computer marketplace, there appears to be a definite "two–tier" marketplace of low–end and high–end system buyers. Among the low–end buyers of "clone" equipment, price played a very important consideration in the buying decision. However, among the high–end system buyers of Apple and IBM equipment, price played a less–important role in the decision–making process.

CURRENT AND FUTURE USES OF PERSONAL COMPUTERS

Primary uses of personal computers installed in libraries are word processing (42.9%), data storage (38.1%), database management (16.1%), on–line connections to data bases (14.2%), budgeting and forecasting (12.0%) and publication indexing (10.4%).

SOURCES USED FOR PERSONAL COMPUTER BUYING DECISIONS

Survey respondents were also asked where they obtained information about personal computers. Overwhelmingly, the respondents turned to the pages of magazines, with 73.5% reporting the magazines as a most–often used source of information. Literature from the computer makers was the second–most quoted source at 63.0%, and associates were the third–most used source of information, at 60.7%. It is interesting to note that trade shows were used by only one in four respondents as a source of information, with 25.9% acknowledging the use of trade shows.

Choose Every New Page if you want the line numbering to start from the beginning on each new page; choose Every New Section to restart from the beginning of each section. Choose Continue if you want line numbering to continue from the last line number of the prior section.

Here is an exercise for adding and viewing line numbers in your sample document:

1. Select Format Section Layout (Alt+T+S). The insertion pointer can be anywhere in the section.

2. Turn on Line Numbering by pressing Alt+L twice (once to get to the Line Numbers dialog box, and once to turn on Add Line Numbering). The default Line Numbers settings can be left as is, or you can change them if you want to experiment.

3. Choose OK twice (or press Enter twice) to put away both dialog boxes.

4. Select File Print Preview (Alt+F+V). On your screen you'll see a representation of how the printed document will look, complete with the line numbers (Figure 5.14).

5. Choose Cancel to exit the Print Preview and return to the document.

Figure 5.14

A document with line numbers in Print Preview mode

Line numbers

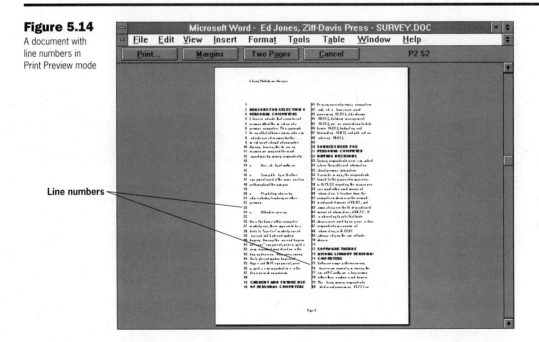

TIP. *If your document contains multicolumn text, the line numbers will appear beside each column. You may want to experiment with the distance value in the From Text box, to get the best arrangement of the line numbers within their respective columns.*

Changing Vertical Alignment

At times you may need to align text vertically on a page. Word lets you do so within a section. Normally, Word aligns text so that the top of the text is vertically aligned with the top margin for the page. You can change this by selecting Format Section Layout (Alt+T+S) and choosing the desired vertical alignment (Top, Center, or Justified) setting:

- Top (the default) aligns the top of each page with the top margin for the page.

- Center places the text for each page of the section between the top and bottom margins. (This is typically done only when a section contains less than a full page of text, and you want the text to be visually centered on the page.)

- With Justify, vertical space is added between lines as needed, so that the first line aligns with the top page margin, and the last line aligns with the bottom page margin. The Justify setting is handy for producing documents that will be bound into book form; by turning on Justify, you can insure that each page has the same visual length and width.

Applying Headers, Footers, and Page Numbers

You can add *headers and footers* to your document with the View Header/Footer command. Headers and footers are typically text, such as page numbers, document or chapter titles, and dates, that appear at the top and bottom of each page. (Do not confuse footers with *footnotes*, which are reference notes that sometimes appear at the bottom of a page. You'll find footnotes explained at the end of this chapter.)

Headers and footers are part of your section formatting because headers and footers apply to a specific section. Word creates headers, footers, and page numbers by inserting special fields into your document (see Chapter 9). By default, Word carries over any headers or footers you establish in a given section to all sections that follow; however, you can easily designate specific headers and footers for any given section, by using the View Header/Footer command once within that section. You can also specify that headers or footers appear on all pages, only on odd pages, or only on even pages. (This lets you place alternating headers on odd and even pages.) And you can specify a different header or footer for the first page of the document. All these settings are explained later in the section.

Tip. If all you need
are page numbers,
select Insert Page
Numbers (Alt+I+U).
From the dialog box,
choose Top of Page
or Bottom of Page
to place the page
numbers vertically,
and choose Left,
Center, or Right to
place the numbers
horizontally. Then
choose OK.

Typically, page numbers are a type of header or footer, and you can add
page numbers to a document in two ways. You can use the Insert Page Numbers command, in which case Word automatically adds a header or footer
that consists of just a page number. Or you can use the View Header/Footer
command to add a header or footer, and include the page number therein.
This next exercise demonstrates the addition of page numbers.

WARNING! *Before adding a header or footer, make sure you are not using
the page view mode of Word. Procedures for editing headers and footers in
page view are different from those in the other view modes of Word. See your
Microsoft Word for Windows documentation for details.*

1. Be sure you are not in page view mode. Then select View Header/Footer
   (Alt+V+H). The Header/Footer dialog box appears, as shown in Figure 5.15.

Figure 5.15

Header/Footer
dialog box

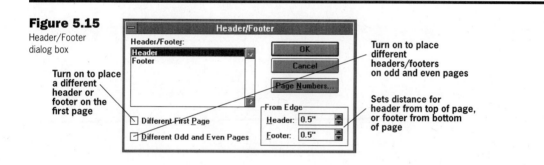

2. Click in the list box (or tab to it and move the highlight) to choose
   Header or Footer. Click on OK or press Enter. The dialog box goes
   away, and the Header/Footer pane and icon bar appears in the lower
   half of your screen, as shown in Figure 5.16. The (S1) you see beside the
   word Header or Footer in the icon bar means you are currently in section 1 of your document (you'll see S2 if you are in Section 2).

When the Header/Footer pane is open, a split bar appears in a vertical scroll
bar. Mouse users can drag the split bar up and down to change the size of the
Header/Footer pane. With the vertical scroll bar, you can scroll the contents
of the pane. This is helpful when you're working with a large header or
footer, such as one that contains a graphics image.

3. Type the desired header or footer in the pane. You are not limited to a
   single line, as is the case with some word processors; you could enter an
   entire paragraph as a header or footer, if desired.

4. When done, click on Close in the pane's icon bar, or press Shift+F10, then C.

Figure 5.16

The Header/Footer pane and icon bar

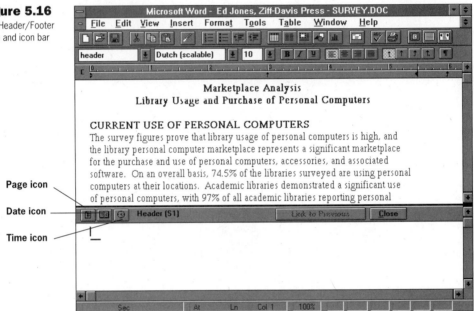

Page icon

Date icon

Time icon

Remember that you can see headers or footers in page view mode, and a representation of them in Print Preview.

Designing the Header/Footer Itself

You can apply character and paragraph formatting to headers and footers just as you do to other text. Simply select the header/footer text, and apply the formatting. For instance, if you want the header/footer centered, press Ctrl+E. To apply boldface or italic, click on the Bold or Italic icon in the ribbon (or press Ctrl+B for Bold or Ctrl+I for Italic). If you want the header/footer to appear flush with the right margin, press Ctrl+R.

In addition to text, you can add the current date, the current time, or the page number to the header or footer. These can be added with the icons of the Header/Footer pane, or with keystroke equivalents. As illustrated in Figure 5.16, the icon containing the calendar is the Date icon; the one with the clock is the Time icon; and the one with the number (#) symbol is the Page Number icon. To add one of these items to your header/footer, click on the appropriate icon, or use the following Shift-key combinations while typing the header or footer:

Keystroke Combination	Effect on Header/Footer
Shift+F10, then D	Adds current date
Shift+F10, then T	Adds current time
Shift+F10, then P	Adds current page number

A "running" page number can also be entered as part of the header or footer. For example, if you want a footer that reads "Section 2, Page *n*," (with *n* being the appropriate page number), select the View Header/Footer command, choose Footer from the list box, type **Section 2, Page** in the Footer pane, and click on the Page icon (or press Shift+F10, then P). Word will add the footer and supply the page number.

TIP. *Word does not limit you to placing only text in a header/footer; graphics can also be used. You can insert any image that has been copied to the Windows Clipboard. While editing the header or footer in the pane, select Edit Paste (Alt+E+P) or the Paste icon in the Toolbar to paste the image from the Clipboard into the header/footer at the insertion pointer location. The image is visible in page view or when using Print Preview.*

Examples of Headers and Footers in a Document

Let's return to the sample document you've been using in this chapter, and practice using Word's various settings for headers and footers. First, be sure you're in Page Layout mode, then add a header and a footer, as follows:

1. Move the insertion pointer to the start of the document, and select View Header/Footer (Alt+V+H).

2. In the dialog box, make sure Header is selected in the list box (it's the default), and then choose OK or press Enter. The Header/Footer pane and icon bar then appear at the bottom of the screen.

3. Enter the words **Library Marketplace Analysis**.

4. Click the Close icon, or press Shift+F10, then C. This completes the process of adding the header.

5. Select View Header/Footer (Alt+V+H).

6. Tab to or click in the list box to highlight and select Footer. Choose OK or press Enter, and the Header/Footer pane and icon bar again appears.

7. Enter the word **Page** followed by a space.

8. Click the Page icon (or press Shift+F10, then P).

9. Press Ctrl+E (or click the Center icon in the ribbon) to center the footer.

10. Click on the Close icon, or press Shift+F10, then C. This completes the process of adding the footer.

If you want, print part of the document to see what the headers and footers look like. Or you can use the File Print Preview command (Alt+F+V) to see an on-screen representation of the printed document, containing the headers and footers. Figure 5.17 shows a printed page from the sample document, with the new header and footer added.

Editing the Header/Footer Options

You can modify certain characteristics of the headers and footers, such as where they are positioned, the format used for page numbering, and the starting page number for the current section.

To change the position of the header/footer, use the Header and Footer text boxes in the From Edge area of the Header/Footer dialog box. (You can enter a measurement value to specify how far the header or footer will be from the edge of the paper.)

WARNING! *Most laser printers will not print information that is within one-half inch of the top or bottom of the page. If you change the From Edge measurement so that the header/footer is less than one-half inch from the top or bottom of the page, your header/footer may not get printed.*

Choose the Page Numbers button from the Header/Footer dialog box to display an additional Page Number Format dialog box, shown below, that lets you change the format used for the page numbers:

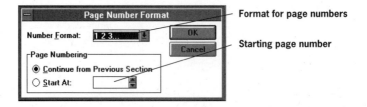

In this dialog box, a Start At text box lets you enter the starting page number (the default is 1). In the Number Format list box, you can choose a format for the page numbers. Word offers you five choices: arabic (1,2,3), lowercase alphabetic (a,b,c), uppercase alphabetic (A,B,C), lowercase roman numerals (i,ii,iii) and uppercase roman numerals (I,II,III). Turn on

Figure 5.17
Page from sample document, containing added header and footer

Library Marketplace Analysis

REASONS FOR SELECTION OF PERSONAL COMPUTERS

Libraries indicate that a number of reasons affect the selection of a personal computer. This approach follows that of home users, who also indicate varied reasons for the selection of a brand of computer. Among libraries, the following reasons are assigned the most importance by survey respondents:

o   Availability of software

o   Compatibility with other equipment used at the same location or throughout the campus

o   Mandatory choice by administrator, teachers, or other persons.

o   Attractive pricing

As in the home-office computer marketplace, there appears to be a definite "two-tier" marketplace of low-end and high-end system buyers. Among the low-end buyers of "clone" equipment, price played a very important consideration in the buying decision. However, among the high-end system buyers of Apple and IBM equipment, price played a less-important role in the decision-making process.

CURRENT AND FUTURE USES OF PERSONAL COMPUTERS

Primary uses of personal computers installed in libraries are word processing (42.9%), data storage (38.1%), database management (16.1%), on-line connections to data bases (14.2%), budgeting and forecasting (12.0%) and publication indexing (10.4%).

SOURCES USED FOR PERSONAL COMPUTER BUYING DECISIONS

Survey respondents were also asked where they obtained information about personal computers. Overwhelmingly, the respondents turned to the pages of magazines, with 73.5% reporting the magazines as a most-often used source of information. Literature from the computer makers was the second-most quoted source at 63.0%, and associates were the third-most used source of information, at 60.7%. It is interesting to note that trade shows were used by only one in four respondents as a source of information, with 25.9% acknowledging the use of trade shows.

the Continue from Previous Section option to tell Word to continue page numbering in sequence from the previous section. Once you have selected all the desired options, choose OK or press Enter to implement the header/footer.

Using the Insert Page Numbers Command

As mentioned earlier, page numbers are a simplified form of header or footer. If you want to add plain, unadorned page numbers with no text of any sort, one way is to use the View Header/Footer command, and insert just the page number as the header or footer. It is probably faster, however, to use the Insert Page Numbers command, which automatically adds a header or footer to your document that contains only a page number.

If you want to try page numbers in your practice document, select Insert Page Numbers (Alt+I+U). You will see this Page Numbers dialog box:

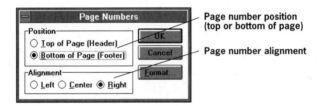

Page number position (top or bottom of page)

Page number alignment

The buttons in the dialog box let you select Top of Page (the page numbers will appear as a header) or Bottom of Page (the page numbers will appear as a footer). You can also designate a horizontal placement of left, center, or right. Select the desired options with the mouse, or with these Alt+key equivalents: Alt+T and Alt+B for top or bottom; Alt+L, Alt+C, and Alt+R for left, center, or right.

From the Page Numbers dialog box, you can choose a Format button to display an additional Page Numbers Format dialog box. This dialog box works in the same manner as described previously for "Editing the Header/Footer Options." Choose a number format from the list box, and specify where the page numbering should begin. Then choose OK or press Enter to implement your selection of page numbering.

Note. If a header/footer already exists and you use the Insert Page Numbers command, the existing header/footer gets replaced with the new page-number header/footer.

Alternating Headers/Footers for Odd and Even Pages

Often, you will need different headers or footers for odd- and even-numbered pages; this technique is common in reports that are printed double-sided, or in book chapters. You use the same procedure as for ordinary headers and footers, except that you supply one header/footer to be used on odd-numbered pages, and another header/footer to be used on even-numbered pages. You do this by means of the Different Odd and Even Pages feature in the View Header/Footer dialog box. You can add alternating headers or footers to any document by performing the following steps; try this now in your practice document.

1. Place the insertion pointer at the start of the document, and then select View Header/Footer (Alt+V+H).

2. In the dialog box, turn on the Different Odd and Even Pages feature (Alt+D). Notice that the header and footer choices in the list box become Odd header, Even header, Odd footer, and Even footer.

3. Select one of these headers or footers, and edit the text as desired in the header/footer pane.

4. Click on Close, or press Shift+F10, then C.

5. Choose View Header/Footer again, and repeat Steps 3 and 4 until you have edited all the desired headers and/or footers.

6. Click on Close (or press Shift+F10, then C) to close the Header/Footer pane and complete the process of adding the alternating headers or footers.

A Special Header or Footer on the First Page

To print a different header or footer on the first page of a document, turn on the Different First Page (Alt+P) option of the View Header/Footer dialog box. When you do so, First Header and First Footer are added to the list box. Then, as you did for Odd and Even headers/footers, select First Header and/or First Footer from the list box, and choose OK to open the pane so you can type the header or footer. When done, close the pane to complete the process of editing the first-page header or footer.

Adding Footnotes

Word's ability to display multiple portions of a document simultaneously makes adding footnotes to a Word document a simple matter. You can look at and work with the text of a footnote in a separate pane, while the related portion of your document remains visible. Word, like most word processors, lets you position footnotes either at the bottom of each page, or collectively at the end of the document (as "endnotes"). However, in Word you can also put a footnote directly beneath the text to which it applies, or at the end of a section.

Footnotes are added with the Insert Footnote command. To add a footnote, first place the insertion pointer where the footnote reference mark (such as a superscript number) is to appear in the text. Select Insert Foot-note (Alt+I+N) and you'll see this dialog box:

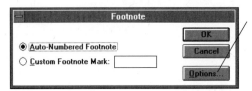

Displays dialog box for control of footnote placement and separators

Here you can specify if you want the footnote to be automatically num-bered by Word (the default), or you can enter a reference mark of your own choosing, such as an asterisk or a number in parentheses. The Options but-ton displays another dialog box that lets you control placement of footnotes, and the separator line used to separate footnotes from the rest of the docu-ment. This dialog box will be explained shortly.

When you choose OK from the Footnote dialog box, a Footnotes pane opens in the bottom portion of the screen (see Figure 5.18), where you type the desired footnote. When the Footnotes pane is open, a split bar appears in the vertical scroll bar. Mouse users can drag the split bar up or down to change the size of the pane. At any time when working with footnotes, you can return to the main part of your document while leaving the pane open, by pressing F6 (Next Pane). When done, you can drag the split bar to close the pane. Keyboard users can select View Footnote (Alt+V+F) to close the Footnotes pane.

You can try adding a footnote to the sample document by doing this next exercise. Then in the sections that follow you'll see how to edit and delete footnote text, position both the reference markers and the footnotes them-selves, and define the separator line at the bottom of the page.

1. Place the insertion pointer at the end of the first paragraph of the sample document.

2. Select Insert Footnote (Alt+I+N).

3. To accept automatic numbering for footnotes, choose OK from the dia-log box. As Figure 5.18 shows, Word places a superscript reference num-ber at the end of the paragraph in the document, and opens the Footnotes pane for the footnote text.

4. Type the following text in the Footnotes pane:

```
Survey responses were taken from the 1990 Library Survey,
provided by ABC Survey Co. Note that an updated survey
will be conducted yearly from 1992 onward.
```

Figure 5.18

Footnote pane open for entry of a footnote, which is marked by superscript reference number at end of paragraph text

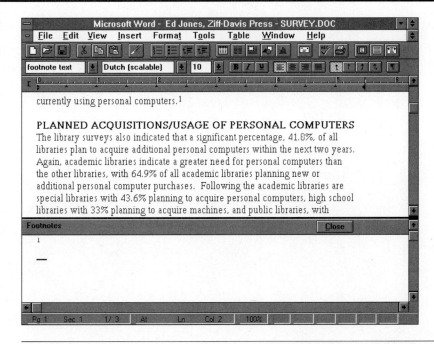

You can return to the document and keep the Footnotes pane open, by pressing F6.

5. Click on Close or select View Footnote (Alt+V+F) to close the Footnotes pane. (The View Footnote command is a toggle, and opens/closes the footnote window.)

You can see the footnotes in your document if you are in the page layout view of Word. Figure 5.19 shows the footnote you added to the sample text, from Word's page layout view.

Editing Existing Footnotes

To edit an existing footnote, first turn off page layout view if necessary, then open the Footnotes pane with the View Footnote command (Alt+V+F). Scroll within the pane, find the desired footnote, and edit it as you would regular text.

TIP. *You can also quickly jump from footnote to footnote with the Go To key (F5). Press F5, and in response to the "Go to?" prompt at the bottom of the screen, enter the letter **F** (for footnote). Then press Enter. Repeat this process to jump through the footnotes until you find the one you want.*

Figure 5.19

Footnote added to end of sample document, shown in page layout view

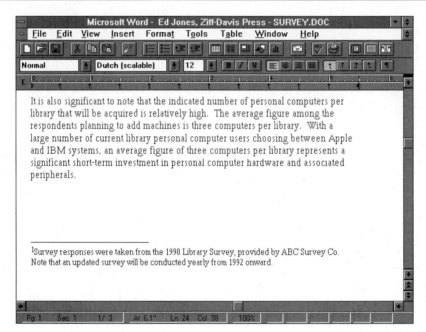

Moving and Deleting Footnotes

Footnotes are indicated by the reference markers in the document, and moving or deleting a footnote is as simple as moving or deleting the reference marker.

- To move a footnote, use your favorite text selection method to select the footnote's *reference marker* within the document, and move it to the desired new location.

- To delete a footnote, select its reference marker, and press Shift+Del or use Edit Cut (Alt+E+T), or the Cut icon in the Toolbar. If you used Word's automatic footnote numbering with any footnote you move or delete, the remaining footnotes will be renumbered accordingly. If you numbered footnotes manually, you'll need to renumber them yourself as necessary.

Using the Insert Footnote Options

As mentioned earlier, when you choose Insert Footnote to add footnotes, the Footnote dialog box that appears contains a button labeled Options. When you click this button, this dialog box appears:

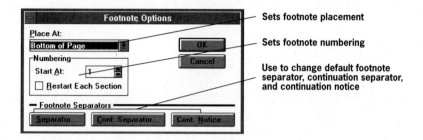

The Place At list box lets you determine placement for the footnotes. The Numbering options let you designate the starting footnote number, and whether numbering should restart within each section. The buttons at the bottom of the dialog box (Separator, Cont. Separator, and Cont. Notice) are used to control the separator lines and continuation notices used for footnotes, as explained in the paragraphs that follow.

Positioning Footnotes

To determine the footnote placement, select Insert Footnote and then Options (Alt+O), and open the Place At (Alt+P) list box. You will have four choices: End of Section, Bottom of Page, Beneath Text, or End of Document. Choose End of Section to put all footnotes for a section at the end of that section. Choose Bottom of Page to place the footnotes for a given page at the bottom of that page. The Beneath Text choice places the footnote directly after the text containing the footnote reference mark, and End of Document places the footnotes at the end of the document.

Suppressing Footnotes

If you choose End of Section for the footnote placement, the Supress Footnotes button becomes available in the Format Section Layout dialog box, and you can then enable this option to prevent footnotes from printing in that section. (When you supress footnotes, Word stores them in memory during the printing process, and they are printed later, at the very next section where footnote printing is not supressed.)

Changing the Numbering

To change the starting number for automatically-numbered footnotes, select Insert Footnote and choose Options (Alt+O), and click in the Start At box (or press Alt+A). Then enter in the text box the number you want for the first automatically-numbered footnote. If you want Word to restart the automatic numbering each time a new section begins, as in for a new chapter or part, mark the Restart Each Section check box.

Changing the Footnote Separators

Normally, Word uses a thin solid line (a series of underline characters) to separate footnotes from the text of the document. For footnotes that continue from one page to another, the line is longer. You can change these lines, and you can also add a message that will print in your document to indicate the continuation of footnotes. These options are available via the buttons at the bottom of the Footnote Options dialog box, illustrated earlier in this section.

Choose the Separator button (Alt+S), and the default separator (a thin line) appears in the Footnotes pane. You can edit the line, or replace it with any desired characters, and then choose Close (Shift+F10, then C) to close the Footnotes pane.

You can use this same procedure to edit the continuation separator or the continuation notice. Continuation separators are used with footnotes that continue from one page to another; continuation notices, such as "Footnote continued next page," indicate the continuation of a footnote. Select the Continuation Separator (Alt+C), or Continuation Notice (Alt+N) button, edit or enter the desired separator or continuation notice in the Footnotes pane, and then click on the Close button (or press Shift+F10, then C) to close the Footnotes pane.

Now that you've explored so many aspects of document formatting, you're probably anxious to try printing some examples of your work. Let's move on to Chapter 6, "Previewing and Printing Your Document."

6

Previewing and Printing Your Document

THIS CHAPTER EXPLAINS THE PROCESS OF PRINTING OF YOUR WORD DOCU-
ments, as well as how you can preview documents before printing
them. Remember—your printer must be set up and ready before you
can print documents. This may seem like an obvious point, but a
surprising number of printer problems are traced to an incorrect printer
setup, or even to the printer's not being turned on and ready. Refer to your
printer's documentation for instructions on setting it up and configuring it to
work with Windows.

Previewing Documents

The handy File Print Preview command lets you see what a document will
look like before it is printed. This is a particularly useful option: You get to
see a representation of how your document will look, without wasting the
time and paper it takes to print a "test" copy. The Print Preview mode shows
the positioning of footnotes, headers, footers, page numbers, and multiple
columns. (In Page Preview mode, even graphics are visible.) You can easily
move between the preview pages, and you can view one or two pages of a
document simultaneously. You cannot edit the text of a document in Print
Preview mode, but you can make certain changes to its format.

File Print Preview
(Alt+F+V) is handy
for getting a quick
idea of how a
document will look
when printed.

To enter Print Preview mode, use the File Print Preview command
(Alt+F+V). You'll see the Print Preview window for the current document,
shown in Figure 6.1. Notice that the status bar is no longer visible. A row of
buttons on the Print Preview screen provides several useful options when
you are in Print Preview mode. Choose these options by clicking them, or by
pressing the underlined letter in the option name. The options perform the
following tasks:

- *Print* (Alt+Shift+P) opens the Print dialog box, so you can print the document after previewing it. This Print option is equivalent to choosing the
  File Print command, or pressing the Print key (Ctrl+Shift+F12).

- *Margins* (Alt+Shift+M) shows the boundaries, indicated by dotted lines, of
  areas occupied by headers, footers, margins, and page breaks, and any
  positioned objects (such as graphics).

- *Two Pages* (Alt+Shift+A) displays two pages side by side. (If you are previewing a single-page document, the second page will be blank.) When you
  choose this toggle option, the name of the button changes to One Page;
  choose it again to switch back to viewing a single page.

- *Cancel* (Alt+Shift+C) lets you exit Print Preview. You are returned to the
  view mode you were using before you chose Print Preview. If you make any
  changes to the format of a document while in Print Preview, the name of the
  Cancel button changes to Close. (See the next section, "Adjusting Margins
  and Objects," for details on changes you can make while in Print Preview.)

Figure 6.1

A document shown within the Print Preview window

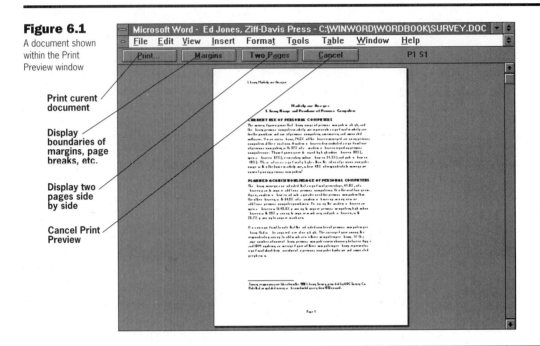

Print current document

Display boundaries of margins, page breaks, etc.

Display two pages side by side

Cancel Print Preview

Tip. A quick way out of Print Preview is to press the Esc key.

■ *Page and Section Numbers* appear to the right of the Cancel button, indicating the current page number (where the insertion pointer is) and the current section number (if your document has multiple sections).

NOTE. *Many commands on Word menus are not available when you're in Print Preview. These commands will, as usual, appear dimmed on the menus. For example, if you open the Edit menu while in Print Preview mode, you will see that all commands except the Repeat command are dimmed, because you cannot edit a document while in Print Preview. Nor can you open files or change windows.*

Adjusting Margins and Objects

Though you cannot edit the text of a document in Print Preview, you can make changes to some aspects of its format. You can adjust the location of page margins, and elements such as headers, footers, and absolutely positioned paragraphs (defined in Chapter 11). These elements are called *objects,* which are the parts of a Word document that can be moved independently of the document itself.

Mouse users have a definite advantage in this area, because you can easily drag the boundaries of page margins and objects to move them. To make these changes with the mouse, click on the Margins button. This causes dotted lines to appear around the margins and objects in the document, as shown in Figure 6.2.

Figure 6.2

A document in Page Preview, with margins and other elements made visible with the Margins button

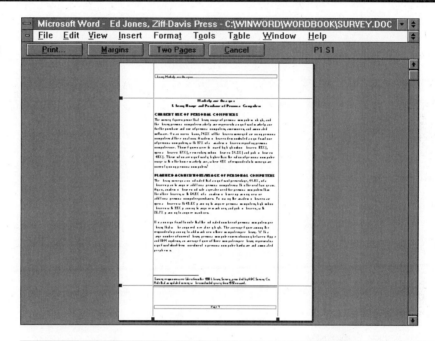

With the dotted margin lines visible, drag the *handle* (the small black square) of each item you wish to adjust. As you move the mouse pointer over a handle, the pointer changes to a small cross-hair. There are no handles for headers and footers, but you can drag the dotted-line box that surrounds the header or footer. To see the result, click anywhere off the picture of the page on the screen. In the case of objects like absolutely positioned paragraphs, just drag the object to the desired location. Note that you can also reposition page breaks or section breaks that are shown in the document.

Keyboard users, too, can move objects in Print Preview, but the process is somewhat more complicated. First choose the Margins button (press M). Then press the Tab key repeatedly until the object you want to move is selected. Use the arrow keys to move the object to the desired location, and press Enter twice.

When you're done with the changes you want to make to the document, choose Close (press C) to exit Page Preview.

Printing a Document

As with any word processor, Word lets you print a document—but you can also print much more. Word lets you print selected portions of a document, or multiple copies of a document. You can also print other information related to a document, such as document summary information, annotations, glossaries, and style sheets.

Word provides a number of different ways to print, as the rest of this chapter will show you. Table 6.1 provides suggestions for deciding on how to print in Word.

Table 6.1   **Printing Technique Guidelines**

Method	Task
Toolbar Print icon	When you want one copy of the current document, without any changes to the default print options
File Print command (Alt+F+P) or the Print key (Ctrl+Shift+F12)	To print multiple copies, a range of pages, or a selection
File Find command (Alt+F+F)	To print several documents consecutively
Print button of File Print Preview (Alt+F+V, then P or Alt+Shift+P)	To visually check appearance of a document, then print it
Tools Create Envelope command or the Toolbar Envelope icon	To print envelopes

---

As described briefly in Chapter 2, you print documents with the File Print (Alt+F+P) command. Once you have readied your printer and chosen your desired options in the Print dialog box, choose OK or press Enter to start printing. Following are descriptions of the options in the Print dialog box (Figure 6.3).

Print

This drop-down list box lets you choose what you want to print. The default choice is the document, but you can also print summary information, annotations, styles, glossaries, and key assignments by selecting the appropriate item from the list box.

Copies

In this text box, you enter the number of copies you want to be printed (the default is 1).

Figure 6.3

The Print dialog box

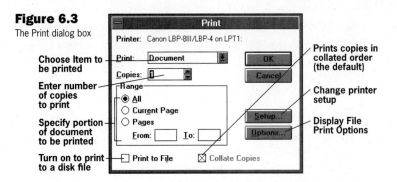

Choose Item to be printed

Enter number of copies to print

Specify portion of document to be printed

Turn on to print to a disk file

Prints copies in collated order (the default)

Change printer setup

Display File Print Options

Range

In this area of the dialog box, you can designate the portion of a document to be printed. Choose All to print the entire document. Choose Current Page to print the page where the insertion pointer is located. If you select text, this button changes to a Selection button. Use the Pages From and To boxes to indicate a starting and ending page number.

TIP. *You can also specify pages of a section to print by typing P for page number, a number, S for section, and then the section number. For example, to print pages 2 through 4 of Section 3, enter P2S3 in the From Box, and P4S3 in the To Box.*

Options

This button displays additional options available for printing; they are detailed in the section "Using the File Print Options" later in this chapter.

Setup

This button lets you choose a different printer from a list of installed printers. See "Changing Your Printer Setup" at the end of this chapter for more on printer setup.

Print to File

This check box tells Word to print to a file on disk. If you mark this option and choose OK, Word will prompt you for a file name.

Collate Copies

This check box tells Word to print the document in page-number order. This option is on by default and dimmed on the screen, unless your printer is able to print multiple, uncollated copies.

TIP. *You can also use the Print key (Ctrl+Shift+F12)—the hotkey for the File Print command. Pressing the Print key causes the Print dialog box to appear; select your print options, and choose OK or press Enter to start printing. Mouse users can also click on the Print icon in the Toolbar, to print one copy of a document. When you use Print from the Toolbar, no dialog box appears; Word assumes you want to print one copy.*

If You Have Problems...

If you have difficulty printing, or if the printer name at the top of the Print dialog box doesn't match the printer that is connected to your computer, choose Setup in the Print dialog box. Make sure that the correct printer is selected in the list box that appears. Choose OK, and try the File Print command again. If the correct printer is selected and you still can't print, the problem is likely to be in the printer itself, or in how Windows is set up on your system.

Word uses the Windows software (specifically, the Windows Print Manager) to manage all printing. If you can't print from another Windows application (like Cardfile or Notepad), you won't be able to print from Word. If you can't print from any application in Windows, refer to your Windows documentation or the *Microsoft Word for Windows Printer Guide* that came with your software. Also, be sure to check the obvious: Make sure the printer is properly connected, turned on, and on line. If you still can't find the source of the problem, there are many helpful troubleshooting tips in the *Microsoft Word for Windows Printer Guide.*

Printing Multiple Documents

Many word processors let you send a series of documents to the printer with a single print command, a process known as building a *print queue*. You can also do this in Word. To print several documents with a single print command, use the File Find File command (described in Chapter 16) instead of the File Print command. Select the desired files in the File Find File dialog box, and then choose the Print button to start printing the files. Here are the specific steps to do this:

1. Select File Find File (Alt+F+F). You'll see the File Find dialog box shown in Figure 6.4.

2. In the File Name list box, highlight the desired files to be printed. (If the files you want are not in the list box, implement a search of the appropriate directories, using the search techniques outlined in Chapter 4.)

   ■ To select files with the mouse, move to the first file you want to print, and click on the file name. Then hold the Ctrl key down, and click each additional desired file.

Figure 6.4

File Find dialog box

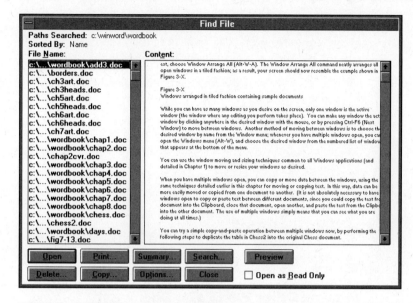

■ To select files with the keyboard, move to the first desired file and press Shift+F8. Use the arrow keys to move the dotted box to the next desired file name. Press the Spacebar. Repeat the last step for all additional files you want to print.

3. With the desired files selected, click on the Print button (or press Alt+P). When the Print dialog box appears, choose OK or press Enter, and Word will print all of the selected files, one by one, in the order you selected them.

Printing a Portion of a Document

You can print a selected portion of a document using either of two methods. You can choose a starting and ending page number, in which case Word prints the starting and ending pages and all pages in between. Or you can select a passage of text to be printed. When you select text, the Current Page button in the Ranges area changes to a Selection button, which you can click to print the selection. Here are two exercises, using both techniques. Before you try them, make sure your printer is ready.

To print one or more pages of a document,

1. With a document open, select File Print (Alt+F+P).

2. Press Alt+G or click the Pages button in the Range box.

3. The cursor moves to the From box; enter the number of the first page you want to print. Tab or click in the To box, and enter the number of the last page you want to print.

4. Choose OK or press Enter, and the specified pages of the document are printed (or queued if necessary).

To print a selection of text,

1. Open a file, and select a passage of text to be printed, using your favorite selection technique.

2. Select File Print (Alt+F+P). Notice that the Current Page button changes to a Selection button.

3. Click the Selection button, or press Alt+E.

4. Choose OK or press Enter to print the selected text.

Printing Other Parts of a Document

Use the Print drop-down list box in the Print dialog box to print parts of a document other than the main body of text. Open and scroll this list box with the usual mouse or keyboard techniques. The various choices are shown here:

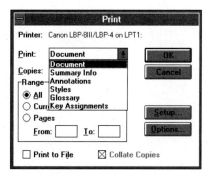

- Document (the default) prints the entire document.

- Summary Info prints just the document summary information (see Chapter 4).

- Annotations prints all annotations you've entered and stored with the document (see Chapter 3).

- Styles prints the style sheet for the document (see Chapter 12).

- Glossary prints the template glossary entries, and then the global glossary entries (see Chapter 13).

- Key Assignments prints the names of macros and the keys they are assigned to (see Chapter 14).

TIP. *You can print summary information and annotations simultaneously with the printing of the document, if desired, with the File Print Options menu discussed later in this chapter.*

Printing Sideways

On occasion you may need to print a document sideways, across the length of the page (in *landscape* orientation). This technique is particularly useful with very wide documents, like those containing tables of numbers. If your printer installed under Windows supports landscape printing, you can easily print Word's documents using this orientation. Figure 6.5 illustrates the difference between regular (*portrait*) and landscape printing orientations. In portrait orientation, text is printed top to bottom down the length of the page.

Figure 6.5
Portrait and landscape printing orientations

Portrait orientation

Landscape orientation

To print a document in landscape orientation, select File Print (Alt+F+P), then choose Setup (Alt+S), and then Setup (Alt+S) again. An alternate method is to select File Printer Setup (Alt+F+R) and choose Setup (Alt+S). Choose Landscape (Alt+L) and then OK from the dialog box that appears. You can then proceed to print the document "sideways" with the File Print command. (If there is no Landscape option in the dialog box that appears, then your printer does not support landscape printing under Windows.)

CAUTION! *When you have finished printing in landscape, don't forget to change the printing orientation back to portrait. Select File Printer Setup (Alt+F+R), and then Setup (Alt+S). Press Alt+P, and choose OK or press Enter. If you do not do this, all successive printing will be in landscape. For additional details about the Print Setup dialog box, see "Changing Your Printer Setup" at the end of this chapter.*

Using the Other File Print Options

The additional printing options in the Print dialog box let you print annotations or summary information along with a document, print in reverse order, and print draft versions of documents. To use the File Print Options, select File Print (Alt+F+P), and click the Options button (or press Alt+O). The dialog box changes to reveal the Options dialog box shown in Figure 6.6. To choose any of the options (explained in the following paragraphs), mark the check box for the option, or press the Alt key plus the underlined letter in the option name.

Figure 6.6

File Print options in the Options dialog box

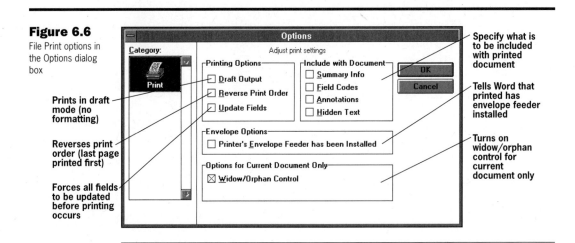

Prints in draft mode (no formatting)

Reverses print order (last page printed first)

Forces all fields to be updated before printing occurs

Specify what is to be included with printed document

Tells Word that printed has envelope feeder installed

Turns on widow/orphan control for current document only

Draft Output

This causes the document to be printed in draft mode, or without any formatting. On many printers (particularly dot-matrix machines), printing without formatting is faster.

Reverse Print Order

This toggle option causes the document to be printed last page first. This is helpful with laser printers based on the first-generation Canon engine (such as the original Hewlett-Packard LaserJet). These machines cause printed pages to come out printed side up, so a multiple-page document winds up stacked with the last page on top (which is usually not how you want it). Turn on the Reverse Print Order option, and the print run will start with the last page and end with the first page, so the document gets stacked in the proper order.

Update Fields

When this option is enabled, Word updates the results of any fields that are in a document before it is printed (see Chapter 9).

Include with Document

Use the checkboxes in this area of the dialog box to specify what you want printed along with the document. You can include a summary information sheet and any annotations added to the document. Turn on Field Codes to print field codes instead of the results of the fields (explained in Chapter 9). Turn on Hidden Text to include any text that was hidden by means of character formatting (with the Hidden option of the Format Character dialog box).

Printing Envelopes

Word has an envelope-printing feature that makes printing envelopes a very simple matter when your printer can handle envelopes. Either the Tools Create Envelope command, or its equivalent Envelope button on the Toolbar, let you quickly create and print an envelope, using a document that contains a mailing address. Try it:

1. If your printer is equipped with an envelope feeder, insert the envelope into the envelope feeder. If your printer is not equipped with an envelope feeder, select Tools Options (Alt+O+O), get into the Category list box (Alt+C), and choose Print. In the dialog box, turn on Printer's Envelope Feeder Has Been Installed, and select OK or press Enter. Then insert the envelope into the manual feeder of your printer.

2. If you already have a document that contains a mailing address for the envelope, open that document. (Don't worry if you don't have this stored in a document; you'll get a chance to enter it later.)

3. Select Tools Create Envelope (Alt+O+E), or click on the Envelope icon in the Toolbar. The Create Envelope dialog box appears.

```
┌─────────────────────────────────────────────────────────┐
│ ─                    Create Envelope                      │
│  Addressed To:                        ┌──────────────┐    │
│  ┌───────────────────────────────┐    │ Print Envelope│    │
│  │ Bill Thompson Industries      │    └──────────────┘    │
│  │ 2000 Watergate Circle         │    ┌──────────────┐    │
│  │ Washington, DC 20017          │    │ Add to Document│   │
│  │                               │    └──────────────┘    │
│  │                               │    ┌──────────────┐    │
│  └───────────────────────────────┘    │    Cancel    │    │
│                                        └──────────────┘    │
│  Return Address:              Envelope Size:               │
│  ┌───────────────────────────┐  ┌──────────────────────┐  │
│  │ Pioneer Systems           │  │ Size 10 (4 1/8 x 9 ½ in) │
│  │ Box 323                   │  └──────────────────────┘  │
│  │ Falls Church, VA 22046    │                            │
│  │                           │  ☐ Omit Return Address      │
│  └───────────────────────────┘                            │
│  Center each envelope face up in your printer's manual feeder. │
└─────────────────────────────────────────────────────────┘
```

This dialog box provides a text box for the return address, and for the mailing address (called Addressed To). A list box lets you select the envelope size you are using.

4. If you opened a document (in Step 2) that contains a mailing address, Word automatically inserts this in the Addressed To box. Otherwise, you'll need to enter the mailing address to be printed on the envelope.

5. In the Return Address box, enter the return address to be printed on the envelope. (The mailing address that's stored in your User Info settings dialog box appears here by default; you can edit this as needed.) To change what is stored in User Info, select Tools Options (Alt+O+O) and select User Info from the Category (Alt+C) list box. If you do not want to print a return address, mark the Omit Return Address check box.

NOTE. *The Add to Document button lets you add the destination and/or return address entered in the Create Envelope dialog box to the current document.*

6. In the Envelope Size list box, select the appropriate envelope size.

7. Choose the Print Envelope button (Alt+P) to tell Word to print the envelope.

If you have difficulty feeding envelopes through your printer, check your printer manual for suggestions. Envelope feeding is by nature a difficult task for the mechanics of printers to handle, and many printers will jam if the envelopes are not loaded properly.

Changing Your Printer Setup

Word provides access to the printer setup facility of Windows, via the Setup button in the Print dialog box, or the File Print Setup command. You can select from among different printers, and change various settings for the printer (such as portrait vs. landscape mode). You can also choose different paper bins, assuming your connected printer supports this.

NOTE. *File Print Setup lets you select a printer that is already installed under Windows; however, you cannot use this command to install a printer. See your Windows documentation if you need to install a new printer to your Windows configuration.*

To change a printer's setup, select File Print Setup (Alt+F+R) or the Setup button in the Print dialog box. You'll get a Print Setup dialog box like the one in Figure 6.7, containing a list box with all printers that you chose when you installed Windows. The contents of the list box in your own Print Setup dialog box will depend on what printers are installed with your version of Windows.

Figure 6.7

Example of a Print
Setup dialog box

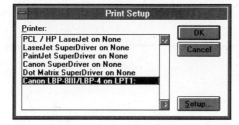

Note. Only one
printer at a time can
use a connection
(printer port). If you
change printers,
remember to
choose Setup from
the File Print dialog
box to change the
active printer.

If you just want to change printers, choose the one you want in the list box (by clicking on the printer name or by highlighting it with the keyboard), and then choose OK or press Enter. If you want to change some printer setup options, choose the Setup button (Alt+S). The dialog box will expand to reveal the available options. An example for a Hewlett-Packard LaserJet II is shown in Figure 6.8.

The contents of this expanded dialog box will vary greatly, of course, depending on the printer you have specified. Because there are literally hundreds of printers on the market, it is impossible to explain all of the possible settings here. Each printer's dialog box will contain the options that are applicable to that particular printer. In addition, most will contain buttons for choosing between portrait (the default) and landscape printing.

Figure 6.8

The expanded
printer setup dialog
box for a Hewlett-
Packard LaserJet II

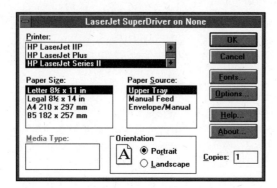

If you are using a laser printer that employs font cartridges, you can select these from a list box in the expanded Print Setup dialog box. Refer to the Microsoft Word for Windows Printer Guide to determine the fonts that can be used with your particular laser printer.

These first six chapters have provided the basics you need to know to work with Word for Windows. In the chapters that follow, more advanced concepts will be demonstrated, starting with the use of Word's table feature in Chapter 7.

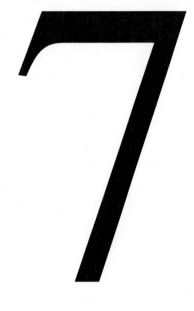

7

Working with Tables

TABLES ARE A COMMON FEATURE OF BUSINESS CORRESPONDENCE, TECH-nical and scientific material, and many other types of documents. Tables in word processed documents have had a reputation for being hard to implement and even harder to modify. Word, however, does not handicap you in this way—Word's table feature makes it a simple matter to insert tables containing varying amounts of text and/or graphics.

Understanding Tables in Word for Windows

A table is any group of information arranged in rows and columns, as illustrated in Figure 7.1. Tables in Word have two or more columns, and one or more rows; each intersection of a row and a column is a *cell* of the table. If you are familiar with computer spreadsheets, you already understand the notion of a cell.

Figure 7.1

A table created in
Word for Windows

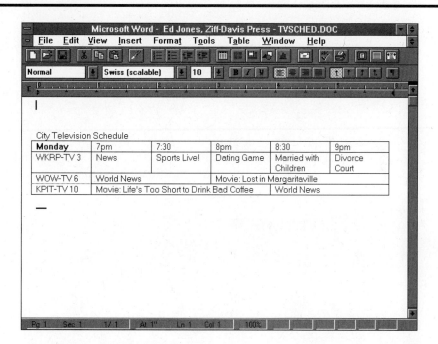

Before Word's table feature came along, tables were typically set up using tabs or indented paragraphs. Although this method works, it can be quite awkward. Consider the following simple example of a table formed with tabs between the text in each column, and a newline character at the end of each line.

Food Arrangements for Ken's Visit With Us

Monday➡ ➡ Pam & Steve➡ Salads➡ Garden Oasis of ↵
➡ ➡ ➡ ➡ ➡ ➡ ➡ Mill Valley
Tuesday➡ ➡ Sandy & Dave➡Mexican➡ Las Casas↵
➡ ➡ ➡ ➡ ➡ ➡ ➡ ➡ Grandes
Wednesday➡ Derek➡ ➡ Chinese➡ N.Aida's↵
➡ ➡ ➡ ➡ ➡ ➡ ➡ ➡ Steak House
Thursday➡ Celita➡ ➡ Pizza➡ Programmer's Pub
Friday➡ ➡ Nikki➡ ➡ Health➡ Mother Nature's ↵
➡ ➡ ➡ ➡ ➡ ➡ Foods➡ Bar and Grill

A table created with tabs, like this one, can be tricky to design whenever some cells of the table contain more than one line, as is the case with most entries in the last column of our example. But the real problem with this table arises when you need to revise it. For example, if you needed to change the name of Friday's restaurant to Mother Nature's Holistic Bar and Grill, your change would add a new line (containing the word Holistic) between the existing two lines of that table entry. This revision would also require you to relocate the word Foods in the last line of the third column, for it would be on the wrong line after the revision. And this is just a relatively simple table! Add more columns, more rows, and more text, and you have a major headache.

By comparison, the cells used by Word's table feature expand as necessary to fit all of your required text and graphics. The only size limit imposed on a cell is that it cannot be larger than a page. You can resize the table columns as desired; you can even resize individual cells. Rows, too, are easily added.

To work with tables, you'll use the various commands of the Table menu.

```
Table
Insert Table...
 Delete Columns
 Merge Cells
 Convert Text to Table...
 Select Row
 Select Column
 Select Table   Alt+NumPad 5
 Row Height...
 Column Width...
 Split Table
√Gridlines
```

The first command on the Table menu, Insert Table, inserts a new table in a document. Mouse users can also use the Table icon on the Toolbar to insert a table. The remaining commands in the Table menu are used for various table operations, and you'll see how these commands function as you work through the chapter. You'll also see how Table menu commands will change as you are working within a table; for example, the Insert Table option changes to Insert Cells or Insert Columns when you are within a table.

As you can see in the example shown in Figure 7.1, Word supplies grid lines surrounding the cells of a table. (These grid lines will not appear if you turn off the Table Grid Lines option in the Table menu, or in the Tools Options dialog box.)

Note. If you do not see grid lines on screen in your tables, select Table Grid Lines option (Alt+A+G).

Grid lines in a table do not print; they appear on screen simply as an aid for entering and editing text in the table. You can, however, add borders to cells or to an entire table; these borders print with the table. Use the Format Border command to add borders, as explained in "Formatting Tables" later in this chapter.

Creating a Table

Tables are added to a document with the Table command's Insert Table option or with the Table icon of the Toolbar. If you select Table Insert Table (Alt+A+I), the Insert Table dialog box appears. Here you'll set up the framework of your table.

In the *Number of Columns* text box, enter the desired number of columns for the table. Word displays 2 as the default, and you can increase this value up to 31. Remember that you can also add columns at any time with the Table Insert Columns option (discussed later), so if you are not sure how many columns you'll need, just make your best guess for the minimum number.

In the *Number of Rows* text box, enter the desired number of rows for the table. It's very easy to add rows as needed with the Tab key, so, enter a number that will give you the minimum number of rows you'll need, as you did with columns.

In the *Column Width* text box, you can enter Auto (the default), or you can type a decimal measurement for the width of the columns. (You can have columns of differing widths; how to set these up is discussed later.) When you enter Auto, Word makes all columns the same width, by dividing all available space between your margins by the number of columns you've selected. Hence, your page margins will affect the maximum width of a table, just as they will affect the width of other text. (See Chapter 5 for details on setting page margins.)

Here are the steps for using Insert Table on the Table menu to create a new table:

1. Place the insertion pointer at the desired location for the table. From the Table menu, select Insert Table (Alt+A+I).

2. Enter the number of columns desired in the Number of Columns text box.

3. Enter the number of rows desired in the Number of Rows text box.

4. Enter a column width in the Column Width text box (or accept the default of Auto).

5. Choose OK to establish your table.

Mouse users can create a table by clicking and dragging the Table icon in the Toolbar. Click on this icon and continue to hold down the left mouse button, and a miniature representation of a table appears, as shown here:

As you drag down or to the right, the number of rows and columns highlighted in the miniature indicate how many rows and columns your table will have. (The illustration shows a selection of 3 rows by 4 columns.) Drag until the miniature has the desired number of rows and columns, and then release the mouse button to place the table at the insertion pointer. This mouse method is fast, but you give up one advantage of using the Table Insert Table command: With the Table icon, you cannot specify a column width. Word automatically determines the column width as described previously for the Auto default. You can, however, change this later with the Column Width option of the Table menu.

Adding Data into the Table Cells

Once you have created the framework for the table, you can proceed to type the table data into each cell. If the text you type will not fit into a cell, Word automatically increases the *row height* (number of lines) in the cell as needed, to accommodate the text. (You can change this row height, or the column width, with the Table Row Height and Table Column Width commands. These will be discussed later, in the section "Formatting Tables.")

Use Tab to move forward from cell to cell; use Shift+Tab to move in reverse. If you press Tab at the end of a table, a new row is added to the table. With a mouse, you can click in any cell to place the insertion pointer in that cell. The arrow keys also move the insertion pointer within the table, as well as into

and out of a table. For a more complete discussion of mouse and keyboard techniques for navigation within tables, see "Navigating in a Table with the Keyboard" and "Navigating in a Table with the Mouse" later in this chapter.

A Simple Example of a Table

As a simple example, let's duplicate the table shown earlier in the chapter, which was originally set up by using tabs. In the exercise that follows, you will duplicate the table using Word's table feature, and you'll see how simple creating and revising tables can be.

1. Open a new document (Alt+F+N), and type the following sentence:

   ```
   Food Arrangements for Ken's Visit With Us
   ```

2. Press Enter to begin a new paragraph.

3. Choose Insert Table from the Table menu (Alt+A+I).

4. In the Number of Columns text box, enter **4**.

5. Tab to or click in the Number of Rows text box, and enter **5**. For now, leave the Column Width option at Auto.

6. Choose OK. The new table appears, containing five rows of four cells each, with the insertion pointer in the first cell.

7. Type the information shown in Figure 7.2, using the Tab key when you're done with each cell. *Do not use the Enter key;* pressing Enter starts a new paragraph (as it does elsewhere in Word), but Enter cannot move you out of a cell. You'll learn later about using paragraphs in table cells.

   You will notice that as you enter longer cell entries that when text is too long to fit on a single line, the cell automatically expands in size. This shows but one advantage of Word's table feature; you do not need to calculate the space needed between rows of a table.

Paragraphs Within Tables

Word's ability to expand a cell as you type text means that you can have as little or as much text as you want in a cell (up to one page in size). Thus you can place entire paragraphs in a cell as needed. For example, move the cursor into the cell containing the restaurant name, Programmer's Pub. Use the End key to get to the end of the existing text, and then press Enter to begin a new paragraph. Type the following text:

```
(Reservations will need to be made in advance if we want
to obtain the best seating.)
```

Note. If you do not see the grid lines, choose Table Gridlines (Alt+A+G); then choose OK.

Note. Remember that you can insert graphics into the cells of a table. Use the cut-and-paste techniques for graphic images you learned in Chapter 2.

Figure 7.2

Sample table of lunch arrangements created with Insert Table

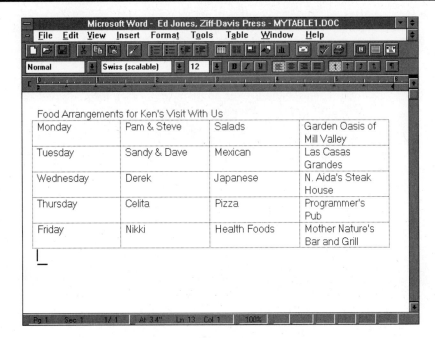

The result, illustrated in Figure 7.3, shows that Word expands the cell as necessary to accommodate the addition. To see an example of this technique with larger amounts of text, look ahead to Figure 7.12 in "Side-By-Side Paragraphs" near the end of this chapter.

Navigating in a Table with the Mouse

Navigation in a table with the mouse works the same way as when you use the mouse in regular text; you point and click where the insertion pointer is needed. In addition, there are some other mouse techniques you'll need to know for using the special selection areas provided in tables for mouse use.

At the left edge of each cell is a selection bar (an area where the mouse pointer changes to an arrow pointing up and to the right). When you click at the left edge of a cell while the pointer is shaped like this, you select the entire cell. You can also double-click in any cell's selection bar, to select the entire row of the table. And you can click and drag across cell boundaries to select a group of cells.

At the top of a table is the column selection area. When you place the mouse pointer above the top border (the topmost dotted line in Figure 7.3), the pointer changes to the shape of an arrow pointing down. This indicates

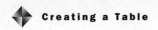

the column selection mode. While the pointer is shaped like this, you can click to select the entire column below the pointer.

Figure 7.3

Lunch arrangements table with new paragraph added

Microsoft Word - Ed Jones, Ziff-Davis Press - MYTABLE1.DOC

<u>F</u>ile <u>E</u>dit <u>V</u>iew <u>I</u>nsert Fo<u>r</u>mat <u>T</u>ools Ta<u>b</u>le <u>W</u>indow <u>H</u>elp

Normal | Swiss (scalable) | 12 | **B** *I* U

Food Arrangements for Ken's Visit With Us

Monday	Pam & Steve	Salads	Garden Oasis of Mill Valley
Tuesday	Sandy & Dave	Mexican	Las Casas Grandes
Wednesday	Derek	Japanese	N. Aida's Steak House
Thursday	Celita	Pizza	Programmer's Pub (Reservations will need to be made in advance if we want to obtain the best seating.)
Friday	Nikki	Health Foods	Mother Nature's Bar and Grill

Pg 1   Sec 1   1/ 1   At 3.8"   Ln 15   Col 1   100%

Navigating in a Table with the Keyboard

Keyboard techniques for moving within a table are helpful to keyboard and mouse users alike. To move from cell to cell within a table, click in the desired cell with the mouse, or use Tab (to move forward through cells) or Shift+Tab (to move in reverse). Within a given cell, use the same keys you use to navigate in any Word document. In addition, you can use the Alt+key combinations defined in Table 7.1.

Adding a Row to the Sample Table

If you press Tab while the insertion pointer is in the last cell of a table, a new row is automatically added, and Word places the insertion pointer in the first cell of the new row. You can also add new rows with the Table Insert Cells command, but it is generally easier to add them as you need them, using the Tab key. You can see how this can be done if you move the insertion pointer to the end of the last cell of the lunch arrangements table, and press Tab. Do so now, and add the following data to the new row that appears:

```
Saturday    Hans & Chani    Thai        Hit or Miss
                                        Exquisite
                                        Thai Cuisine
```

Save the completed sample table with the File Save command (Alt+F+S), and name it MYTABLE1.

Table 7.1   **Keyboard Navigation Within Tables**

Keystrokes	Insertion Pointer Action
Tab	Moves to next cell; if at last cell in table, adds a new row and moves to first cell there
Shift+Tab	Moves to prior cell
Alt+Home	Moves to first cell in current row
Alt+End	Moves to last cell in current row
Alt+PgUp	Moves to top cell in current column
Alt+PgDn	Moves to bottom cell in current column
Alt+5 (on numeric keypad)	Selects entire table
Arrow keys	Move within a cell and between cells; if at edge of table, arrow keys move in or out of the table
Shift+arrow keys	Select text in a cell, entire cells, rows, and columns with keyboard

---

The tables you've seen so far have been pretty plain, but Word lets you apply a variety of formatting options to a table. You can change the width of individual columns or the spacing between columns, and you can add borders around the cells. These options are explored in "Formatting Tables" later in the chapter.

Editing Tables

In this section you'll explore the options on the Table menu that allow you to edit your tables by inserting and deleting rows and columns. You can also merge the contents of a group of cells into a single cell. And you can split a table horizontally, at a point between any given rows, into two tables.

Inserting and Deleting Columns and Rows

When you need to add or remove cells, rows, or columns in a table, you can do so with the Insert and Delete commands of the Table menu. (These commands appear on the Table menu only when the insertion pointer is within a table.) If you have selected an entire row or column of a table before opening the Table menu, the Insert and Delete commands change to Insert Rows and Delete Rows, or Insert Columns and Delete Columns, as explained below.

When you choose the Insert option on the Table menu (Alt+A+I), the Insert Cells dialog box appears:

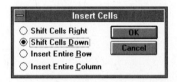

Tip. You can insert multiple rows or columns by selecting a number of existing rows or columns where you want to insert blank ones. Then select the Insert Rows or Insert Columns option on the Table menu. For example, if you select three existing rows and choose Insert Rows, Word inserts three new rows above the selected rows.

Here, you choose Shift Cells Right, Shift Cells Down, Insert Entire Row, or Insert Entire Column. In the case of the first two options, the cells that get shifted depend on whether you select a certain number of cells at the time you issue the command: If nothing is selected, only one cell gets inserted; if you select two existing cells and issue the command, the selected cells are shifted and two blank cells are inserted; select three cells, and three cells get shifted and inserted; and so on. Choose Shift Cells Right if you want the insertion to push existing cells to the right; choose Shift Cells Down if you want the insertion to push existing cells down. Choose Insert Entire Row or Insert Entire Column if you want to add a whole new row or column, respectively. New rows are added above the row containing the insertion pointer (or the selected cells), and new columns are added to the left of the column containing the insertion pointer (or the selected cells).

NOTE. *If you select an entire row or column, the Insert command on the Table menu changes to Insert Rows or Insert Columns. The Delete command changes to Delete Row or Delete Column. (Word assumes that, since you have selected an entire row or column, you want to insert or delete an entire row or column.)*

A command that works in a similar fashion (but with the opposite results) is the Delete command on the Table menu. When you choose Table Delete (Alt+A+D), the Delete Cells dialog box appears:

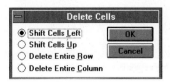

Here, you choose Shift Cells Left, Shift Cells Up, Delete Entire Row, or Delete Entire Column. Again, with the first two options, the cells that get shifted depend on your selection at the time you issue the command: If nothing is selected, only one cell is deleted. If you select two cells and issue the command, two cells are deleted; select three cells, and three cells are deleted; and so on. Choose Shift Cells Left if you want the deletion to pull existing cells to the left; choose Shift Cells Up to pull existing cells up. Choose Delete Entire Row or Delete Entire Column if you want to remove a row or column, respectively; any adjacent rows or columns are moved up or to the left to fill the space left by the deleted row or column.

Selecting Cells in a Table

To select cells within a table, use the same selection techniques that you learned in Chapter 2. You can click and drag across text in one or more cells with the mouse, or you can hold the Shift key down while using the arrow keys. You can also use the Shift key along with any of the Alt+key combinations shown in Table 7.1. While selecting, as you move the insertion pointer past the end of text in a particular cell, text in the adjacent cell is selected. If there is no text in a cell, the entire cell is selected as you drag through it, or move through it with the Shift key held down. Select past a paragraph marker, and an entire row is selected.

Examples of Inserting/Deleting Cells

How the insertion or deletion of cells affects the table depends on which cells you delete or add, and whether you choose to shift the remaining cells horizontally or vertically. There are many possibilities, and the results are best illustrated by example.

Consider the following table:

uno! (1)	seis! (6)
dos! (2)	siete! (7)
tres! (3)	ocho! (8)
cuatro! (4)	nueve! (9)
cinco! (5)	diez! (10)

In the examples that follow, cells 3 and 4—tres and cuatro—are selected. If you select cells 3 and 4 and choose Insert Cells on the Table menu, and then choose Shift Cells Right from the dialog box, the inserted new cells are

inserted at the selection location, and the existing cells are moved to the right, as shown here:

uno! (1)	seis! (6)	
dos! (2)	siete! (7)	
	tres! (3)	ocho! (8)
	cuatro! (4)	nueve! (9)
cinco! (5)	diez! (10)	

If you select cells 3 and 4, then choose Table Insert Cells and then Shift Cells Down, the blank cells are inserted at the selection location, and the existing cells are moved down, like this:

uno! (1)	seis! (6)
dos! (2)	siete! (7)
	ocho! (8)
	nueve! (9)
tres! (3)	diez! (10)
cuatro! (4)	
cinco! (5)	

If you select cells 3 and 4, then choose Table Delete Cells and then Shift Cells Left, the selected cells are deleted, and cells to the right move left to fill in the empty space, like this:

uno! (1)	seis! (6)
dos! (2)	siete! (7)
ocho! (8)	
nueve! (9)	
cinco! (5)	diez! (10)

If you select cells 3 and 4, then choose Table Delete Cells and then Shift Cells Up, the selected cells are deleted, and cells underneath move up to fill in the empty space, as shown here:

uno! (1)	seis! (6)
dos! (2)	siete! (7)
cinco! (5)	ocho! (8)
	nueve! (9)
	diez! (10)

Merging Cells

A group of horizontally adjacent cells can be merged into a single cell, using the Merge Cells command of the Table menu. (This command is available only after you have selected two or more adjoining cells in the table.) As an example, consider the simple table shown in Figure 7.4.

Figure 7.4
Table before cells are merged

These cells	will be merged
in this simple example	of a table.

If you select the two cells in the top row of this table, and choose Merge Cells on the Table menu, the result will be the table in Figure 7.5, where the selected cells are merged into one. Notice how the text in the cells is merged into a single entry.

Figure 7.5
Table after cells are merged

These cells will be merged	
in this simple example	of a table.

Splitting a Table into Two Tables

You can split a table into two tables with the Ctrl+Shift+Enter (New Column/Split Table) key-combination. This is often helpful if you want to insert text (such as a key definition or a note) between the rows of an existing table, and you do not want the text to be a part of the table. With the insertion pointer within the table, press Ctrl+Shift+Enter, and the table is split in two horizontally just above the insertion pointer. Hence, if the insertion pointer is in the third row of a table, the split occurs between the second and third rows. Figure 7.6 shows a table before being split, and Figure 7.7 shows the same table after being split with Ctrl+Shift+Enter; in this example, text has been added at the split location.

Figure 7.6
Table before
splitting with
Ctrl+Shift+Enter

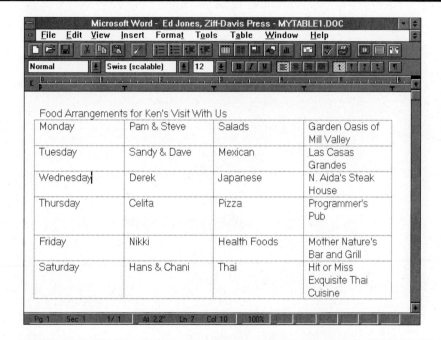

Formatting Tables

In Word, you can format the text contents of your tables, and you can format the tables themselves. Formatting is applied to the contents of tables in the same way you apply formatting to characters or paragraphs in Word, as explained in Chapter 4. For example, to apply Bold character formatting to a portion of text in a table, you select the desired text and press Ctrl+B to apply the formatting.

If you want to format the structure of the table itself (as opposed to its contents), use the various options of the Table and Format menus. With the Row Height and Column Width options of the Table menu, you can control elements such as column width, minimum row height, space between columns, row indentation, and row alignment. With the Format Border command, you can determine whether borders appear around individual cells or around the entire table. These commands are described in the following paragraphs.

Figure 7.7

Table after splitting with added text between

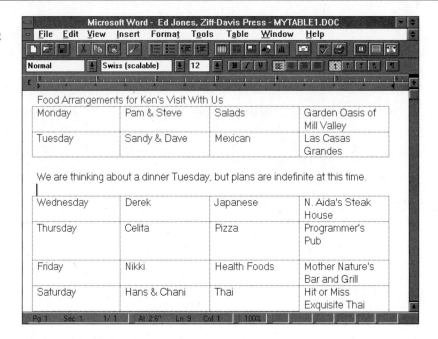

Setting Column Width

You can set column width in either of two ways. Keyboard users can use the Table Column Width command. Mouse users can drag the table gridlines or the table's column indicators in the ruler to the desired location.

When you choose Column Width on the Table menu (Alt+A+W), the Column Width dialog box appears:

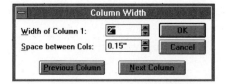

In the Width of Column text box, Word suggests a column width based on the page margins. You can change this to specify the width of one or more cells of the table. If you select more than one cell in the table before you choose the command, the width you enter applies to those selected cells, which are identified next to the text box. If you select no cells, the width you enter will apply to the cell containing the insertion pointer. You can also

assign a width to one column, and then move your selection to the next or previous column by choosing Next Column (Alt+N) or Previous Column (Alt+P) command buttons from the dialog box. By repeatedly using Next Column and Previous Column, you can assign different widths to various columns throughout a table.

Mouse users have the option of changing column widths by dragging the table gridlines, or dragging the table column indicators around on the ruler. (The table column indicators resemble boldfaced upside-down Ts; when the insertion pointer is in the table, the Ts appear on the ruler directly above the dotted lines indicating column borders.) Place the pointer directly over the column gridline, and drag the gridline as desired. Or, click on a table column indicator and drag it, and you will see the column width change accordingly. If you select no tables before you drag the indicator, you change the column width for the entire table. If you make a selection first, you will change the width of the columns within that selection.

Setting Space Between Columns

Choose Table Column Width and use the Space Between Cols text box to adjust the space Word places between the text of adjacent cells. (The default amount is 0.15 inches.) With cells selected, the spacing amount you enter applies to the cells in all rows of the current selection. If no cells are selected, the column spacing applies to all cells of the row that contains the insertion pointer.

Setting Row Height, Row Indentation, and Row Alignment

You can set the row height, row indentation, and row alignment of one or more row in a table, with the Row Height command (Alt+A+H) on the Table menu. For all these elements, the measurement you enter applies to all rows in the current selection, or to the row containing the insertion pointer if no rows are selected. When you select this command, you see this dialog box:

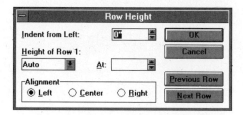

Use the Indent From Left text box to indent one or more rows of a table. The rows will be indented from the left page margin by the decimal amount that you enter; for example, enter 0.5" to indent the rows one-half inch. You can enter a negative value to shift the rows to the left, past the left margin. Figure 7.8 shows the effects of indentation on the rows of a table.

Figure 7.8

Indentation applied to the rows of a table

This row is not indented.		
	This row is indented,	by one inch.
This row is indented,	by minus one-half inch.	

Note. Cells can have differing widths, but all cells in a given row of a table must have the same height.

Use the Height of Row text box to set the minimum height of one or more rows. The number after Height of Row indicates the selected rows. The default for this element is Auto, which means the row will be high enough to contain any text in the row. If you choose At Least and enter a decimal value, Word makes the rows at least as tall as the value you enter. If any text within a cell is larger than the minimum height, Word increases the height as needed to accommodate the text. Exactly specifies an exact height, regardless of the size of the text.

Use the Left, Center, and Right buttons of the Align Rows area of the dialog box to determine the alignment of table rows in relation to the page margins. This can be compared to the alignment options of the Format Paragraph dialog box. As with paragraphs, you can left-align, center, or right-align the rows of your table. The selected rows are left-aligned by default; this means the left edge of the row will be aligned with the left margin unless you have specified an indentation. Choose Center to center the rows, or choose Right to align the right edge of the row with the right page margin.

Of course, for the Row Alignment options to have any visible effect, your table must be narrower than the space between the left and right page margins. If you used the default options in the Insert Table dialog box when you created the table, then the table is already as wide as the space between the page margins, and choosing an alignment option will have no visible effect. The alignment options are useful when you have designed your own widths for the table columns (rather than letting Word automatically size the table), and you want to place the table in a specific location. Figure 7.9 demonstrates the effects of row alignment on a table.

Figure 7.9

Various alignment options applied to the rows of a table

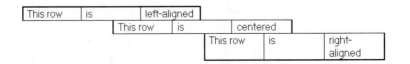

This row	is	left-aligned			
	This row	is	centered		
		This row	is	right-aligned	

Remember that the Alignment settings move the *horizontal position* of the entire row, not the text within the row. Thus, if you choose Center for the row alignment, the row will be centered within the page margins, but individual text within the cells will not necessarily be centered. To left-align, center, or right-align text within a cell, you must select the text and then use the alignment options of the Format Paragraph command (or the keyboard or ribbon equivalents).

Applying Borders

Use the Format Border command (Alt+T+B) to place borders around a cell or a group of cells of the table. The borders that you place with this command will be printed, unlike the table grid lines; these borders are added directly atop the table gridlines. Figure 7.10 shows sample borders available with the Format Border command.

Figure 7.10

Types and positions of borders

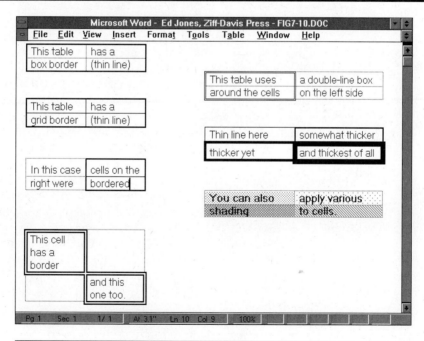

How borders are applied depends on the selections you make in the Border Cells dialog box that appears when you choose Format Borders, and on how much of the table is selected when you choose the command. If no cells are selected, the borders you add will apply only to the cell containing the insertion pointer. If a selection exists, the borders are applied to all cells in the selection.

When you choose Format Borders, the Border Cells dialog box appears:

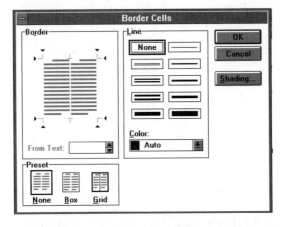

Tip. If you want to apply borders to the entire table, use Table Select Table (or press Alt+5 on the numeric keypad) to select the entire table, and then use Format Borders.

The Border diagram at the left of the dialog box displays border markers representing the border options that you choose. In the Preset area, you can choose None (Alt+N), Box (Alt+B), or Shadow (Alt+H), to have no border, a box border drawn with a thin line, or a shadow border around the selected cells. If you select more than one cell, the name of the Shadow option changes to Grid. Grid adds the border to all sides of the selected cells, rather than just to the outside edges of the selection as a unit.

The Line (Alt+L) style buttons let you implement a particular type of line as the border; as you choose a line type, a representation of it appears in the border diagram. Use the Color (Alt+C) list box to choose a color different from the default for the border. (Of course, your hardware must support color display or color printing for your color choice to be visible on screen or in the printed copy.)

You might want to shade a specific row or column in a table, to emphasize the text contained within that row or column. To do this, choose the Shading button (Alt+S) to display this Shading dialog box:

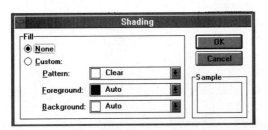

Here you can select a shading pattern for the cells selected. First choose Custom (Alt+C), and then select the desired settings from the Pattern (Alt+P), Foreground (Alt+F), and Background (Alt+B) list boxes. In the case of Foreground and Background, the default setting of Auto uses the colors that are specified as default foreground and background colors in your Word Setup. You'll see a sample of what you've chosen in the Sample box.

Once you have chosen all the border settings you need, choose OK. The borders and shading will then be applied to your selection within the table.

An Exercise in Laying Out a Complex Table

You can utilize many of the options provided by the various commands of the Table menu and the Format Border command to duplicate the fictitious television schedule shown in Figure 7.11. Try the exercise, and you'll get to practice most table creation techniques.

Figure 7.11

Sample television schedule

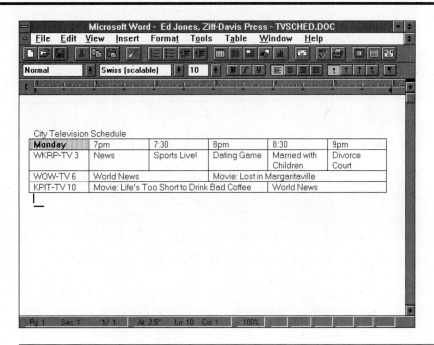

1. Open a new document with the File New command (Alt+F+N, and then OK).

2. Type the heading, **City Television Schedule**, and press Enter to begin a new paragraph.

3. Choose Insert Table on the Table menu (Alt+A+I).

4. In the Insert Table dialog box, enter **6** for the Number of Columns, **4** for the Number of Rows, **1** for the Initial Column Width, and then choose OK or press Enter.

5. If you are not already using a 10-point type style, choose Table Select Table (Alt+A+A) to select the entire table. Then open the Format Character dialog box (Alt+T+C), and select 10 from the Points list box. Choose OK.

6. Move the insertion pointer to the first cell of the table. Press Ctrl+B to apply boldface. Type **Monday**. Then press Ctrl+B again to turn off the boldface.

7. Press Tab to move to the next cell. In the remaining five columns, type the following cell entries, pressing Tab after each one to move to the next cell:

   7pm   7:30   8pm   8:30   9pm

8. After pressing Tab following the last column entry (9pm), the insertion pointer will be in the first cell of the second row. Type **WKRP-TV 3**. Press Tab to move to the next cell.

9. In the remaining five columns, type the following cell entries, pressing Tab after each one to move to the next cell:

   News   Sports Live!   Dating Game   Married with Children   Divorce Court

10. Press Tab after typing the last cell entry, to move the insertion pointer to the first cell of the third row. Type **WOW-TV 6** and press Tab to move to the second cell of the third row.

11. Select Table and choose Delete Cells (Alt+A+D); then choose Shift Cells Left; then click OK. Again, select Delete Cells on the Table menu (Alt+A+D) and choose OK. Doing this twice deletes two cells. Alternatively, you could select these two cells and then use the Table Delete Cells option.

12. With the insertion pointer still in the second cell of the third row, select Column Width in the Table menu (Alt+A+W). In the Width of Column box, enter **2**, and choose OK.

13. Press Tab once to move to the third column of the third row. Select Table Column Width (Alt+A+W). In the Width of Column box, enter **3**, and choose OK.

14. Press Tab once to move to the last column of the third row. Select Delete Cells in the Table menu (Alt+A+D), and choose OK.

15. Use Shift+Tab or the mouse to place the insertion pointer in the second cell of the third row. Type **World News**, press Tab once, and then type **Movie: Lost in Margaritaville**.

16. Press Tab to move the insertion pointer to the first cell of the last row. Type **KPIT-TV 10**, and press Tab to move to the second cell of the last row.

17. Use your preferred selection method to select the second, third, and fourth cells in this row of the table. Then choose Table Delete Cells (Alt+A+D) and click OK. When done, you will have just two unused cells remaining in the last row of the table.

18. With the cursor in the second cell of the last row, select Column Width in the Table menu (Alt+A+W). Enter **3** in the Width of Column box, and choose OK.

19. Enter this text in the cell **Movie: Life's Too Short to Drink Bad Coffee**. Then press Tab to move the insertion pointer to the last cell of the last row.

20. Select Table Column Width (Alt+A+W) again. Enter **2** in the Width of Column box, and choose OK. Enter **World News** in the last cell.

All that remains is to add borders to the cells of the table, using the Format Borders command.

21. Choose Table Select Table (Alt+A+A), and then Format Border (Alt+T+B).

22. Select the Grid (Alt+G) option, and choose OK.

23. Place the insertion pointer in the first cell of the top row of the table (the one containing Monday).

24. Select Format Border (Alt+T+B) again, and click the Shading button (Alt+S).

25. In the Shading dialog box, choose Pattern (Alt+P) and scroll to 25% in the list box. Then choose OK twice to close both dialog boxes.

Side-by-Side Paragraphs

Word's ability to store up to a page of text in any column of a table makes it easy to set up *side-by-side paragraphs* using the table feature. Side-by-side paragraphs are paragraphs of text that appear in columns beside each other, but are not necessarily related. Newspaper columns are a good example of side-by-side paragraphs. (There are other ways to do side-by-side paragraphs, and Chapter 11 provides details on this format, as well as other desktop-publishing topics.)

To create side-by-side paragraphs, simply insert a table with two or more columns, and use the Format Table dialog box to size the columns as desired. Then, type the desired text into the columns, keeping in mind the rule that a table cannot extend beyond the length of a single page. The table will automatically lay out the paragraphs of text side by side on your screen. You can add borders, as described in the foregoing exercise, to differentiate the cells.

Figure 7.12 on the next page shows a document with side-by-side paragraphs, set up within the boundaries of a table. In this example, the table has one row and two columns; the left column is set to a width of two inches, and the right column is set to a width of 4 inches. A thick border has been added to the left cell of the table, giving the text the look of a "sidebar" (an enclosed box of text commonly used on newspaper pages and in magazine articles).

Converting Text to Tables

Word lets you convert text that is typed or arranged in tabular form into Word-format tables. This is helpful when someone else has created a table using tabs, and you want to work with it using Word's table feature. You can also use this technique to convert data from databases in "comma-delimited format" into Word tables. (See your database management software documentation for directions on creating comma-delimited files.) Text that is separated by tabs, by commas, or by paragraph marks can be converted into a Word table.

To convert text into a table, first open the file in Word with File Open. If it is a foreign-format text file, a dialog box may ask you which type of file you're importing. Once the file is open, select the text, and then choose the Convert Text to Table option on the Table menu (Alt+A+T). If the Insert Table dialog box appears, in the Convert From area choose Paragraphs, Tab Delimited, or Comma Delimited (as appropriate based on the text to be converted). Choose OK, and Word recommends entries in the Number of Columns and Number of Rows boxes, based on the appearance of the text you are converting. (You can change these recommendations by entering any desired values in the text boxes.) To complete the conversion of the text to a table, choose OK from the dialog box.

Figure 7.12

Side-by-side paragraphs within a two-column table

CURRENT USE OF PERSONAL COMPUTERS	REASONS FOR SELECTION OF PERSONAL COMPUTERS
The survey figures prove that library usage of personal computers is high, and the library personal computer marketplace represents a significant market-place for the purchase and use of personal computers, acces-sories, and associated software. On an overall basis, 74.5% of the libraries surveyed are using personal computers at their locations. Academic libraries demonstrated a significant use of personal computers, with 97% of all academic libraries reporting personal computer use. Those figures were followed by high school libraries (83%), special libraries (67%), ele-mentary school libraries (51.5%) and public libraries (48%). These ratios are significantly higher than the ratios of personal computer usage within the home marketplace, where 43% of respondents to surveys are currently using personal computers.	Libraries indicate that a number of reasons affect the selection of a personal computer. This approach follows that of home users, who also indicate varied reasons for the selection of a brand of computer. Among libraries, the following reasons are assigned the most importance by survey respondents: • Availability of software • Compatibility with other equipment used at the same location or throughout the campus • Mandatory choice by administrator, teachers, or other persons. • Attractive pricing As in the home–office computer marketplace, there appears to be a definite "two–tier" marketplace of low–end and high–end system buyers. Among the low–end buyers of "clone" equipment, price played a very important consideration in the buying decision. However, among the high–end system buyers of Apple and IBM equipment, price played a less–important role in the decision–making process. **CURRENT AND FUTURE USES OF PERSONAL COMPUTERS** Primary uses of personal computers installed in libraries are word processing (42.9%), data storage (38.1%), database management (16.1%), on–line connections to data bases (14.2%), budgeting and forecasting (12.0%) and publication indexing (10.4%).

As an example, consider the text in Figure 7.13. (You can easily duplicate this example if you want to, by opening a new document and typing the text shown, using tabs between columns and pressing Enter at the end of each line.)

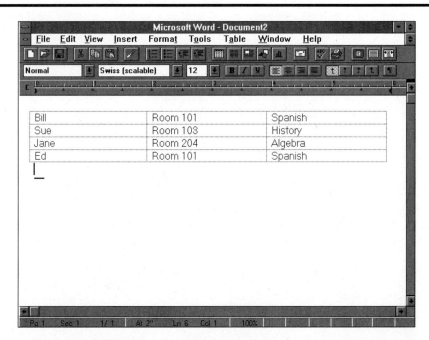

Select all four rows of the text, and invoke the Insert Table command. Then use the Table Column Width command to change the column widths to two inches. The results are similar to those shown in Figure 7.14.

Sorting

There will likely be times when you want to arrange a list of data (often within a table) in alphabetical or numerical order. Word's Tools Sorting command can be used for this task. Because tables often contain the type of data you might want to sort, sorting is covered in this chapter. Keep in mind, however, that the Tools Sorting command is by no means limited to tables. You can use the command to sort any list of data, whether it is in table form or a simple typed list with lines separated by paragraph markers.

When Word sorts a list, it rearranges the list entries in alphabetical or numeric order. Using options in the dialog box that appears when you select the Tools Sorting command, you can sort in ascending or descending order, and choose a sort based on all characters (alphanumeric), on numbers, or on dates.

Sorting a list, whether it is in a table or not, is a simple matter. First select the information you want to sort. (If the information is in a table, you can select all of the table, or as much of it as you want to sort.) Next choose Tools Sorting (Alt+O+I), and the sorting dialog box appears:

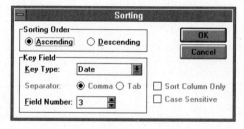

- In the Sorting Order box, specify Ascending (Alt+A) or Descending (Alt+D).

- The Key Type (Alt+K) list box provides choices of Alphanumeric (ordinary text that may be letters mixed with numbers), Numeric, or Date; choose the key that matches what you are sorting.

- The Separator buttons are needed only when you are sorting lists that are *not* stored within tables; mark Comma (Alt+C) or Tab (Alt+T) to indicate that items in the list are separated by commas or tabs.

- The Field Number list box is used only with tables; here you specify the number of the column that you want to sort.

- Mark the Case Sensitive option to tell Word to include case in the sort; uppercase letters will appear first in the list, followed by lowercase letters.

- The Sort Column Only option also applies only to tables; after selecting just one column of a table, you can mark this check box to tell Word to sort only that column, without rearranging the remaining columns. (Typically, you would not want to do this, but there may be rare instances where you want to sort one column of a table while leaving the adjacent columns unchanged.)

Once you have chosen your desired sort characteristics, choose OK from the dialog box, and Word will sort the list.

TIP. *If you perform a sort and the results are not what you want, you can undo the sort with the Undo Sort option on the Edit menu. (As with all Undo commands, you must choose it immediately after executing the Tools Sorting command; once you perform another action, this changes the name of the last command to be undone.)*

An Example of a Sort

You can see how easily Word can sort a table of information by performing the following steps:

1. Create a new document with File New (Alt+F+N, and then OK).

2. Select the Table Insert Table command (Alt+A+I) to insert a new table; specify **3** columns and **5** rows. Leave Column Width set at Auto.

3. Add the following data to the table, using your preferred method of navigating within cells:

Smith	construction	5/15/85
Jackson	accounting	6/22/87
Appelby	construction	8/19/79
Williams	operations	10/14/91
Shaw	construction	12/1/86

4. For this first example, do a sort based on the employee's name. With the insertion pointer anywhere in the table, choose Table Select Table (or press Alt+5 on the numeric keypad) to select the entire table.

5. Choose Sorting on the Tools menu (Alt+O+I). Since the sort is based on the first column (the one containing the surnames), leave the default field number (1) in the Field No. box. Leave Ascending marked as the desired sort order.

6. Choose OK. The results of the sort will resemble this table:

Appelby	construction	8/19/79
Jackson	accounting	6/22/87
Shaw	construction	12/1/86
Smith	construction	5/15/85
Williams	operations	10/14/91

7. Now try a sort based on the employee's hire date (the last column). With the table still selected from the last operation, choose Tools Sorting (Alt+O+I).

8. Since you are sorting dates, press Alt+K to move to the Key Type list box, and select Date. Also, the sort must be based on the third column, so specify 3 in the Field No. box. Again, leave Ascending selected as the desired sort order.

9. Choose OK. this time the sorted data looks like this:

Appelby	construction	8/19/79
Smith	construction	5/15/85
Shaw	construction	12/1/86
Jackson	accounting	6/22/87
Williams	operations	10/14/91

10. You can exit this document without saving; it will not be needed later in this text.

The sorts you've just done provide only an idea of the power of the Tools Sorting command. Keep in mind that you must select the proper Key Type in the Sorting dialog box to obtain the proper results. For example, if you want to sort a list based on dates, but you leave Alphanumeric selected as the Key Type, you will not get the sort that you want.

This chapter has given you an introduction to all the major features of tables. The flexibility provided by Word's table feature means that you can likely apply tables to many facets of your work in Word. In Chapter 11 you'll find some additional tips on how tables, along with various other features of Word, can be used to create documents typical of desktop publishing.

8

Working with Outlines

FOR MANY WHO WORK WITH WORDS, AN OUTLINE IS THE FIRST STEP IN getting thoughts and ideas down on paper. With even the earliest of word processors, simple outlining was possible by using tabs and manually typed headings. Word, however, offers *automatic outlining*, and with it come significant advantages. In addition to aiding the organizing process, Word's outlining feature lets you automatically number headings, and create tables of contents based on an outline. And when you create an outline in Word, you can easily rearrange parts of the outline without giving thought to precise formatting.

Understanding Word Outlines

In Word, outlining is "built into" a document; as you create a document, you can create an outline of that document at the same time. With Word, the only difference between a normal document and an outline is the view that you use to examine the document. When you are in normal, draft, or page layout view, you are looking at the document in its normal (nonoutline) form. Turn on the outline view, however, and you look at the document in the entirely separate form of an outline. Figure 8.1 shows an example of a document in outline form; in an exercise later in this chapter you will duplicate this document.

In outline view, a document can contain two types of text: headings and body text. A *heading* is any paragraph that has been assigned one of the special paragraph styles Word provides specifically for the creation of outlines. There are nine of these predefined styles, called Heading 1 through Heading 9. The numbers define the importance of the heading in the outline; a top-level heading is assigned the Heading 1 style, the next level heading is assigned the Heading 2 style, and so on. Word automatically places all top-level headings at the left margin by default, and indents each successive level of heading incrementally.

Body text is any text within an outline that hasn't been given a heading style. Word also uses the term *subtext* to refer to all subheadings and body text that appear below a particular heading. Body text, too, is assigned a style, called Normal.

Figure 8.2 demonstrates the difference between each level of heading and its associated body text. Although the figure shows only four levels of headings, remember that Word lets you have up to nine levels.

Figure 8.1

Sample document viewed in outline form

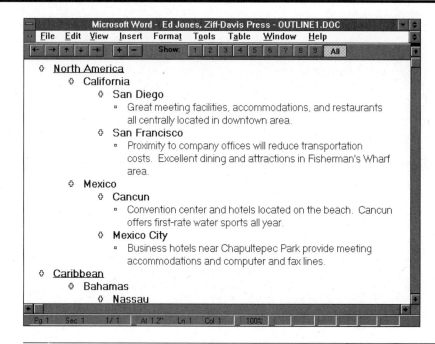

Working in Outline View

You work with a document in outline form by using the View Outline command. Within outline view, Word gives you additional tools to aid in structuring the outline. A special toolbar, called the Outline bar, appears at the top of the screen, and the ruler goes away. The Outline bar contains the buttons you need for working in outline view. In addition to the Outline bar, small selection icons appear to the left of each heading and subtext paragraph. Icons shaped like plus symbols indicate headings; icons shaped like small squares indicate body text. You can see the Outline bar and the selection icons in both Figures 8.1 and 8.2.

Word's outlining feature is flexible—you can use it with a document at any time. You can create the document, and later come back to it and structure the document in outline form. Or you can create the document in outline form as you go along. Additional portions of a document, from headings to body text, can be added to the document at any time. Also, you can split a window, using the techniques explained in Chapter 3, and turn on outline view in one window and normal view in the other. This lets you see the document in outline form and in normal form at the same time, and watch how changes you make in the outline view will affect your entire document.

(Because you are working with a single document, any changes to text you make in one window will appear in the other.)

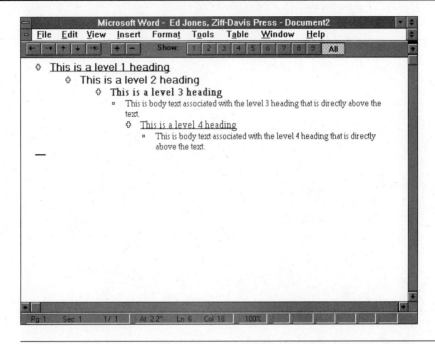

Figure 8.2

Outline with four levels of headings and accompanying body text

You can change the structure of an outline as you work with it, by promoting a paragraph (heading or body text) to a higher level, or demoting it to a lower level of importance. You can also "expand" and "collapse" an outline to display and/or put away the subtext of headings, allowing you to focus on a particular area of thought when necessary. You can move headings around to reorganize a document, and you can collapse headings so that you can more easily navigate through a document. (All of these techniques will be demonstrated throughout this chapter.)

Using the Outline Bar

When working on the structure of a Word outline, you generally select the desired paragraph, and then choose an outline tool from the Outline bar (or use a keystroke equivalent). The Outline bar has the following buttons, as shown in Figure 8.3.

Figure 8.3
The buttons of the
Outline bar

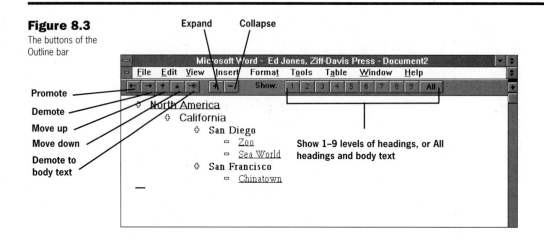

- Use the Promote button (←) to promote a heading to a higher level in the outline, and the Demote button (→) to demote a heading to a lower level.

- The Move Up and Move Down buttons (↑ and ↓) let you move a paragraph up or down to a new location in the outline.

- With the Demote to Body Text button (→ >), you can convert a heading to body text.

- Use the Expand button (+) to show all text under a heading, and the Collapse button (–) to hide the text under a heading so that only the heading shows.

- The numbered Show buttons let you control which levels of the outline are displayed. Use the All button to tell Word to display all levels of headings and body text.

For keyboard users, there are Alt+Shift keystroke equivalents for every button in the Outline bar. These are mentioned at appropriate places in the chapter, and summarized in Table 8.1.

Note to Laptop Users
The Alt+Shift+5 key-combination for converting headings to body text does not work on some keyboards, including those of many laptops. This is due to the compromises made in designing laptop keyboards; these keyboards often give up the numeric keypad, and combine all numbers with the character keys. There is no easy way out of this problem. If you are using a laptop and you plan on doing much work with Word outlines, consider adding a mouse so you can use the Outline bar.

Table 8.1 **Keyboard Equivalents for Outline Bar Buttons**

Key	Purpose
Alt+Shift+Left Arrow	Promote paragraph to higher level
Alt+Shift+Right Arrow	Demote paragraph to lower level
Alt+Shift+Up Arrow	Move paragraph up in outline
Alt+Shift+Down Arrow	Move paragraph down in outline
Alt+Shift+Plus	Expand (show) body text under a heading
Alt+Shift+Minus	Collapse body text so that only heading shows
Alt+Shift+5 (on numeric keypad)	Convert heading to body text (Num Lock must be off)
Alt+Shift+1 through Alt+Shift+9 (on keyboard)	Show heading levels 1 through 9
Alt+Shift+A	Show all headings and body text

Selecting Text in Outline View

When you are in outline view, selecting text works much the same as it does in other Word tasks. There are, however, differences you should be aware of. The most significant one is that you lose the ability to select a full paragraph along with part of another paragraph. If you use either mouse or keyboard methods to select past the boundary of a paragraph and into the following one, the entire second paragraph becomes selected. As you drag across additional paragraphs, each one becomes selected in its entirety. This makes editing a bit more difficult in outline view. (You can, of course, get around this by turning off outline view while you do your editing of the outline text.)

Another difference involves the technique for selecting a heading and all of the subtext below it. You can do this by double-clicking the mouse while the pointer is beside the heading, in the selection bar area. Unfortunately, there is no equivalent for this mouse action from the keyboard; you can, however, accomplish the same result by selecting the heading and its subtext with a combination of Shift and the arrow keys. You can also select a heading by clicking on its selection icon.

CAUTION! *When you drag to select text, be careful not to drag the selection icon for the heading or body text. (The mouse pointer changes to a ✛.) Doing so causes the heading or body text to be repositioned within the outline, rather than selected.*

Creating and Organizing Outlines

This chapter teaches you a number of techniques used in building outlines. They include

- Promoting and demoting headings to different levels in the outline

- Converting headings to body text and vice versa

- Expanding and collapsing outline headings to display/hide their subtext

- Moving headings within the outline

- Applying numbering to the headings of an outline

- Creating a table of contents from an outline

Promoting and Demoting Headings

You can use the Promote (←)and Demote (→) buttons, or the equivalent key-combinations, to change a heading's level within the outline.

- To promote a heading to another level with the mouse, select the heading and click on the Promote button in the Outline bar, or drag the heading's icon to the left. From the keyboard, first select the desired heading. Then press Alt+Shift+Left Arrow.

- To demote a heading level with the mouse, select the heading and click on the Demote button in the Outline bar, or drag the heading's icon to the right. Using the keyboard, select the heading and press Alt+Shift+Right Arrow.

When you promote a heading, it gets assigned the next highest heading level, and is outdented one level to the left. The opposite happens when you demote a heading; it gets assigned the next lower level, and is indented one level to the right. In Figure 8.4, the heading San Diego has been promoted to the same level as the heading above it, California. (In the figure, the text was selected before being promoted; hence, it remains highlighted.) As a result of the promotion, San Diego's subtext paragraphs, Zoo and Sea World, have also been promoted one level, to the same level as San Francisco. In Figure 8.5, the heading San Diego has been demoted one level to the same level as Chinatown. Once again, the subtext under San Diego has been demoted along with the heading.

Converting Headings to Body Text and Vice Versa

Another reorganizing task you'll need to do is to demote a heading and change it to body text. To do this with the mouse, click on the Demote to Body

Text (→>) button in the Outline bar, or drag the heading's selection icon to the right. From the keyboard, select the heading and press Alt+Shift+5, using the 5 on the numeric keypad. (If you're using a laptop, see the note earlier in this chapter about Alt+Shift+5 on laptop keyboards.)

Figure 8.4

A heading and its subtext that have been promoted

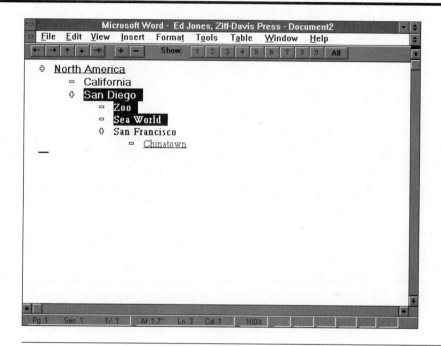

In the other direction, you can convert body text and make it a heading simply by promoting it. When body text is promoted, it is converted to a heading that has the same level as the heading above it. With the mouse, select the body text and click on the Promote button, or drag the heading's selection icon to the left. From the keyboard, select the desired body text and press Alt+Shift+Left Arrow.

Expanding and Collapsing Outline Headings

As an aid in organizing your thoughts, Word lets you *expand* or *collapse* an outline. When a heading in an outline is expanded, all of its subtext (lower-level headings and body text) is made visible. In comparison, when a heading is collapsed, all its subtext is hidden from view. In Figure 8.6, a sample outline has its body text collapsed; the lines that appear under the headings indicate the presence of collapsed subtext. Figure 8.7 shows the same outline with body text expanded.

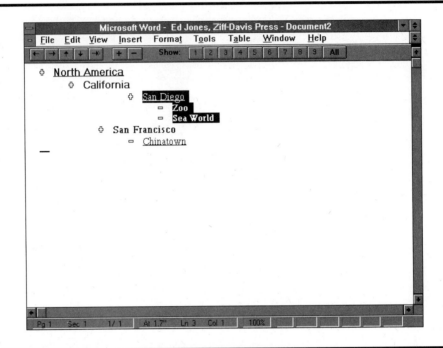

Figure 8.5
A heading and its subtext that have been demoted

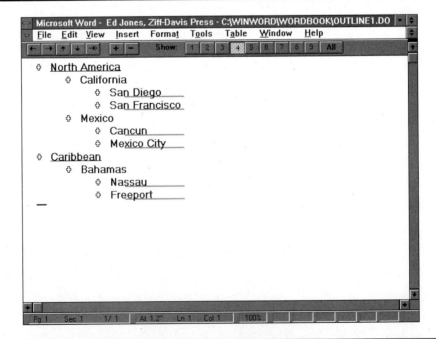

Figure 8.6
Outline with body text collapsed

Figure 8.7
Outline with body text expanded

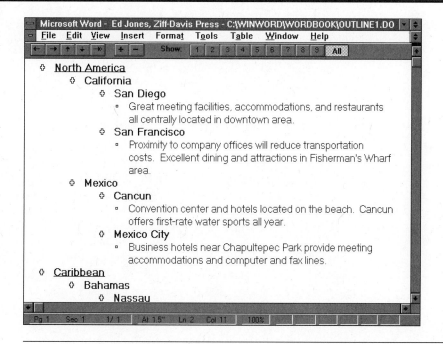

There are several methods available to you for expanding and collapsing the headings of an outline.

To expand a heading with the mouse, select the heading and click the Expand (+) button in the Outline bar. To collapse a heading, select the heading and click the Collapse (–) button. From the keyboard, select the heading and press Alt+Shift+Plus to expand, or Alt+Shift+Minus to collapse.

NOTE. *Many keyboards have two minus keys and two plus keys; one set is located on the numeric keyboard. In outline view, and if Num Lock is off, Word recognizes either set; you can use either in the Alt+Shift key-combinations.*

Mouse users can also expand or collapse headings by double-clicking on the heading's selection icon. The icon acts as a toggle, so double-clicking once expands the heading; double-clicking again collapses the heading; and so on.

Tip. You can also press the * key on the numeric keypad to expand all headings and body text, or collapse all body text.

You can also use the numbered Show buttons of the Outline bar (or the equivalent key-combinations) to collapse or expand the entire outline to a specific level. The numbers on the Outline bar correspond to all the possible heading levels within an outline. Choosing the Show 1 button, for example, causes level 1 headings and subtext to be visible; choosing Show 2 causes all headings and subtext at level 1 and level 2 to be visible; Show 3 causes everything at levels 1, 2, and 3 to be visible, and so on. Conversely, if you have all levels up to level 4 visible, choosing Show 2 causes levels 3 and 4 to collapse, so that only levels 1 and 2 are visible. Choosing All displays all headings and all body text in the outline.

You can click on a Show button with the mouse, or you can press Alt+Shift and the desired heading level number, or Alt+Shift+A to choose All.

Moving Headings Within the Outline

Word provides considerable flexibility for the task of moving headings and their associated subtext. You can move a heading up and down in an outline, with or without its associated subtext. And you can move multiple headings and associated subtext, simply by selecting more than one heading prior to the move operation.

Tip. Moving headings with associated subtext is easiest if you first collapse the heading and then move it to its new location.

To move a heading, first select it. If you select an expanded heading *without* selecting its visible subtext, Word moves the heading but leaves the subtext in its current position. If the heading is collapsed, moving the heading causes the associated subtext also to be moved, even though only the heading is selected. If you want to move only the subtext without moving the heading, select just the subtext. You cannot move a portion of a subtext unit; you must move it all.

Once you have selected the heading to be moved:

- Click on the Move Up or Down arrow buttons in the Outline bar to move the heading up or down in the outline.

- Mouse users have another option for moving headings: You can drag the heading's selection icon up or down in the outline to the new desired location. When you position the mouse pointer over the selection icon, it changes to the shape of a cross with four arrowheads (✛). As you click, the pointer becomes a two-headed arrow pointing up and down. Drag the heading to the new location.

- From the keyboard, press Alt+Shift+Up Arrow to move the heading up, or press Alt+Shift+Down Arrow to move the heading down.

An Exercise with an Outline

To get to know the concepts used in building outlines, do the following exercise:

1. Select File New, and choose OK from the dialog box to create a new document.

2. Select View Outline (Alt+V+O) to switch to outline view.

3. Type the following text exactly as shown, pressing Enter—not newline—
   after each line. These will become the headings for your sample outline.

   ```
   North America
   California
   San Diego
   San Francisco
   Mexico
   Cancun
   Mexico City
   Caribbean
   Bahamas
   Nassau
   Freeport
   ```

4. Move the cursor to the line that reads California, and click the Demote
   button (or press Alt+Shift+Right Arrow).

5. Repeat Step 4 for Mexico and Bahamas.

6. Move the cursor to San Diego, and demote this line twice, by pressing
   Alt+Shift+Right Arrow twice or by clicking on the Demote button twice.

7. Move the cursor to San Francisco, and repeat Step 6 to demote this line
   twice. Then do the same for Cancun, Mexico City, Nassau, and Freeport.

At this point, the structure of your sample outline is apparent; it will resemble the outline in Figure 8.8.

Now you can begin adding body text to various parts of the outline.
As you work, keep in mind that you do not necessarily have to create
your outlines in this same manner. This example follows the common technique of creating outline headings first, and then filling in the details; however, you can create headings and body text as you go along, if that works
better for your task.

8. Move the cursor to the end of the line that reads San Diego, and press
   Enter to begin a new line. Note that the selection icon for the new line
   aligns with the existing San Diego line; hence, the new line is at this
   point a heading. Before you begin typing, you'll want to convert it to
   body text.

9. Click the Demote to Body Text (→>) button in the Outline bar, or
   press Alt+Shift+5 (using the 5 on the numeric keypad). Then type the
   following text:

   ```
   Great meeting facilities, accommodations, and restaurants
   all centrally located in downtown area.
   ```

Figure 8.8

The initial headings in a sample outline

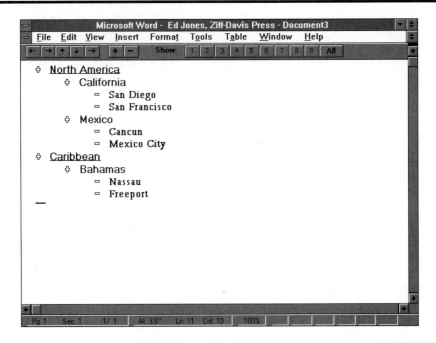

10. Move the cursor to the end of the San Francisco line, and press Enter to begin a new line. Demote this line to body text as described in Step 9. Then type the following text:

    Proximity to company offices will reduce transportation costs. Excellent dining and attractions in Fisherman's Wharf area.

11. Move the cursor to the end of Cancun, and press Enter to begin a new line. Demote the line to body text (Step 9), and type

    Convention center and hotels located on the beach. Cancun offers first-rate water sports all year.

12. Move the cursor to the end of Mexico City, and press Enter to begin a new line. Demote the line to body text (Step 9), and type

    Business hotels near Chapultepec Park provide meeting accommodations and computer and fax lines.

13. Move the cursor to the end of Nassau, and press Enter to begin a new line. Demote the line to body text (Step 9), and type

```
Great hotels with meeting facilities located on the beach,
in Cable Beach area.
```

14. Finally, move the cursor to the end of Freeport, and press Enter to begin a new line. Demote the line to body text (Step 9), and type

```
Shopping, excellent golf, and water sports readily
available.
```

15. Save the outline with File Save (Alt+F+S), and call it OUTLINE1. At this point, your outline should resemble Figure 8.9.

This example demonstrates some outlining techniques, such as the demotion of heading levels to body text, and the demotion of headings to lower-level headings. In the next section, you'll experiment with some additional outline features.

Figure 8.9

Sample outline with body text inserted

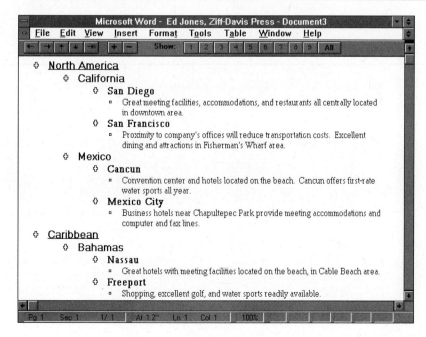

Expanding and Collapsing Headings in the Example

It's often helpful to collapse an outline so you can look at the major points without being distracted by lower-level headings and other subtext. An easy way to do this for the entire outline is with the Show buttons of the Outline bar, or their keyboard equivalents. Try this with the OUTLINE1 sample.

1. Click on the Show 1 button (or press Alt+Shift+1) to show only level 1 headings in the outline. When you do this, only North America and Caribbean are visible.

2. Click on the Show 2 button (or press Alt+Shift+2). The level 2 headings, California, Mexico, and Bahamas, become visible underneath the level 1 headings.

3. Click on the Show 3 button (or press Alt+Shift+3), and all the city names at level 3 become visible beneath the level 2 headings.

4. Finally, click on the All button (or press Alt+Shift+A). The body text appears, and the entire outline is thus displayed.

Of course, you can also show or hide the subtext of individual headings using the Expand (+) and Collapse (–) buttons of the Outline bar (or their keyboard equivalents). To see how this works, place the cursor anywhere in the Mexico heading. Click on the Collapse (–) icon or press Alt+Shift+Minus. Notice that the Cancun and Mexico City headings collapse underneath, hiding their body text. Click on the Expand (+) button (or press Alt+Shift+Plus), and the subheadings expand again, revealing the body text underneath.

Promoting and Demoting Headings in the Example

You can use the Promote (←) and Demote (→) buttons of the Outline bar (or their keyboard equivalents) to promote and demote headings. Remember that body text for a heading gets promoted or demoted along with the heading, but subheadings do not. To see how this works, use your preferred selection method to select the San Francisco heading and the subtext below it. Then, click on the ← button in the Outline bar (or press Alt+Shift+Left Arrow). Notice that the San Francisco heading is promoted to the same level as the California and Mexico headings. While this heading and subtext remain selected, click on the → button of the Outline bar (or press Alt+Shift+Right Arrow) to demote the heading and subtext back to its original level.

Moving Headings in the Example

Use the Move Up (↑) and Move Down (↓) buttons of the Outline bar (or their keyboard equivalents) to move headings (paragraphs) up or down within an outline. Remember, if any related subtext is collapsed, the subtext moves with the heading. If subtext is visible, it moves with the heading only if it has been selected along with the heading.

To demonstrate this operation, place the insertion pointer in the Mexico City line. Click on the ↑ button in the Outline bar (or press Alt+Shift+Up Arrow). You will see the Mexico City heading move up in the outline by one line. However, the associated body text remains in its original location. While Mexico City is still the selected paragraph, click on the ↓ in the Outline bar (or press Alt+Shift+Down Arrow) to restore the heading to its proper location.

Next, use your preferred selection method to select the Mexico City heading *and* its subtext. Click on the ↑ button twice in the Outline bar (or press Alt+Shift+Up Arrow twice). The heading and its subtext move above the Cancun heading and its subtext, as shown in Figure 8.10.

Figure 8.10
Result of moving a heading and its subtext up twice

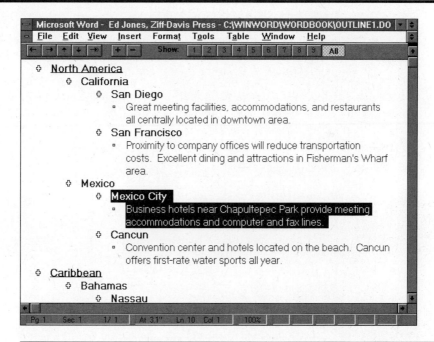

TIP. *When moving headings, in most cases you'll want the associated body text to move, too. To accomplish this, it is usually easiest to first collapse the outline to the level of the heading to be moved (using the Show buttons or their keyboard equivalents). Once the outline has been collapsed, you can move headings without needing to select their subtext; the subtext will automatically follow the headings.*

Applying Numbering to Outline Headings

Occasionally you may want to number the headings of an outline. Of course, you can manually number an outline by typing the numbers as you type the headings. But a major drawback to this technique is evident when you need to rearrange the outline by adding, deleting, or moving headings; you must then manually renumber the headings. You can avoid this problem if you use the Bullets and Numbering option on Word's Tools menu to apply numbering to your outline headings. (Tools Bullets and Numbering can apply numbers to more than just outlines; see Chapter 3 for more details on using this command.)

To number your sample outline, perform the following steps:

1. Collapse or expand the outline so that only the headings that you want to number are visible. (Word will number any visible paragraphs, so if all headings and body text are visible, the entire outline will be numbered, which is probably not what you want.)

2. Select the paragraphs (headings and subtext) that you want to number. If you want to number the entire document, select the entire document by pressing Ctrl+5 (using 5 on the numeric keypad).

3. Choose Bullets and Numbering on the Tools menu (Alt+O+B), and you'll see the dialog box shown here. (Refer to Chapter 3 for more about this dialog box.)

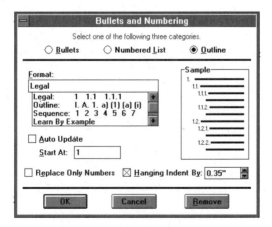

4. Press Alt+L to choose Numbered List, and select the desired numbering format from the Format list box. Leave the other settings in their default state.

5. Choose OK, and paragraph numbers appear beside the headings and subtext.

You can remove paragraph numbering from the outline at any time, by choosing the Tools Bullets and Numbering command (Alt+O+B) and selecting Remove from the dialog box.

NOTE. *If you insert, move, or delete headings, the numbering of your outline may not be correct. You will have to use the Tools Bullets and Numbering command again to renumber the headings—or you can turn on the Auto Update option in the Bullets and Numbering dialog box. This option tells Word to create the numbers using fields, which are automatically updated if you change the order of the headings.*

Creating a Table of Contents from an Outline

One of Word's most useful features is the ability to quickly generate a table of contents based on the headings of an outline. After your document exists in outline form, you can use the Insert Table of Contents command to create and insert a table of contents in your document. This command does most of the work for you. Word will insert the table of contents at the insertion pointer.

Select Insert Table of Contents (Alt+I+C), and you'll see the dialog box shown here:

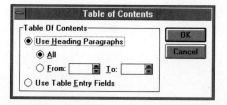

To create a table of contents from an outline, leave the Use Heading Paragraphs option turned on (the default). (The Use Table Entry Fields choice lets you create a table of contents using a special type of field called TC entries, discussed in Chapter 10.)

Choose the All (Alt+A) button if you want Word to include all outline headings in the table of contents. Or you can specify a range of heading levels in the From and To list boxes. For example, to include only level 1, 2, and 3 headings in the table of contents, select From, enter 1 in the From box, and enter 3 in the To box. To include level 1 heads only, enter 1 in both boxes.

Try the following exercise to add a table of contents to OUTLINE1.

1. With the OUTLINE1 file open, choose View Normal (Alt+V+N) to turn off outline view.

This allows you to add a page break, so you can put the table of contents on the first page of the document; you cannot add page breaks while in outline view. To create the table of contents, it does not matter whether you are in outline view or not, as long as the headings are in the document.

2. To insert a page break, first press Ctrl+Home to get to the start of the document. Press Enter once to add a blank line, and then press Ctr+1+Enter to insert the page break. Press Ctrl+Home again to get the insertion pointer back to the start of the document.

You can now create the table of contents on this new first page of the document; the remainder of the outline will begin on page 2.

3. Select Insert Table of Contents (Alt+I+C).

4. In the dialog box, leave the default options, Use Heading Paragraphs and All, selected.

5. Choose OK.

Figure 8.11 shows the resulting table of contents that is inserted into the document. Since the entire outline is on page 2, all topics of the outline are listed in the table of contents as being on page 2. If your sample document were longer, Word would assign the proper page numbers automatically.

If you change the contents of an outline so that its page numbers change, you'll want to remember that any related table of contents is *not* updated automatically. You must update the table of contents by selecting the entire document and then pressing F9, Update Fields. (The entries in the table of contents are based on fields; you will learn more about fields in Chapter 9.)

NOTE. *Word performs some other tricks with tables of contents. Chapter 10 of this book is devoted to tables of contents and indexes, and contains the details you'll need on this subject.*

A Note About Printing

Although you print outlines in the same way you print any other document, keep in mind that printed results will vary depending on what view you are using. Just as a document looks different on screen when you are in outline view, so will the document print differently.

In outline view, the document prints much as it appears on the screen. The only items that don't appear on the printed copy are the outline selection icons. Word uses whatever tabs are in effect for the document to indent

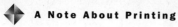

the headings and body text. If you are not in outline view, the headings are still indented, but less so. And body text is printed at the left margin, without any indentation.

Figure 8.11

Sample outline with a table of contents added

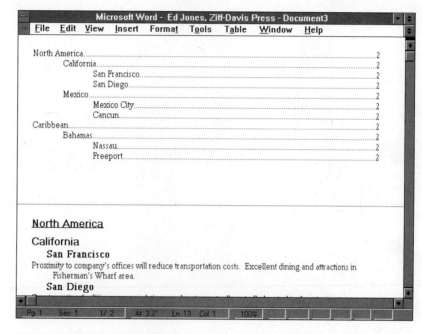

You may want to try printing the sample outline you created in this chapter, with outline view turned on and then with outline view off, and examine the differences in their appearance.

9

Working with Fields and Form Letters

What's in a Field?

Working with Fields

Common Uses for Fields

Using Word's Print Merge Facility

Creating Data Files Using Excel Spreadsheets

Creating Data Files Using Other Software

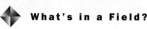

I N WORD, A FIELD IS A SPECIAL SET OF INSTRUCTIONS THAT TELLS WORD TO insert certain information at a given location in a document. The basic difference between fields and normal text is that with fields, the computer provides the information for you. Using fields does more than just save you the effort of typing in the information, however. Fields are *dynamic*; they can change as circumstances change.

You have already used fields at various places in the exercises of this book; for example, when you insert page numbers in a document, you are using a type of field. Also, in Chapter 8 the paragraph numbering and the table of contents were both generated based on fields. You can even use fields to add graphics to your documents.

Word has dozens of field types. Some, like page numbers and the current date, are simple to understand and use. Others are more complex, and are beyond the scope of this book. (You can refer to the Fields chapter in your *Microsoft Word User's Guide* for details on fields not covered in this text.) But all fields, no matter their type or complexity, are inserted into a document and updated using the same procedures, as you'll learn in this chapter. You can work effectively with fields after learning four skills: how to insert fields in a document, how to update fields so they show the most current results, how to view fields, and how to move between fields.

You'll insert fields using the Insert Fields command; this command's dialog box lets you choose among the many fields available in Word. In this chapter you'll most often use the Insert Fields command for this task, but there are other ways to insert fields in Word. You can also use the Insert Field key (Ctrl+F9), which is often used to insert fields for operations involving tables of contents and indexes, as discussed in Chapter 10. And many Word commands, such as Insert Page Numbers, Insert Index, and Tools Bullets and Numbering, insert fields automatically.

Updating fields is accomplished with the Update Field (F9) key, viewing field codes with the View Field Codes command, and moving between fields with the Next Field and Previous Field keys. These techniques, and more, are explained later; first, let's examine the contents of fields.

What's in a Field?

A field has three parts: field characters, a field type, and instructions. Shortly, you will see how to insert fields like the following one, which produces a date, and how to view them as shown in this example:

```
{ date \@ M/d/yy }
```

The *field characters* are the curly braces that enclose the field. These braces cannot be typed using the corresponding keyboard characters; rather, you must produce these characters by using a command or a key-combination specifically designed to insert fields, such as the Insert Field command. *Exception*: One type of field, for print merge operations to produce repetitive documents like form letters, is not enclosed in curly braces; these print merge fields appear within double angle brackets (<< >>).

The *field type* is the first word that appears after the left field character. In the above example, the word *date* is the field type; a date field tells Word to insert the current date, based on the computer's clock, into the document.

The *instructions* follow the field type, and tell Word exactly how the information specified by the field type (which is the field *result*) will be displayed. Instructions are optional, depending on the field type; most, but not all field types have instructions. In the above example, \@ M/d/yy is an instruction that tells Word to display the current date using the American numeric format with the month, day, and year separated by slashes. Field instructions are often somewhat cryptic, but Word usually inserts the proper instructions for you automatically, based on field type.

The field type and instructions together are called the field *codes*.

Working with Fields

This section shows you how to insert and edit fields, view the codes of fields, move among fields, and update results of fields.

Inserting Fields

Since Word uses fields for so many purposes, many of Word's commands insert fields indirectly. When you use Insert Page Numbers or Insert Table of Contents, for example, you are inserting fields to produce the page numbers or the table of contents. The Tools Bullets and Numbering command also inserts fields to accomplish its results. To insert fields directly yourself, you'll select the Insert Fields command (Alt+I+D), and use the Field dialog box shown here:

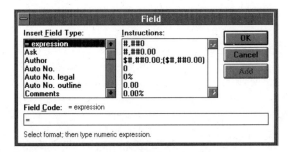

The Field dialog box contains two list boxes, titled Insert Field Type, and Instructions. You use the Insert Field Type list box on the left to select the field you wish to insert into your document. You can use the scroll bars or the arrow keys to navigate among the possible field types. For most field types, the Instructions list box on the right will display various instructions that apply. (Some field types can have only one set of instructions; for these, the Instructions box will be empty.) As an example of instructions, if the Create Date field type is highlighted in the Insert Field Type list box, a variety of possible date formats appear in the Instructions box. To insert a field, you first choose the desired field type, then select from among the possible instructions (if available), and choose OK to insert the field.

The Field Code text box at the bottom of the dialog box displays whatever field is selected in the Insert Field Type list box; just above the text box you'll see what type of field it is. (You can also use this text box to type in the name of the desired field yourself; however, it's generally easier to pick the field by name from the list box.)

In addition to the usual OK and Cancel buttons, this dialog box also contains an Add button. The Add button becomes available whenever you choose a field type that displays a variety of possible instructions. You can use the Add button to add multiple instructions to a single field, a technique that is at times useful with some field types.

NOTE. *As mentioned, Word also provides an Insert Field Characters key-combination (Ctrl+F9). Press this, and Word inserts the field characters (curly braces), enabling you to enter manually the field type and instructions. This method of inserting fields is typically used by programmers familiar with the programming language, WordBasic, that is built into Word. Unless you are very familiar with fields and their instruction syntax, you will likely find it easier to add fields with the Insert Fields menu command.*

An Example of Fields in a Document

To see how fields can be used within a document, first open a new document in the usual manner, and then try the following exercise:

1. Select Insert Fields (Alt+I+D).

2. In the Insert Field Type list box, click on or highlight Create Date. Then click on the MMMM d, yyyy option in the Instructions list box, or tab over to the box and highlight the MMMM d, yyyy option. Then choose OK.

The creation date for the document, as measured by your computer's clock, appears at the insertion pointer. (If, instead of the date, you see the field type and instructions, select View Field Codes (Alt+V+C) to turn off the View Field Codes option; this command will be explained in more detail shortly.)

Tip. The author name that Word uses is based on what you entered for a user name when Word was installed. To change the author name, select Tools Options, and choose User Info from the Category list box. Then you'll have to exit and restart Word to effect the change.

3. Press enter twice, type the following words, and add a space after the colon:

```
This document was written by:
```

4. Select Insert Fields (Alt+I+D). In the Insert Field Type list box, click on or highlight Author. (Note that there are no instructions available for this type of field.) Choose OK to insert the result (the author name) in the document.

5. In the document, type a period after the author name. Start a new sentence, and type these words, with a space after the last word:

```
The document contains
```

6. Select Insert Fields (Alt+I+D). In the Insert Field Type list box, click on or highlight No. of Words, and choose OK to insert the field. You'll see a value indicating the number of words so far in the document.

TIP. *If you are using the keyboard rather than the scroll bar, you can quickly get near the desired field type by typing its first letter. For example, typing N will bring you to the first entry in the list box that starts with N.*

7. Add a space after the word count just inserted, and finish the sentence by typing the following:

```
words, and the time of day is now:
```

8. Select Insert Fields (Alt+I+D). In the Insert Field Type list box, click on or highlight Time. In the Instructions list box, choose H:mm to indicate hours and minutes without the a.m./p.m. designation. Then choose OK to place the field.

At this point, your document will resemble the one shown in Figure 9.1. Of course, your author name, date, and time will be different, and if you have varied your screen text from the example text, the word count may differ as well.

Viewing Field Codes

By default, when you insert a field in a document, you see the results of that field; for example, when you insert a date field, you see the current date. However, when editing documents, you may at times find it useful to see the actual field codes (type and instructions), rather than a field's results. You can do so with the View Field Codes command. This command is a toggle, so choosing it repeatedly turns on or off the view of the field codes. To see an example, with the document you created earlier still open, choose View Field Codes (Alt+V+C). The document now resembles the one shown in Figure 9.2.

Figure 9.1

Sample document
containing inserted
fields for date,
author name, word
count, and time

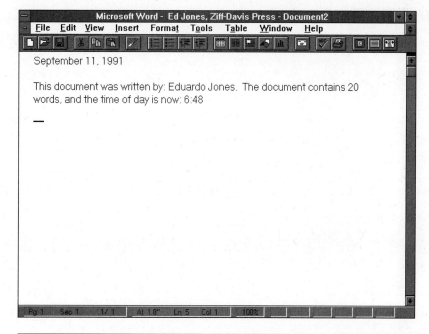

Tip. To move
forward from field to
field of a document,
use the Next Field
key (F11 or Alt+F1).
Use Previous Field
(Shift+F11 or
Alt+Shift+F1) to
move in reverse.

You can also view the codes of an individual field by using the Field Codes key (Shift+F9). This key lets you switch between a field's results and its code contents. Place the insertion pointer anywhere in the desired field, press Shift+F9, and you will see the display of the field change from codes to results or vice versa. Note that some fields do not have results, but instead supply Word with needed information for other tasks. Such fields are not normally visible on your screen. On these fields, the Field Codes key has no effect.

Updating Fields

When you update fields in Word, you are asking Word to use the field's instructions to provide new results based on the latest available information. Think of updating as a type of "recalculation" of a field. Some fields, like those used in page numbering, are automatically updated whenever you print or repaginate a document. Other fields, however, are not necessarily updated unless you tell Word to do it. You can see this by looking at the {numwords} field in the sample document; though it says 20, there are more than 20 words in the document. When you need to update field results, use the Update Field key (F9).

Figure 9.2

Sample document with View Field Codes turned on

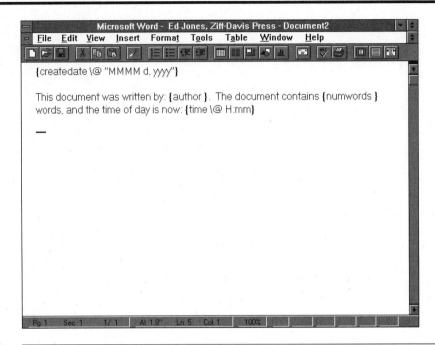

To update a single field, place the insertion pointer anywhere in the field, and press Update Field (F9). To update all fields in the entire document, first select the entire document (choose Edit Select All, or use Ctrl+5 on the numeric keypad), and then press Update Field (F9). Try these operations now in the sample document (choose View Field Codes first to change back to viewing the field results). When you update the fields for this document, you will see that the word count and the current time are updated.

Note that some fields are not affected by the Update Field key. These include fields used for automatic numbering, and some other special fields commonly used in WordBasic programming.

TIP. *If you are working with a large document that contains a number of fields, you may find it helpful to split the document into two panes, using the window techniques covered in Chapter 3. You can then turn on View Field Codes in one pane, and leave the field results showing in the other pane.*

Locking Fields from Updating

At times, you will want to lock a field so its results will not be updated. A good example is the current date; perhaps you want the date in a letter to remain fixed as the date of its creation, and not be updated every time you print the letter. To lock a field, place the insertion pointer anywhere in the field and press Lock Field (Ctrl+F11 or Alt+Ctrl+F1). If need be, you can later unlock the field, by again placing the insertion pointer in the field and pressing Unlock Field (Ctrl+Shift+F11 or Alt+Ctrl+Shift+F1).

Another way that you can freeze a field's results is to convert the field results into ordinary text, a process known as "unlinking" a field. To do this, position the insertion pointer anywhere in the field, and press Unlink Field (Ctrl+Shift+F9). Suppose you need to insert the current date into an existing document, and you don't want that date to change. Use Insert Field and choose Date, select your desired date format, and then choose OK. Next, move the insertion pointer back into the date field, and press Unlink Field (Ctrl+Shift+F9). If you need to do this often, you can save these keystrokes to a macro; see Chapter 12 for details on macros.

Before proceeding, you can close the current example document without saving it; you will not need it later in the chapter.

Formatting a Field's Results

You can apply formatting to a field's results just as you would apply formatting to any other text in a Word document. Select the field, and then apply the formatting you want. For instance, in the sample document you just created, you might select the author's name and press Ctrl+B to apply boldface, or you could select the time and press Ctrl+I to apply italic.

Common Uses for Fields

You'll find fields to be useful in many word processing tasks. Although this chapter cannot cover all possible uses for fields, some of their more common functions are described in the following paragraphs. Each of the fields named is available from the list box of field choices that appears when you use the Insert Fields command.

Time and Date Information

Use the various time and date fields to insert the current time or date, in the format you choose. Create Date inserts the document's creation date; Date inserts a field containing the current date; Save Date inserts a field containing the date the document was last saved; Print Date inserts a field containing the date the document was last printed.

Summary Information

Use these fields to insert in the document various facts normally stored in the Summary Info dialog box. (To change the information within the Summary Info dialog box, use the File Summary Info command.) Use Author, Comments, Keywords, and Title fields to insert the contents of these boxes from Summary Info. Use No. of Chars, No. of Pages, or No. of Words fields to insert a count for the document's characters, pages, or words, respectively.

Automatic Numbering

You can insert fields that cause automatic numbering of the paragraphs in a document. Although you can use the Auto No., Auto No. Legal, and Auto No. Outline fields that are available with the Insert Fields command, you will likely find numbering to be easier if you use the Tools Bullets and Numbering command, as discussed in Chapter 3. This command automatically inserts the proper fields at the start of all selected paragraphs in your document. If you do decide to use the Insert Fields command, use Auto No. to add a paragraph number field at the insertion pointer; use Auto No. Legal to add a paragraph number field using legal numbering format at the insertion pointer; and use Auto No. Outline to add a paragraph number field using outline numbering format at the insertion pointer.

Tables of Contents and Indexes

The TC, TOC, Index, and Index Entry fields are used in the creation of tables of contents and indexes. You'll find a complete discussion of these fields in Chapter 10.

Merge Printing

A number of fields (including Data, Next, and MergeRec) are used in the print merge process. The following section discusses how you can make use of these fields.

Using Word's Print Merge Facility

One common application of fields is in Word's Print Merge facility. This feature lets you print multiple copies of a document, where certain aspects change for each copy. A typical example of this technique is illustrated by form letters sent by businesses. In a form letter, much of each copy of the document is identical, but certain aspects, such as the recipient's name and address, are tailored for each letter. Word lets you create form letters (and other repetitive documents such as mailing labels) by combining (merging) two types of documents: a *main document* containing the text that is identical for each printed copy, and a *data document* containing the text that is specific to each copy. Figure 9.3 illustrates this concept.

Figure 9.3

Merging of main document and data document into form letter

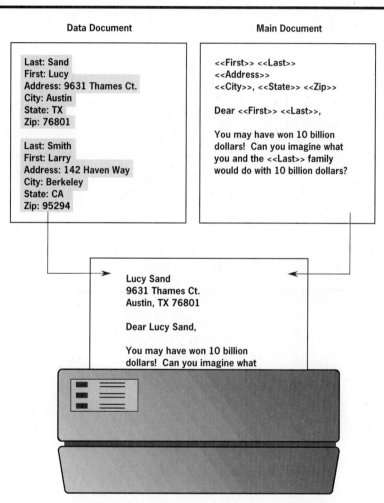

An Overview of the Print Merge Process

When you prepare the main document for a merge, you type the text that will not change for each letter printed. In addition to this text, you insert the fields that tell Word where to find the variable information stored in the data document. These fields in the main document are referred to as *merge fields*.

As you type the main document, you can insert the merge fields at the appropriate locations.

In the data document (or file), type the information that Word will use to fill in the merge fields of the main document. For example, if your main document contains fields that use a name and address, the data file will contain all the names and addresses for each document to be printed. The first line of a data file normally contains a header record; this is a single line that identifies the order in which you place the data in the data document.

The items contained in the data document (both the field names in the header and the actual data contents of the fields) can be placed into the cells of a Word table; in fact, using a table is the easiest way to set up a data document in Word. If you do not use a table, the data elements must be separated either by tabs or by commas, and you must end each row with a paragraph marker (by pressing Enter). To illustrate, Figures 9.4, 9.5, and 9.6 show three different examples of a data document; all three examples contain the same information. In Figure 9.4, the header and accompanying data have been stored in the form of a Word table. In Figure 9.5, tabs are used to separate the header and accompanying data. In Figure 9.6, commas are used as the separators.

Figure 9.4

Data document stored in Word table

```
Microsoft Word - Ed Jones, Ziff-Davis Press - C:\WINWORD\WORDBOOK\NAMES.DOC
 File   Edit   View   Insert   Format   Tools   Table   Window   Help
```

title	first	last	address	city	state	zip
Ms.	Jamie	Allen	118 Main St.	Reston	VA	22091
Mrs.	Norma	Roberts	6210 Brandon Ave.	Chicago	IL	60617
Mr.	Larry	Smith	142 Haven Way	Berkeley	CA	95294
Ms.	Lucy	Sand	9631 Thames Ct., Apt. 2	Austin	TX	76801

```
Pg 1   Sec 1   1/1   At 1"   Ln 1   Col 1   100%
```

Figure 9.5

Data document
using tabs

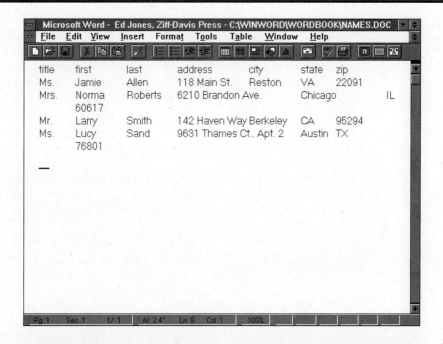

Figure 9.6

Data document
using commas

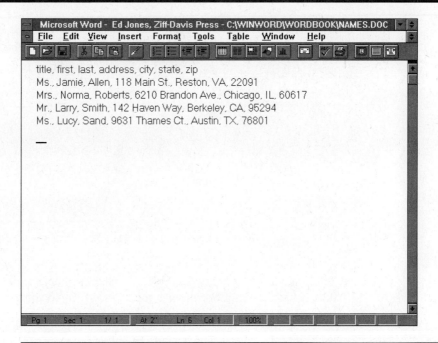

Data documents can be created directly, by typing the information into a Word document screen. You can also create data documents using information stored as a database, within a spreadsheet (as in Excel or Lotus 1-2-3), or stored using database management software (such as dBASE or Paradox). At the end of this chapter you will see how you can create a data document using data both stored in a spreadsheet and in a database.

Once the data document and the main document both exist, you can merge them and print multiple copies of the main document, based on the data contained in the data document. When you print the file, Word reads the first record in the data document, inserts the fields of that record into the main document, and prints a copy. It repeats this process for as many records as are contained in the data document; hence, if a data document has five lines containing the name and address for five individuals, a print merge operation will print five copies of the document, each addressed to a different individual.

Print Merge Toolbar

When you select the File Print Merge command and specify a data file, another toolbar, called the Print Merge toolbar, is added above the workspace. The buttons and icons in this toolbar, illustrated below, provide fast access to the commands commonly used in a print merge operation.

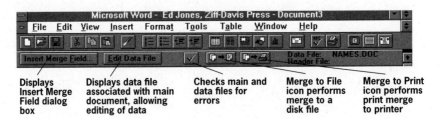

Displays Insert Merge Field dialog box | Displays data file associated with main document, allowing editing of data | Checks main and data files for errors | Merge to File icon performs merge to a disk file | Merge to Print icon performs print merge to printer

- The Insert Merge Field button (Alt+Shift+F) displays the Insert Merge Field, where you choose the fields (stored in the data document) that you want to use in your main document.

- The Edit Data File button (Alt+Shift+E) displays the data file, so you can view or edit its data. This is essentially a fast way of switching between the documents; you can accomplish the same task with the Next Window (Ctrl+F6) key, or with the Window menu.

- The Checkmark button (Alt+Shift+K) checks the main document and data file for errors. For example, the main file might contain a field whose name does not exist in the header of the data file.

- The Merge To File icon (Alt+Shift+N) merges documents, separated by section breaks, in a single file. This choice is useful if you don't have a printer attached to your PC, and you want to create a file of merged documents that you can print elsewhere.

- The Merge to Print icon (Alt+Shift+M) displays the Print dialog box; there you can choose OK to print the merged documents.

- At the far right end of the toolbar appears the name of the data file associated with the main document. In the section that follows, you'll learn how to associate a data file with a main document.

The Steps in the Print Merge Process

Following is a description of the specific steps in the overall print merge process. In the next section, you'll get a chance to try a print merge exercise.

1. Create a Data Document Open a new document in the usual manner, and type the header as the first line of the document; this header contains the names of the fields. You can use any field names up to 20 characters, including the underscore character, but using no spaces. The easiest way to store data in a data document is in a Word table, because Word automatically considers each cell of the table to be a different field. If you do not use a table, you must use tabs or commas to separate the field names and the contents of the actual fields, as illustrated in Figures 9.5 and 9.6. Save the document under a helpful file name. It does not matter whether you leave the data document open or closed, but it must be saved before you can perform the print merge operation.

2. Create a Main Document Open a new document in the usual manner.

3. Choose File Print Merge (Alt+F+M) You'll see the Print Merge Setup dialog box.

4. Attach the Data Document In the Print Merge Setup dialog box, choose Attach Data File. In the list box of files that next appears, choose the data document by name and select OK. When you do this, the Print Merge toolbar appears. Mouse users can use this toolbar as an alternate way of choosing commands associated with the print merge operation (detailed throughout this chapter).

Mouse users can click on the Insert Merge Field button in the Print Merge toolbar, and choose a field from a list box.

5. Type the Main Document To insert fields at the appropriate locations within the document, choose select Field (Alt+I+D). Choose Merge Field from the Field Types list box; then tab over to the Instructions box and choose the desired field.

Mouse users can click on the Merge to Printer icon in the Print Merge toolbar, and choose OK from the resulting Print dialog box to begin printing.

6. Issue the Print Merge Command   From the keyboard, select File Print Merge (Alt+F+M), and in the dialog box that appears, choose Merge (Alt+M). In the Print Merge dialog box, change any necessary options, and then choose OK. In the Print dialog box that appears next, choose OK to begin printing.

An Example of a Print Merge Operation

To demonstrate the use of Word's Print Merge facility, the following exercise helps you combine a data document with a main document to generate form letters. Start by creating the data document.

1. Open a new Word document in the usual manner.

2. Select Table Insert Table (Alt+A+I). In the dialog box that appears, enter **7** for the number of columns, and **5** for the number of rows. Then choose OK.

3. In the first line of the table, type the following, pressing Tab at the end of each word:

   Title   First   Last   Address   City   State   Zip

   This first row of the table makes up the header at the start of the data document. The names you type here will be the same names that you will use later to identify the fields in the main document.

4. Start with the cursor at the beginning of the second row of the table, and type the following data, using Tab after every cell entry.

Ms.	Jamie	Allen	118 Main St.	Reston	VA	22091
Mrs.	Norma	Roberts	6210 Brandon Ave.	Chicago	IL	60617
Mr.	Larry	Smith	142 Haven Way	Berkeley	CA	95294
Ms.	Lucy	Sand	9631 Thames Ct., Apt. 2	Austin	TX	76801

5. Save the data file (Alt+F+S) and name it NAMES.DOC.

6. Choose File Close (Alt+F+C) to put away the data file. It does not need to be open on the screen to be used later in the print merge operation.

Now that the data document exists, you are ready to create the main document.

1. Open another new document in the usual manner.

2. Select File Print Merge (Alt+F+M). You'll see the Print Merge Setup dialog box:

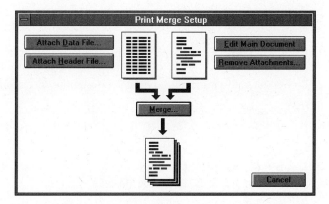

3. Choose Attach Data File (Alt+D) and a dialog box appears showing the files in the current directory.

4. Highlight NAMES.DOC, the data file you saved earlier, in the list box. Then choose OK. Notice that the Print Merge toolbar is then added to the screen.

5. Press Enter once to move the insertion pointer down one line. Choose Insert Field (Alt+I+D). In the Insert Field Type list box, choose Merge Field. In the Instructions list box, choose First (the name you chose for the first name field), then click OK. (Or click on the Insert Merge Field button in the Print Merge toolbar, choose First from a list box, and click OK.)

The designation <<first>> appears at the insertion pointer in the document, indicating that the contents of the data field called First will be printed at this location in the main document.

6. Type a space after the first name field. Then use Insert Field or the Print Merge toolbar, as explained in Step 5, to choose Merge Field as the field type and Last as the instruction.

7. Press Enter once. Then use Insert Field or the Print Merge toolbar, as explained in Step 5, to choose Merge Field as the field type and Address as the instruction.

8. Press Enter once. Then use Insert Field or the Print Merge toolbar (Step 5) to choose Merge Field as the field type and City as the instruction.

9. Type a comma, and add a space. Then use Insert Field or the Print Merge toolbar (Step 5) to choose Merge Field as the field type and State as the instruction.

10. Add two spaces. Then use Insert Field or the Print Merge toolbar (Step 5) to choose Merge Field as the field type and Zip as the instruction.

11. Press Enter twice, and type the word **Dear** followed by a space. Use Insert Field or the Insert Merge Field button in the toolbar (as described above) to add a merge field called Title at the insertion pointer.

12. Type a space, and use Insert Field or the Insert Merge Field button in the toolbar to add a merge field called Last at the insertion pointer.

13. Add a comma, and press Enter twice. Type the following text, using the Insert Field command or the Insert Merge Field button on the toolbar to add the named fields in the locations indicated.

```
You may have won 10 billion dollars! Can you imagine what you and the <<last>> family
would do with 10 billion dollars? A new car... a new home... your own savings and
loan... a trip to Paris... purchase the Eiffel Tower... all this and more can belong
to the <<last>> family of <<city>>, <<state>>.

Just return the entry form. And remember, <<first>>, there's no obligation. Ed
Superstar will announce your name on television when you win our grand prize of 10
billion dollars!
```

14. Save the main file with File Save (Alt+F+S); call it FORMLET1. (This is not a requirement for performing a print merge operation, but saving files regularly is simply a good habit.)

With both the field data and the main document available, you can now proceed to print the merged documents. Make sure your printer is turned on and ready. If you are using the mouse, click on the Merge to Print icon in the Print Merge toolbar (*not* the Print icon in the regular toolbar!), and when the Print dialog box appears, choose OK to begin printing. Or, from the keyboard, choose File Print Merge (Alt+F+M), and in the dialog box that appears, choose Merge (Alt+M). When the Print Merge dialog box appears, choose OK to accept the default options; then choose OK from the Print dialog box to begin printing. Figure 9.7 shows the results of the print merge operation.

Figure 9.7

Results of print
merge operation

Jamie Allen
118 Main St.
Reston, VA 22091

Dear Ms. Allen,

You may have won 10 billion dollars! Can you imagine what you and the Allen
family would do with 10 billion dollars? A new car... a new home... your own
savings and loan... a trip to Paris... purchase the Eiffel Tower... all this and more
can belong to the Allen family of Reston, VA.

Just return the entry form. And remember, Jamie, there's no obligation. Ed
Superstar will announce your name on television when you win our grand prize
of 10 billion dollars!

Norma Roberts
6210 Brandon Ave.
Chicago, IL 60617

Dear Mrs. Roberts,

You may have won 10 billion dollars! Can you imagine what you and the Roberts
family would do with 10 billion dollars? A new car... a new home... your own
savings and loan... a trip to Paris... purchase the Eiffel Tower... all this and more
can belong to the Roberts family of Chicago, IL.

Just return the entry form. And remember, Norma, there's no obligation. Ed
Superstar will announce your name on television when you win our grand prize
of 10 billion dollars!

Lucy Sand
9631 Thames Ct., Apt. 2
Austin, TX 76801

Dear Ms. Sand,

You may have won 10 billion dollars! Can you imagine what you and the Sand
family would do with 10 billion dollars? A new car... a new home... your own
savings and loan... a trip to Paris... purchase the Eiffel Tower... all this and more
can belong to the Sand family of Austin, TX.

Just return the entry form. And remember, Lucy, there's no obligation. Ed
Superstar will announce your name on television when you win our grand prize
of 10 billion dollars!

Larry Smith
142 Haven Way
Berkeley, CA 95294

Dear Mr. Smith

You may have won 10 billion dollars! Can you imagine what you and the Smith
family would do with 10 billion dollars? A new car... a new home... your own
savings and loan... a trip to Paris... purchase the Eiffel Tower... all this and more
can belong to the Smith family of Berkeley, CA.

Just return the entry form. And remember, Larry, there's no obligation. Ed
Superstar will announce your name on television when you win our grand prize
of 10 billion dollars!

Creating Data Files Using Excel Spreadsheets

If you have a database stored in the form of an Excel spreadsheet, you can easily create a table in Word based on that data. (In fact, the process is much easier with Excel than with most other software.) When all or a part of an Excel spreadsheet is selected and copied into a Word document, the Excel data automatically appears in the form of a table. You can then add a header and save the table as a data document, and use it with a main document in a print merge operation as described earlier.

Here's how to transfer data from an Excel spreadsheet into a Word document:

1. Start Excel and open the spreadsheet you want to use.

2. Using Excel selection techniques, select the spreadsheet range that contains the desired data.

3. From the Excel menus, choose Edit Copy (Alt+E+C) and copy the selected data into the Clipboard.

4. Exit Excel (or leave it running if you have sufficient memory), and start Word. Open a new document in Word (to become the data file).

5. Select Edit Paste (Alt+E+P). The Excel data appears in table form within the Word document.

6. Use the Table Insert Cells command to add a new row to the start of the table, and enter the header information into this row. (This step may not be necessary if the spreadsheet range you copied had column names in the first row; you can use these column names as the header.)

Once the Excel data exists in a Word table, you can incorporate it with a main document as outlined in this chapter to complete the print merge operation.

Creating Data Files Using Other Software

Throughout this chapter, you've used data documents that were created by typing the data directly into a Word table or by importing Excel data into a Word table. There are significant advantages to this method, but there may be times when you'll want to set up a data document using tabs or commas, rather than a table. A common example is when the needed data is already stored in another software package, such as in a non-Windows spreadsheet's cells, or with a database manager like dBASE. Most DOS spreadsheets and nearly all database managers can export a file in a file format known as *comma-delimited*. This file format can then be imported as text into a Word document, and used as the data document for a print merge operation.

(See your spreadsheet or database software documentation for details on how to create a comma-delimited file.)

You already know that when setting up a data document to be used in a print merge, data not stored in table form must contain either tabs or commas to separate the fields. A paragraph marker at the end of each line is used to indicate the end of each record. If you use commas as field separators, you can also include quotation marks around each field. These are not required, but many database managers automatically add quotation marks around each field when producing comma-delimited files.

All versions of dBASE and most dBASE-compatible database managers can produce comma-delimited files resembling the following example:

```
"Johnson","Linda",2890.30,"Carrollton","TX"
"Johnson","Martin",2495.00,"Fort Worth","TX"
"Smith","Karen",2075.40,"Dallas","TX"
"Williams","Greg",1890.50,"Arlington","TX"
"Klien","Samuel",1775.00,"Carrollton","TX"
"Roberts","Jerry",1740.00,"Dallas","TX"
"Robertson","Henry",1534.60,"Garland","TX"
"Martin","Lydia",1390.00,"Fort Worth","TX"
"Sanders","Anette",1170.20,"Dallas","TX"
```

In this database (exported from dBASE), all character-based fields are surrounded by quotation marks. Word can work with this file as is; to be used as a data document, you need only add a header to indicate the names of the fields.

10

Building Tables of Contents and Indexes

THIS CHAPTER COVERS TWO ELEMENTS OF A DOCUMENT THAT ARE SIMI-lar in many ways: automatically created tables of contents and indexes. Both are essentially lists, arranged in slightly different ways. A table of contents is a list of the major portions of a document (such as sections of a report), including the page numbers for each section. By comparison, an index is a list of important words or subjects in a document, with page numbers where the subjects can be found. Word lets you avoid much of the work of preparing both. With the Insert Table of Contents command, you can automatically create tables of contents and other lists in similar form (such as lists of illustrations or photographs in a document). With the Insert Index command, you can let Word automatically build your index based on special fields you insert while writing the document. Besides saving you all that typing and formatting time and labor, Word will even automatically update the table of contents and index to reflect the changes you make to the document.

This chapter shows you two ways to build a table of contents, and how to build and expand an index. Exercises are included so you can practice with both these document elements.

Building Tables of Contents

There are two methods for building a table of contents in Word documents. The first method is to base the table of contents on outline headings. This method is easier, but requires that you structure your document in outline view, as discussed in Chapter 8. In fact, an example of using an outline to create a table of contents was included in that chapter. The overall technique is briefly explained here, but you may also want to review the more specific example in Chapter 8. A second method of building a table of contents, using entries called TC fields, is discussed later in this chapter. Though a bit more complex, this technique does not require the use of outline headings.

You can update and format your tables of contents, too, using some familiar commands and techniques. You'll see this as you work through the chapter.

Tip. You can quickly convert an ordinary title or section heading to a heading in outline view by placing the insertion pointer anywhere in the heading and pressing Alt+Shift+←. See Chapter 8 for more details on this topic.

Tables of Contents Based on Outline Headings

When you have a document with headings in outline view, you can quickly build a table of contents based on the headings in your outline. Outline headings are paragraphs that use the special paragraph styles, Heading 1 through Heading 9 (see Chapter 8 for details). Get into outline view, place the insertion pointer where you want the table of contents in the document, and then perform the following steps.

1. Select Insert and choose Table of Contents (Alt+I+C). You'll see the dialog box shown here:

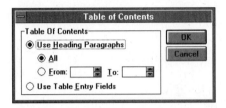

2. In the Table of Contents dialog box, select the Use Heading Paragraphs option (the default). This tells Word to build the table of contents using the outline headings in your document.

3. Choose the All (Alt+A) button (the default) if you want the entries in the table of contents to include all levels of the headings in the outline. Or you can click the button beside the From (Alt+F) text box, and then enter a range of levels in the From and To boxes, to specify what outline heading levels you want included in the table of contents. (For example, to include levels 1, 2, and 3, enter 1 in the From box, and enter 3 in the To box. To include only level 1 headings, enter 1 in both boxes.)

4. Choose OK, and Word inserts the table of contents at the insertion pointer.

Note. If View Field Codes is turned on, you will see the TOC field that builds the table of contents, rather than the table of contents itself. Turn off View Field Codes by choosing the View Field Codes toggle (Alt+V+C).

Besides ease of use, an advantage of the outline view method is that the resulting table of contents automatically follows the structure of the outline. Figure 10.1 shows a sample table of contents created using the outline method. Note that some items in the table of contents are indented, matching the heading level structure of the outline. (If you want to create an outline along with the table of contents shown here, you can do the exercises in Chapter 8 again.)

Tables of Contents Based on TC Fields

The second method for building a table of contents involves the addition of special entries called *TC fields* to your document. TC (an abbreviation for table of contents) fields can be inserted using either the Insert Field command or the Ctrl+F9 (Insert Field) key-combination. This chapter stresses the use of Ctrl+F9, because it takes fewer keystrokes than using the Insert Field command.

In general, the overall technique has two steps:

■ First, identify each item to be included in the table of contents. You do this by inserting a TC field in your document at the location of the item. For example, to have a certain heading in a document appear as an entry in the table of contents, insert a TC field on the line with that heading, usually at the start or the end of the line.

Figure 10.1

Table of contents based on outline headings

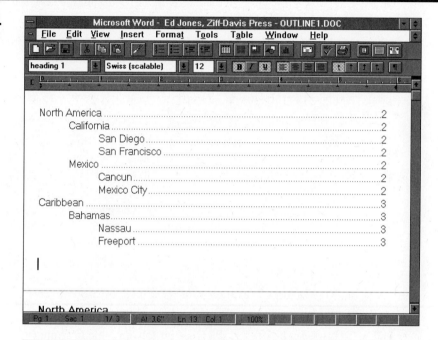

■ Second, place the insertion pointer in the document at the desired location for the table of contents, choose Table of Contents on the Insert menu, and turn on the Use Table Entry Fields option in the dialog box. Word then generates the table of contents based on the TC fields throughout your document.

TIP. *By default, TC fields are stored as hidden text. If you find TC fields difficult to enter when you cannot see what you are typing, you can make hidden text visible while you are making the entries. Choose Tools Options (Alt+O+O), select View in the Category list box (Alt+C), and turn on the Hidden Text option (Alt+I) in the dialog box that appears. After making the entries, you will probably want to turn off the Hidden Text option, so your TC fields (as well as other hidden text) will again be hidden.*

As in a table of contents based on outline headings, this TC-based table of contents is built by a Word field called the TOC field. If you make changes to the document that change the pagination, you can easily update the table of contents to reflect those changes. Just place the insertion pointer anywhere within the table of contents, and press Update Field (F9).

Remember that TC entries are also fields. If you want to delete or move a TC field to another location, select the entire field, and move it or delete it as you would move or delete any text in Word.

To insert TC fields in a document, and generate the table of contents, perform the following steps:

1. Make sure the Hidden Text option is enabled. Choose Tools Options (Alt+O+O), select View in the Category list box, turn on Hidden Text (Alt+I), and choose OK.

Tip. A good place for TC entry fields is right after the section titles or headings in your document.

2. Place the insertion pointer at the location in the document where you want to insert a TC field.

3. Press Ctrl+F9 to insert an empty TC field. You will see the field characters, with the insertion pointer placed between them, like this:

   { | }

4. Type **TC** (upper- or lowercase), then a space, then an opening quotation mark, then the entry that you want to appear in the table of contents, and finally, a closing quotation mark. Here's an example:

   {tc "Unpacking Your New Lawn Mower"}

5. Repeat steps 2 through 4 for each table of contents entry desired.

6. When all the TC fields have been inserted in the document, move the insertion pointer to the location for the table of contents, and choose Table of Contents on the Insert menu. In the dialog box that appears, mark Use Table Entry Fields (Alt+E). This tells Word to base the table of contents on the TC fields that you have added to the document.

Note. If View Field Codes is turned on, you will see the TOC field that builds the table of contents, rather than the table of contents itself. Turn off the View Field Codes by choosing the View Field Codes toggle (Alt+V+C).

7. Choose OK, and Word builds the table of contents at the insertion pointer location.

An Exercise with TC Fields

You can see how easily a table of contents can be built with TC fields by performing the following exercise. (If you have a sizable document on file, you may want to apply these steps to that document, and use its headings in place of the sample headings in the exercise.)

1. Choose File New and then OK to create a new document.

2. Type the following lines, pressing Ctrl+Enter after each line to insert page breaks:

```
Principles of Flight
Aircraft and Engines
Flight Instruments
Navigation
```

3. Make sure the Hidden Text option is turned on. Choose Tools Options (Alt+O+O), select View in the Category list box (if necessary), turn on Hidden Text (Alt+I), and choose OK.

4. Place the insertion pointer at the end of the first line of text. Press Ctrl+F9, and then type

```
tc "Principles of Flight"
```

5. Move the insertion pointer to the end of the next line of text, press Ctrl+F9, and type

```
tc "Aircraft and Engines"
```

6. Move the insertion pointer to the end of the next line of text, press Ctrl+F9, and type

```
tc "Flight Instruments"
```

7. Move the insertion pointer to the end of the next line of text, press Ctrl+F9, and type

```
tc "Navigation"
```

8. Press Ctrl+Home to return to the start of the document. Press Enter once to add a new line, and then Ctrl+Enter to insert a page break. Press Ctrl+Home again to return to the start of the document.

9. Now you need to add the table of contents (the TOC field) on what is now page one of the document, with the remainder of the document appearing on the following four pages. Choose Table of Contents from the Insert menu (Alt+I+C).

10. Mark the Use Table Entry Fields option (Alt+E), and choose OK.

Figure 10.2 shows the TC fields you've entered, as well as the resulting table of contents that is inserted into the document.

About Formatting

Once a table of contents exists in a document, you can format it as desired, using the same formatting techniques used for other Word text. For example, here's a tip: The outline-based table of contents is based on a Word field called the TOC field, so if you make changes to the document that change the pagination, there's an easy way to update the table of contents. Return to normal view mode, place the insertion pointer anywhere within the table, and press Update Field (F9).

Figure 10.2

A sample table of contents based on TC fields

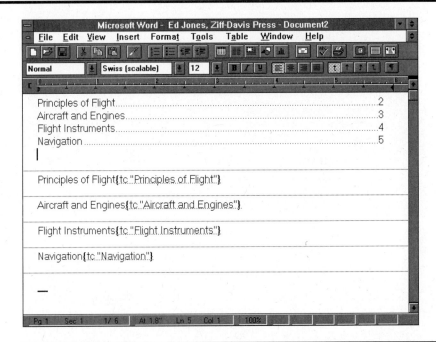

Remember, also, that Word produces the entire table of contents using a single field. (Choose the View Field Codes command, and you can see the TOC field.) This design trait of Word places some formatting limitations on a table of contents; since the table of contents does not actually exist as separate characters, you cannot always do character formatting, although you can easily apply formatting to the table of contents as a whole. For example, you can select the table of contents and apply bold or italic formatting to it, using the ribbon or the Format Character command. You can change the individual page numbers by selecting and editing them, but you cannot change the style of dot leaders used.

Adding Multiple Levels to a Table of Contents

You can use the *level switch* (a backslash followed by the letter *L* and a number) to indicate levels of indentation in a table of contents. This switch may be needed with tables of contents based on TC fields, as the entries won't be automatically indented as are tables of contents based on outline headings. To insert the level switch, type **\L**, followed by a number from 1 to 9 indicating the level of indentation, at the end of the TC field. The number 1 indicates flush left, 2 indicates indentation by one default tab stop, 3 indicates indentation by two tab stops, and so on. If a level switch is not included, Word assumes flush left for the TC entry.

As examples, consider the following TC entries; the first three are on page 5 of a document, and the second three are on page 6:

```
{tc "Traveling to the Caribbean"}
{tc "Traveling by Air" \L2}
{tc "Scheduled Flights" \L3}
{tc "Chartered Flights" \L3}
{tc "Traveling by Cruise Liner" \L2}
{tc "On the Islands"}
```

Tip. Once you have inserted a table of contents (or an index), you can select it and apply formatting to it, just as you would format any other text in Word.

These TC fields result in the following table of contents entries when you invoke the Insert Table of Contents command:

```
Traveling to the Caribbean..........................5
    Traveling by Air............................. 5
        Scheduled Flights..............................5
        Chartered Flights..............................6
    Traveling by Cruise Liner.......................6
On the Islands.....................................7
```

Multiple Tables of Contents from a Single Document

At times you'll want to have more than one table of contents based on the same document. You might need, for example, a main table of contents based on chapter or subject headings, and a list of illustrations, and a list of photographs, as well. To create multiple tables of contents, you include the \F switch in your TC fields, as well as add it to the TOC field that builds the table of contents.

First, let's examine the \F switch in the TC field. It is followed by a single character (parameter) that identifies the specific table to which this entry should be added. Later, when you insert the TOC field that builds the actual table of contents, you'll include this same \F parameter as part of that field. You can use any character you want, but you may find it helpful to use a letter that suggests the type of list. Microsoft suggests the following letters as identifiers:

Type of List/Table	\F Switch Parameter
Contents	C
Figures	F
Illustrations	I
Tables	T
Photographs	P
Graphs or charts	G
Authorities	A

When inserting a TC field with an \F switch, type **tc**, then type the text of the entry (in quotes), add a space, type **\f**, add another space, and type the desired list parameter. As an example, an entry for a table of photos might look like this:

```
{tc "Beach at Luquillo" \f p}
```

Another entry in the same document for the main table of contents might read as follows:

```
{tc "Vacationing in Puerto Rico" \f c}
```

Once you have inserted all needed TC fields (with the \F switch included), you are ready to insert the TOC fields to generate the tables of contents. When creating multiple tables of contents for the same document, you will need a separate TOC field for each one. The easiest way to accomplish this is not with the Insert Table of Contents command, but with the Insert Field (Ctrl+F9) key instead, so you can manually type the TOC field along with the \F switch and its parameter. Place the insertion pointer at the location for the table of contents, and press Ctrl+F9 to insert a field. Type the letters **TOC** followed by a space, a backslash, the letter *F*, another space, and the same parameter you used for the TC fields. For example, if you used P to identify TC entries for a table of photographs, the TOC field would look like this:

```
{toc \f p}
```

After manually inserting the TOC field, you'll need to update it to generate the actual table of contents. With the insertion pointer anywhere in the field, press Update Field (F9), and Word will generate the table. You can repeat this process for each table needed in the document, using the appropriate parameter after the \F switch in each TOC field.

Building Indexes

Building an index in a Word document works very much the same as the second method described in the foregoing section for building a table of contents. You insert special XE fields called *index entries* into the document, at locations where the indexed topics are discussed. Word provides a command (Insert Index Entry) for just this purpose, so you won't need to use the Insert Field (Ctrl+F9) key, although you can use it if you prefer. Once all the index entries have been inserted, place the insertion pointer in the location for the index, and use the Insert Index command to generate the Index field. As with a table of contents, the index that Word generates is based on a field. This lets you easily update the index as the document changes, by updating the field with F9.

Word offers you considerable control over the index. You can generate an index for the entire document, or for a range of letters in the alphabet. Index entries can all appear flush left in the index, or they can be indented to several levels. And you can easily add bold or italic formatting to the page numbers in the index entries.

Tip. If you plan to build large indexes (particularly those with 4,000 or more entries), you may have to build the index in multiple parts. See "Building Large Indexes" later in this chapter for details.

Inserting the Index Entries

Every item that is to appear in the index must have an index entry (XE) field. Here's how to insert XE fields:

1. Select the text in the document that will be used for the text of the index entry, or place the insertion pointer immediately after the desired text.

2. Choose Index Entry from the Insert menu (Alt+I+E). The Index Entry dialog box appears, with the first 64 characters of the text selected in Step 1 displayed in the Index Entry text box, as shown in Figure 10.3. (Rather than selecting text for the index entry, you can type it in the Index Entry box. Whatever text is entered in this box will be the text of the entry in the index.)

3. Turn on Bold (Alt+B) and/or Italic (Alt+I) if you want to apply these format characteristics to the page number for the index entry. (Leave the remaining Page Number option, Range, blank for now. Its use is explained later in this chapter.)

4. Choose OK. Word inserts the XE field in the document, at the insertion pointer location.

NOTE. *Like the fields used to produce tables of contents, index entry fields are stored as hidden text. You will not see them in the document unless you choose Tools Options (Alt+O+O), select View in the Category list box, and turn on the Hidden Text (Alt+I) option.*

Figure 10.3

The Insert Index
Entry dialog box
appears after text
is selected and the
command is
chosen.

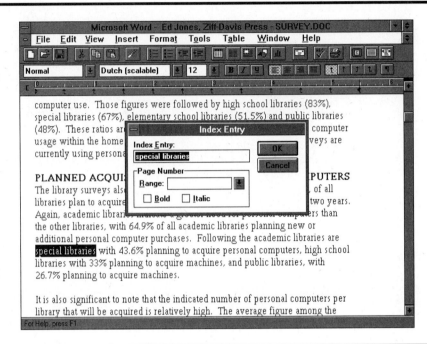

For those who despise menus, there is an alternate way of inserting index entries. Since an index entry is a field, you can insert it with the Insert Field key (Ctrl+F9). To do so, press Insert Field (Ctrl+F9), type the letters **xe** followed by a space, and then type the index entry text surrounded by quotation marks. If you want the page number of the index entry to be in boldface or italic, add a **\b** switch for bold, or **\i** for italic (you can apply both in the same XE field). Assuming the Tools Options Hidden Text option is enabled, a sample index entry might resemble the following:

```
{xe "Adding Oil to the Lawn Mower" \b}
```

Positioning Index Entries

It's important that index entries follow the topic to which they refer in the text; that is, the index entry should be placed immediately *after* the sentence that concludes the subject being indexed. (If you select the index entry text before using the Insert Index Entry command, rather than using Ctrl+F9 and typing the index entry, Word automatically places the XE field immediately after the selection.) This positioning of the field is significant; if you were to place the index entry *before* the subject being indexed, and the subject were near the bottom of the page, Word might place a page break between the index entry and the text. The end result would be an index entry with an incorrect page number.

Building the Index

After inserting all desired index entries, you use the Insert Index command to place the index in the document. Use the following steps:

1. Place the insertion pointer at the desired location for the index. (Indexes are customarily placed at the end of a document.)

2. Choose Insert Index (Alt+I+I). The Index dialog box is shown here:

3. Select the desired options from the dialog box. (These options are explained in the paragraphs that follow.)

4. Choose OK, and Word generates the index.

Note. If View Field Codes is turned on, you will see the field that builds the index, and not the index itself. You can turn off View Field Codes by choosing View Field Codes (Alt+V+C).

Let's take a look at the options in the Index dialog box: Normal Index tells Word to place subentries on an indented level; Run-in Index places subentries on the same line as the main entry. (See "Creating Multilevel Index Entries" later in this chapter for more information on index subentries.) If you have created index entries that are all the same level, it does not matter which of these options is selected.

The Heading Separator buttons let you choose what type of separator you want between the alphabetical sections of the index. If you choose None (the default), the sections are not separated, as illustrated here:

```
Gallery menu, 143
Get Info command, 41
Go To command, 62
Gridlines command, 145
Hardware, 19
Help menu, 12
Hewlett-Packard LaserJet, 188
```

The Blank Line option, when turned on, causes a blank line to appear as the separator between alphabetical groups, as shown here:

```
Gallery menu, 143
Get Info command, 41
Go To command, 62
```

```
Gridlines command, 145

Hardware, 19
Help menu, 12
Hewlett-Packard LaserJet, 188
```

Choose the Letter option if you want letters of the alphabet to appear as the separators between groups, as shown here:

```
G
Gallery menu, 143
Get Info command, 41
Go To command, 62
Gridlines command, 145
H
Hardware, 19
Help menu, 12
Hewlett-Packard LaserJet, 188
```

An Exercise in Building an Index

You can try the following exercise to practice building an index.

1. Select File Open (Alt+F+O) and open the CHESS.DOC document you created in the first chapter.

2. Place the insertion pointer at the end of the first paragraph, and press Ctrl+Enter to add a page break between the first and second paragraphs.

3. Place the insertion pointer at the end of the first paragraph (after the word *pieces*), and choose Index Entry on the Insert menu (Alt+I+E).

4. In the Index Entry text box, enter **Number of pieces**, and choose OK.

5. Select the word *King* in the first paragraph, and choose Insert Index Entry (Alt+I+E). Because *King* is selected, it automatically appears in the Index Entry text box. Choose OK.

6. Again select the word *King*, but this time from the second paragraph. Choose Insert Index Entry (Alt+I+E), and then OK.

7. Repeat Step 6 for the words *Pawn*, *Rook*, *Bishop*, and *Queen*.

8. Press Ctrl+End to move the insertion pointer to the end of the document.

9. Press Ctrl+Enter to add a page break and start a new line. You'll place the index on this new last page of the document.

10. Select Insert Index (Alt+I+I). Leave the Normal Index option marked.

11. Press Alt+B to choose Blank Line as a heading separator; then choose OK.

The index appears in the document as shown in Figure 10.4. Notice that because you added two *King* entries that were on two different pages, the index contains references to both pages 1 and 2 for that word. You can close the index document without saving it (Alt+F+C, then No). This modified version of the CHESS.DOC file will not be needed again in this text.

Figure 10.4

Index based on index entries added to CHESS.DOC document

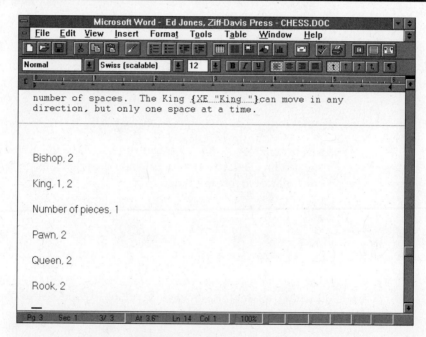

number of spaces. The King {XE…"King…"}can move in any direction, but only one space at a time.

Bishop, 2

King, 1, 2

Number of pieces, 1

Pawn, 2

Queen, 2

Rook, 2

Creating Multilevel Index Entries

You can insert index entries that contain multiple levels, or subentries. As an example, the following excerpt from an index is designed using two levels:

```
Data
    Copying, 104
    Definition, 251
    Deleting, 92
    Editing, 91
    Linking, 216
    Reporting, 251
```

```
Data Menu, 64, 216
Database
    Attributes of, 251
    Creating, 216
    Criteria, 23Ø
```

To create an index with multiple levels, you simply separate the levels by adding a colon when typing the XE field for the index entry into the Index Entry dialog box. Here are the steps to do this:

1. In the document to be indexed, place the insertion pointer at the end of the text for which you are creating the index entry.

2. Choose Index Entry on the Insert menu (Alt+I+E).

3. In the Index Entry text box, type the first level of index entry, then a colon, and then the second level subentry. For any additional subentries, type a colon and then the text of the subentry.

4. Choose OK to insert the index entry field.

As an example, to add index subentries like those illustrated previously under the heading Database, you would add the following index entries at the appropriate places in the document:

```
Database:Attributes of
Database:Creating
Database:Criteria
```

By specifying subentries, you will thus have a choice of index structures when you use the Insert Index command to build the index. As mentioned earlier, the dialog box for this command contains the options Normal Index and Run-In Index, which tell Word how to set up a multilevel index. Leave the default of Normal Index selected, and the resulting index will have indented sublevel entries like these:

```
Database
    Attributes of, 251
    Creating, 216
    Criteria, 23Ø
```

On the other hand, if you select the Run-In Index option, Word inserts all index subentries in the same paragraph as their higher-level entry. The first two items are separated by a colon, and all remaining items are separated by semicolons. The index entry shown just above would thus look like the following in a Run-In Index:

```
Database: Attributes of, 251; Creating, 216; Criteria, 23Ø
```

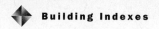

Using Index Entry Page Number Ranges

When a subject covered by an index entry spans two or more pages of a document, you may want the reference in the index to include the entire range of pages that are applicable. In the portion of an index shown just below, the entries for "Go To command" and for "Hardware" both span a range of pages:

```
Get Info command, 41
Go To command, 62-65
Gridlines command, 145

Hardware, 19-20
Help menu, 12
```

With the techniques described so far for inserting index entries, you can refer only to the first page of the subject of the index entry—even if you select multiple pages of text before invoking the Insert Index Entry command. If you want to have a range of page numbers in your index entry, like those shown above, you must do things a little differently. You will need to select the range of text and insert a *bookmark* that refers to the selection. Then, when you invoke the Insert Index Entry command, you enter the bookmark name in the Page Number Range list box. This process involves the following steps:

See Chapter 3 for more about bookmarks.

1. Use your preferred selection method to select the range of text you want the index entry to reference.

2. Choose Bookmark from the Insert menu (Alt+I+M). In the Bookmark dialog box, type a name for the bookmark and choose OK.

   Figure 10.5 shows a portion of selected text that in total spans two pages, along with the Bookmark dialog box that appears as a result of the Insert Bookmark command. In this example, bm1 has been entered as the bookmark name.

3. Choose Index Entry from the Insert menu (Alt+I+E). In the Index Entry text box, type the text for your index entry.

4. Tab to the Page Number Range list box. Type the bookmark name for the selection, or choose a bookmark name from the list box. In the illustration below, the bm1 bookmark has been entered in the Range box:

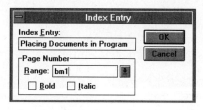

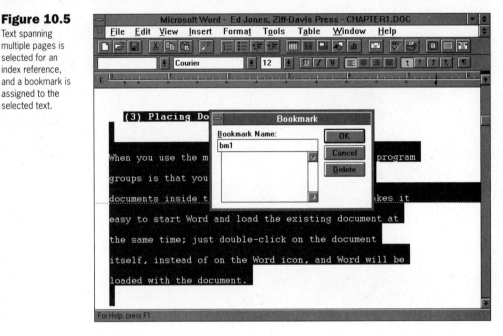

Figure 10.5

Text spanning multiple pages is selected for an index reference, and a bookmark is assigned to the selected text.

5. Choose OK to insert the index entry field.

The index entry created in the above example will look like this:

```
Placing Documents in Program Groups, 7-8
```

Building Large Indexes

If you are generating a large index (one with 4,000 entries or more), Word may run out of memory when you attempt to use the Insert Index command. Microsoft recommends that you generate indexes for very large documents in multiple steps. For example, first you build an index that contains entries for A through L; then build an index for M through Z. You can do this by using the Insert Field command (rather than the Insert Index command) to insert a separate field for each portion of the index, and using the \p switch in the Index field. (Switches used in fields were discussed in earlier sections of this chapter.) If you want to try this, first add all of your desired index entries into the document, or use an existing document with many index entries, and then perform the following steps:

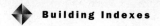

1. Place the insertion pointer at the location in the document for the index.

2. Select Insert Field (Alt+I+D).

3. Click in the Field Code box and delete any entry that's there.

4. Type the word **index** followed by a space, a backslash, the letter **p**, another space, and a range of letters separated by a dash (such as **A-L**).

5. Choose OK to insert the first index field into the document. If the Hidden Text option under Tools Options is turned on, the field will resemble the following:

   ```
   {index \p A-L}
   ```

6. Move the insertion pointer to the right of the existing index field, and press Enter to start a new line.

7. Repeat steps 2 through 5 for each additional range of letters needed.

A Note About Additional Index Options

There are additional switches available for use in the Index Entry (XE) fields in Word, to add sophistication to your indexes. These features include changing the separator character used between ranges of page numbers (normally a hyphen), and restricting an index to only include index items that begin with a certain letter. These special index switches are beyond the scope of this book, but you can find more information about them in your *Microsoft Word User's Reference*.

Desktop Publishing with Word

THIS CHAPTER SHOWS HOW A NUMBER OF DIFFERENT TECHNIQUES IN Word for Windows Version 2.0 can be used in the area of desktop publishing. Earlier versions of Word for Windows came close to offering true desktop publishing power, but some needed features were lacking. For example, Versions 1.0 and 1.1 did not give you the ability to insert frames into any location in a document. With Version 2.0, you can insert frames, and you can place graphics or text within those frames. The frames can then be positioned anywhere in the document, and other text can be made to flow around the frames. This feature is common to desktop publishing packages like Aldus PageMaker and Xerox Ventura Publisher.

With Version 2.0 of Word for Windows, you acquire a fuller range of desktop publishing capabilities.

Version 2.0 of Word for Windows also adds significant drawing and charting tools to your repertory, via the Microsoft Draw and Microsoft Graph programs. These utilities let you create business graphs (also called charts) and drawings which, along with similar graphic enhancements created with programs like Lotus 1-2-3 and Corel Draw, can be inserted into your Word documents.

The first part of this chapter shows how to import graphics into a Word document, and how to work with frames. The second part of the chapter discusses the organizational tools that aid desktop publishing. These tools exist throughout Word and have been introduced in prior chapters, but it is their combined use that gives your documents a polished, professional look. Finally, at the end of the chapter you will find examples of how all these techniques have been combined in some documents typical of desktop publishing, such as newsletters and brochures.

About Graphic Images

Word's ability to import graphic images from other software adds much to your desktop publishing capabilities. Word can import any of the following image files:

File Type	File Name Extension
AutoCAD 2-D Format	.DXF
AutoCAD Plot File	.PLT
Computer Graphics Metafile	.CGM
DrawPerfect	.WPG
Encapsulated PostScript	.EPS
Hewlett-Packard Graphics Language	.HGL
Lotus 1-2-3 Graphic	.PIC
Micrografx Designer/Draw	.DRW
PC Paintbrush	.PCX
Tagged Image Format	.TIF
Windows Bitmap	.BMP
Windows Metafile	.WMF

Word uses built-in *graphic filters* to convert these graphics files into the images that appear in your document. When you install Word, it is possible to omit graphic filters that aren't needed, to save disk space. When you import a picture file, the Insert Picture command (detailed shortly) presents a list of files and formats according to the graphic filters that are installed. If you need a file in a format that isn't installed, you will need to run Word's installation program and reinstall the graphic filter for that image file format. See your Word documentation for details.

In addition to importing graphics, you can also create your own graphics, directly from Word. While Word itself cannot create graphics, Microsoft includes with Word a program called Microsoft Draw (MS Draw) that can create many of the graphics you need, and that can be started from within Word. You start MS Draw within a separate window by clicking on the Draw icon in the Toolbar, or by selecting Insert Object and choosing Microsoft Drawing in the dialog box that appears. You can then use MS Draw to draw the desired picture, or you can load one of the ready-to-use images, called *clip art,* stored with MS Draw. Once you have an image within MS Draw, you use its File Update command to transfer the picture into your Word document. An example later in this chapter shows how this is done. For more specifics on using MS Draw, refer to Appendix C.

In Windows, there are two kinds of graphic images: *bitmap images,* which are created in paint programs, and *object images,* created in drawing programs. Since each type of image has its own advantages and disadvantages (and having both MS Draw and Windows Paintbrush means that you can create either type), you will want to be familiar with both.

Bitmap Images

Bitmap images are composed of a collection of dots, or *pixels,* on the screen. Bitmaps are so called because their image is literally defined within the computer by assigning each pixel on the screen to a storage bit (location) within the computer's memory. Paint programs create bitmap images. Your copy of Windows comes with a free paint program, Paintbrush; the sample CHESS document used throughout this book contains a bitmap image loaded with the Windows Paintbrush program.

Bitmap images can also be purchased from various software suppliers, or found on computer bulletin boards. Disks of bitmap images typically contain collections of useful graphics such as business caricatures, sports and game logos, and images of animals and nature settings. You can import bitmap files in any of the file formats named in the previous section into a Word document. Figure 11.1 shows a screen full of ready-to-use bitmap images from a clip-art collection.

Figure 11.1

Examples of clip-art images

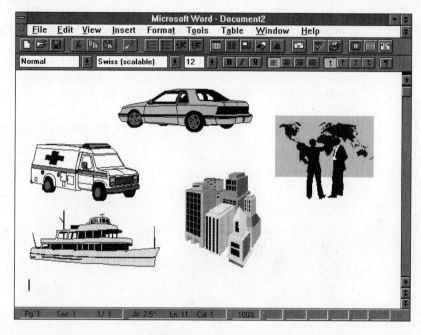

Photographs are also stored as bitmap images. If you have access to a scanner, you can scan photographs and store them on disk as bitmaps; the scanner's directions will tell you how. The bitmap of the photo can then be imported into your Word document. Bear in mind that black-and-white photos typically scan with greater clarity than color. Figure 11.2 shows an example of a photograph scanned into a bitmap image.

Bitmaps have one major advantage, and one major drawback. The strength of bitmaps is that they can easily be extensively modified. Most paint programs (including Paintbrush) let you modify existing parts of a bitmap image by selectively adding or deleting bits; you can "zoom in" on the image, as if it were under a magnifying glass, and change individual pixels to black, white, or any one of a range of colors. The disadvantage to using a bitmap is that you typically cannot modify its size by *scaling* (stretching or shrinking the image in one or more directions).

Object Images

Object images are based on a collection of geometric objects—lines, arcs, circles, rectangles, and so forth. Object images are created by drawing programs such as MS Draw, provided with Word. Other popular draw packages that run under Windows include Corel Draw and Micrografx Draw; you may be using one of these. Drawing programs are preferred for the creation of line drawings like company logos, maps, and images of objects with "clean" lines (buildings, cars, planes, bridges, and so on). However, these packages typically do not do well with images you might sketch without a ruler, such as a portrait of a person's face. Such tasks are usually better left to paint programs.

Figure 11.2

Scanned photo inserted as a bitmap in a Word document

The difficulty paint programs have with object images is the forte of drawing programs. In packages such as MS Draw, objects can easily be scaled—since the object is based on a collection of straight and curved lines, the software simply expands or contracts the lines to expand or contract the entire image. An object image cannot, however, be modified as easily as a bitmap. Though you can select any of the objects that make up the image (such as one line in a drawing of a building), and stretch, shrink, or redraw that line, this is a tedious task. And with complex drawings, it may be difficult to get the results you want when modifying an existing image.

Most drawing programs (including MS Draw) have the capability to load a bitmap and covert it to an object image, but the difference in how the two images are stored means that the results may be less than spectacular. Curved lines in a bitmap are stored as jagged or "stepped" patterns of light and dark pixels, and if you bring a bitmap into a drawing program and then try to scale it, the stepped patterns change disproportionately. The result is often an image with some distortion.

Inserting Images into Word

Chapter 2 taught you how to insert a portion of a Windows Paintbrush image using the Clipboard, and this technique is a handy one to have in your collection. But for importing images from a wide range of software, you'll need to use the Insert Picture command. It's easy to insert a graphic into your document using Insert Picture. Begin by placing the insertion pointer where you want the image to appear. Select Insert Picture (Alt+I+P), and the Picture dialog box appears, as shown in Figure 11.3.

Figure 11.3
The Picture dialog box appears when you invoke the Insert Picture command.

Enter name of picture file to import, or choose a file from the list box

Change drive and/or directories

Insert a picture file as a Word field

Displays the selected picture file in the Preview Picture box

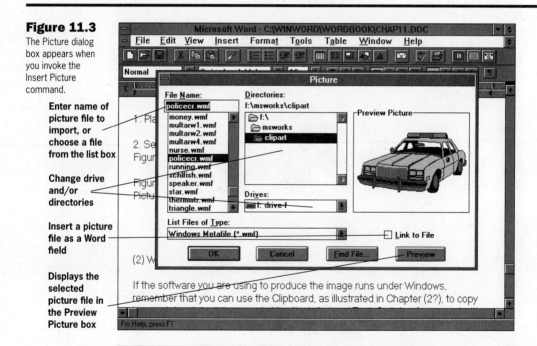

Specifying the image file you want is a familiar process—one you have used in many similar dialog boxes in Word for Windows. In the File Name text box (Alt+N), you can enter the name of an image file, or select one by name from the list box. To work with files of a particular type, press Alt+T to open the List Files of Type list box, and choose your image file format from the list. Use the Directories (Alt+D) and/or Drives (Alt+V) list boxes when you need a file from a different directory, or on a different drive.

Once you've highlighted the desired file in the File Name box, you have the following options:

Tip. The Preview button in the Picture dialog box is a handy way to examine a collection of clip art stored on a disk. In the File Name list box you can highlight each file one at a time, and select Preview to see the image that's stored in the file.

- Choose Preview (Alt+I) to see the image in the Preview Picture box, like the image of the police car in Figure 11.3.

- The Find File button brings forth the Find File dialog box (discussed in Chapter 16), which can be used to search for other image files.

- If you want to link an image in Word to the graphics file, mark the Link to File check box (Alt+L). Word then inserts the image as a field in the document. Then, if you later change the picture in the program that was used to create the image, you can use the Update Field key (F9) to update the picture.

- The Cancel button closes the Picture dialog box.

Once you've captured your picture, choose OK (or press Enter). This closes the Picture dialog box and inserts the image into your Word document, at the insertion pointer location. Figure 11.4 shows an example of a clip-art image (from MS Draw) pasted into a Word document using this technique.

Figure 11.4

Clip-art image inserted into Word document

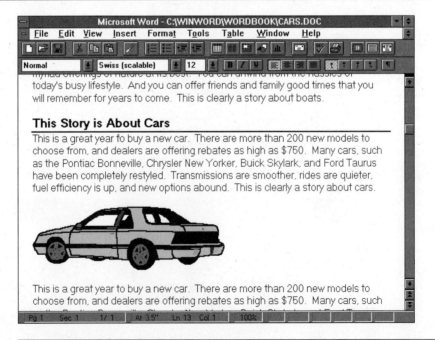

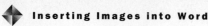

Using Frames Around Objects

Normally, you can think of an image in your document as a single, large character, such as a giant letter *A*. As such, you cannot place text around the image, because the image takes up one giant line of text. You can, however, insert a frame that surrounds the image, and then position the frame containing the image anywhere in your document. The other text in the document then automatically repositions itself around the frame (this will be visible only in page layout view). See "Working with Frames in Word" later in this chapter for details. Also later in the chapter is an example that shows how you can create an image using MS Graph, insert it into a document, and surround it with a frame.

Adding Text

Often, you will want to add text (callouts or captions) to the images you insert into your documents. There are many ways to do this, but one easy way is to use Word's table feature. Add a table with the Insert Table command, and insert the image into one cell of the table. Then type the text of your callout or caption into an adjacent cell of the table, and format the table as needed so that the text is designed and located as you want it. See Chapter 8 for more information about using tables.

Using Reverse Type

For some applications, *reverse type* is popular; many newsletters make use of this technique—white letters on a black background—to make a headline or subhead stand out. The line of text shown here is in reverse type:

November, 1991   The Guide to the Best Videos   Issue 9

You can create reverse type in Word by assigning the color white to the text, and then designating a border with a black background. (For more about borders, see the following section, "Scaling, Cropping, and Adding Borders.") Here are the steps to try this out:

1. Type the text that is to be displayed as reverse type. (You may want to apply boldface or use a larger font, as reverse type displays better when wider-than-normal characters are used.)

2. Select the text to be displayed as reverse type. (If you are creating a heading like the one above, select the entire heading.)

3. Choose Character on the Format menu (Alt+T+C). In the Color list box (Alt+C), change the color to White, and select OK. For the time being, the text will not be visible, because you now have white letters placed on a white background.

4. Choose Border on the Format menu (Alt+T+B), and in the dialog box, choose Shading (Alt+S). In the Background list box (Alt+B), choose Black, and then choose OK twice.

5. Move the cursor out of the paragraph to deselect it, and you will see the effect of the reverse type, like that shown in the above illustration.

Word has some difficulty displaying reverse type correctly in outline view and Print Preview; in these modes, reverse type text appears as a blank line. In normal view and page layout view, however, the text appears correctly. Also keep in mind that extensive use of this technique increases wear on your printer, because larger quantities of ink or laser toner are required.

Inserting with the Clipboard

If the software you are using to produce your graphics is a Windows-compatible application, remember that you can also use the Clipboard, as illustrated in Chapter 2, to copy images into a Word document. Here are the steps:

1. Use the Windows Task Switcher (press Ctrl+Esc) to bring up the Program Manager, and start your painting or drawing program in another window in the usual manner. (If Word is running and you have less than 2Mb of memory installed, you will probably need to exit Word before you can run another Windows application.)

2. Display the desired image within the paint or draw program, and use the appropriate selection tool to select the needed portion of the image.

3. Invoke the Edit Copy command that is available in all Windows applications.

4. Restart Word, if necessary. Press Ctrl+Esc to bring up the Task Switcher, open Program Manager, and start Word in the usual manner.

5. Open the Word document that will receive the image, and place the insertion pointer at the desired location for the image. Choose Edit Paste, and the image from the other program will be inserted.

Scaling, Cropping, and Adding Borders to Images

Once an image has been inserted into a document, Word provides the powerful capability to change the size of that image, by scaling (resizing) and cropping (trimming). These movements are accomplished more easily with a mouse than with a keyboard. Mouse users can scale and crop images by selecting the image and dragging sizing handles that appear around it, but keyboard users must use the Format Picture command and enter dimensions in a dialog box. With the Format Border command (detailed in Chapter 4), you can also apply borders to an image.

Scaling an Image

To scale (resize) an image, you must first select it. When you select an image by clicking on it with the mouse, sizing handles are displayed. (In the illustration below, the sizing handles are the small black squares at the corners and in the centers of the sides of the image.) Keyboard users can select an image by placing the insertion pointer at the start of the image (its immediate left), holding down the Shift key, and pressing the → key once.

Sizing
handles

To scale with the mouse, simply click and drag one of the sizing handles until the image reaches the desired size. Dragging a handle at the center of either side resizes the width of the image; dragging a handle at the center of the top or bottom resizes the height of the image. Dragging any of the corner handles resizes *both* the width and height of the image.

To scale with the keyboard, choose Format Picture (Alt+T+R) (remember to select the picture first). The Picture dialog box appears.

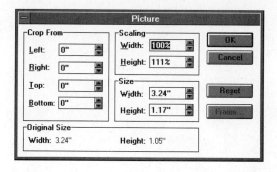

Here you can change the scaling in one of two ways: Enter a percentage value in the Scaling Width and Height text boxes, which makes the Size

Mouse users, too, can use the Reset button in the Picture dialog box, to restore an image to its original size.

Width and Height measurements change accordingly. Or you can enter a measurement value in the Size Width and Height text boxes, which makes the Scaling percentages change accordingly. The Reset button lets you restore a scaled image to its original size. (Word remembers the original size of an image, regardless of how you scale or crop it.) When you have made your scaling changes, choose OK or press Enter.

Cropping an Image

To crop an image, you must select it first, using either mouse or keyboard as described just above for the scaling procedure.

To crop using the mouse, hold down the Shift key while dragging one of the handles. Dragging a handle at the center of either side crops the image on that side. Dragging a handle at the center of either the top or bottom crops the image from the top or the bottom. Dragging any of the corner handles crops from the side nearest that corner, *and* from the top or bottom nearest that corner. Figure 11.5 shows an image in its original form, after scaling, and after cropping.

To crop using the keyboard, choose Format Picture (Alt+T+R) (remember to select the picture first). You'll again see the Picture dialog box, as you did for scaling. Use the Crop From boxes to enter the measurement amounts by which you want to crop the image. Enter values in the Left and Right boxes to specify how much to crop from the left and right sides; enter values in the Top and Bottom boxes to specify how much to crop from the top and bottom. You can enter crop measurements for just the width, or just the height, or for both. Use the Reset button to restore a cropped image back to its original size. When you have finished cropping as needed, choose OK or press Enter.

Adding Borders

Note. You cannot apply shading to an image as you can to a paragraph; when a picture is selected and you choose Format Border, the Shading button that normally appears in the dialog box is dimmed.

You can put borders around graphic images with the Format Border command. To apply a border, first select the image. Then choose Format Border (Alt+T+B). From the dialog box, select the type of border you want. (For more details about the border options in this dialog box, see Chapter 4.) In the illustration below, a shadow border has been added around the car by choosing Format Border, then Shadow, and then OK.

Figure 11.5

Examples of scaling and cropping applied to a graphic image

The image below is the original.

The image below has been scaled to 135 percent of its original width.

The image below has been cropped by cutting off a portion of the bottom.

NOTE. *You cannot apply shading to an image as you can to a paragraph; when a picture is selected and you choose Format Border, the Shading button that normally appears in the dialog box is dimmed.*

Editing Images in Word

For details about the use of MS Draw, refer to Appendix C.

Once you have placed an image into a Word file, you can edit it using MS Draw. Double-click on the image or select it with the keyboard, and choose Edit Picture. (This command appears on the Word Edit menu only when you have selected a graphic image. If the image was created using MS Draw, the command changes to Edit Microsoft Drawing Object.) The image appears inside an MS Draw window, and you can then use that program's editing techniques as necessary. When you're done, choose File Exit (Alt+F+X) from the MS Draw menu, and answer Yes (Alt+Y or Y) to the "Update document?" prompt that appears. The modified image then appears in your Word document.

NOTE. *Remember that MS Draw is an object-based drawing program, so you may get unsatisfactory results if you import a bitmap into a Word document and then modify it with MS Draw.*

Inserting Graphs into Word Documents

You can insert graphs into Word documents by using MS Graph, a program designed for the creation of business graphs (see Appendix D). You can also insert graphs created from spreadsheets such as Lotus 1-2-3, Excel, and Microsoft Works; how to do this is described shortly. But first, here's the procedure for inserting a graph from MS Graph into a Word document:

- Click on the Graph icon in the Toolbar, or select Insert Object (Alt+I+O) and choose Microsoft Graph from the dialog box. Then choose OK (or press Enter) to open the MS Graph window.

- Enter the desired category titles and values in the MS Graph Datasheet to create your graph. Use the Gallery menu to change the graph type. (For more details, refer to Appendix D.)

Tip. You can use the Clipboard techniques detailed in Chapter 2 to copy information from any Windows application into a Word document.

- When you've completed your graph, choose File Exit (Alt+F+X) from the MS Graph menu, and answer Yes (Alt+Y or just Y) to the "Update document?" prompt. The graph will be pasted into the Word document, at the insertion pointer.

Whenever it is started, MS Graph shows a simple bar graph by default, so let's use that graph to practice inserting a graph into a document. Try the following exercise.

1. In Word, open the document you saved earlier in the book as SAMPLE2. (If you did not create this sample document, open any document containing a paragraph or more of text.)

2. Place the insertion pointer at the end of a paragraph, and press Enter to begin a new line.

3. Click on the Graph icon in the Toolbar, or select Insert Object (Alt+I+O) and choose Microsoft Graph from the dialog box that appears. Choose OK (or press Enter) to open the MS Graph window.

A default bar graph (Figure 11.6) appears in the MS Graph window. This is the graph that you will insert into the document.

Figure 11.6

Default bar graph displayed when MS Graph is started

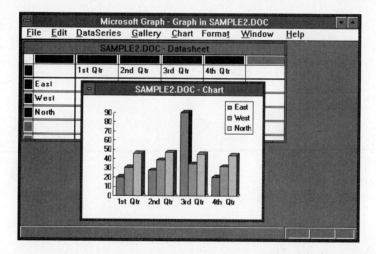

4. Select File Exit (Alt+F+X).

5. In response to the "Update graph in SAMPLE2.DOC?" prompt that appears, answer Yes (Alt+Y or just Y).

The graph appears in the SAMPLE2 document, as shown in Figure 11.7. For now, leave the document open on your screen; you will use it in an upcoming exercise with frames.

NOTE. *If you are using Microsoft Excel, Microsoft Works, or another Windows application, you can use the copy-and-paste techniques of the Clipboard (Chapter 2) to copy graphs from those programs into your Word documents. In Excel or in Works, perform the usual commands needed to display the* *graph in a window; then choose Edit Copy (Alt+E+C). Exit the other program, and load Word in the usual manner. Place the insertion pointer at the desired location for the graph, and choose Edit Paste (Alt+E+P) to insert the graph into your document.*

Figure 11.7
SAMPLE2 document with bar graph inserted from MS Graph

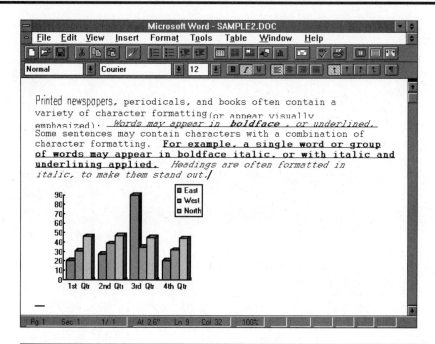

Working with Frames

At times, you will want a certain object in a document to appear in a very specific location on the page. With Word, you can do this by placing the object in a *frame.* The object that you insert into the frame can be a graphic image, a table, or text. Once the object has been framed, you can position the frame and its contents anywhere you want within the document. When you move a frame, everything within it moves as a single unit. Then, once you place a frame in its location, you can decide how you want text outside the frame to wrap around it.

If you are already familiar with desktop publishing software, you might think of frames as places to insert graphics, but frames in Word can accommodate more than just pictures. In addition to serving as placeholders for graphics, another popular use for frames is to place *absolutely positioned* paragraphs of text (paragraphs that occupy a specific, fixed location in a document).

TIP. *As you work with frames, it is a good idea to use Word's page layout view. Text wrap (around a frame) is visible only in page layout view. Also, this view helps you to see how your frames relate to other text or objects on the page.*

Inserting a Frame Around an Existing Object

It's easy to place a frame around an existing object, by selecting the object and then using either the Insert Frame command or the Frame button on the Toolbar. Here's how:

■ Select the text, table, or image that you want to enclose with a frame.

■ Click the Frame button on the Toolbar, or choose Insert Frame (Alt+I+F). If you are not already in page layout view, Word will ask if you want to switch views. Choose Yes from the dialog box; the frame is inserted, and your screen view changes to page layout.

■ Once Word inserts the frame, the framed object remains selected, and you can resize or move it as needed. (See "Sizing Frames" and "Moving Frames" later in this chapter.)

NOTE. *By default, Word places a single-line border around frames. If you remove the frame, the border remains, as a single-line border around the object. You can remove the border, if necessary, with the Format Borders command.*

With the SAMPLE2 document still open from the last example, try this exercise to insert a frame around the graph you just added to the document.

1. Select the graph (click on it; or place the insertion pointer to the immediate left of the graph, hold Shift, and press the → key). The selected graph is enclosed in a visible border, and sizing handles (the small black squares) appear at the edges.

2. Click the Frame icon on the Toolbar, or choose Insert Frame (Alt+I+F).

3. If you are not already in page layout view, you will see the following dialog box:

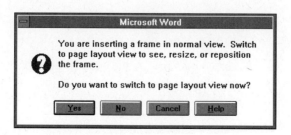

Choose Yes (Alt+Y, or just Y) or just press Enter. Word places a frame around the graph.

Inserting an Empty Frame into a Document

Suppose you need an empty frame so that you can enter new text into it. This is the most common (and the easiest) method for producing an absolutely positioned paragraph at a fixed location in the document. Once you insert the empty frame, you can type within it, and your text will automatically wrap within the frame. To insert an empty frame, perform the following steps:

1. Make sure no text or object is selected.

2. Click on the Frame button on the Toolbar, or choose Insert Frame (Alt+I+F). (If you are not already in page layout view, Word asks if you want to switch views; choose Yes from the dialog box.) The pointer then changes to a large plus sign.

3. *With the Mouse:* Move the converted mouse pointer to the location where you want the frame. Hold down the left mouse button, drag the frame to the desired size, and release the mouse button. *With the Keyboard:* Use the arrow keys to place the pointer in the location where you want the upper-left corner of the frame, and press Enter. Use the arrow keys to resize the frame, and then press Enter again.

An Exercise: Placing an Absolutely Positioned Paragraph Within a Frame

As an exercise, use the three steps listed above to place an absolutely positioned paragraph in a frame. As you work through the steps, make these adjustments:

- In Step 1, remember to move the insertion pointer *away* from the existing graph, so that it is not selected.

- In Step 3, place the frame at the start of the document, and size the frame so it is roughly two inches square.

  Then, with the insertion pointer in the new frame, type the following text:

  ```
  Character formatting can call attention to your message.
  ```

As you type the text, watch how it automatically wraps within the frame. Figure 11.8 shows the sample document containing the frame with the newly entered text.

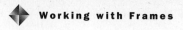

Figure 11.8
SAMPLE2
document with new
frame inserted,
containing an
absolutely
positioned
paragraph

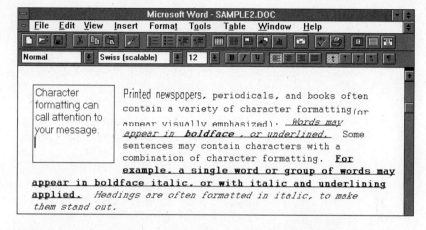

Working with the Format Frames Dialog Box

Once you have placed a frame in a document, you may need to control various aspects of the frame, such as its location, its size, and whether adjacent text will be permitted to wrap around the frame. Mouse users can accomplish most of these tasks using the mouse, but for the few tasks that can't be done with a mouse (and for keyboard users), Word provides the Format Frame command. When a frame is selected and you invoke Format Frame (Alt+T+F), this Frame dialog box appears:

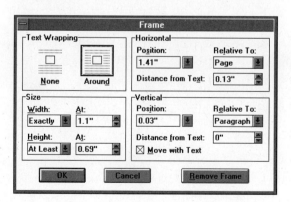

The options in this dialog box will be demonstrated in the exercises that follow, but for now, here is a summary:

Horizontal and Vertical Placement   The Horizontal and Vertical areas of the dialog box contain text and list boxes for entering measurements and other specifications for the location of the frame. Enter measurement values in the Horizontal Position and Vertical Position boxes. As usual, you can enter inches, centimeters, points, etc. Then, in the Relative To list boxes, tell Word that the measurement is relative to a margin, a page, a column, or a paragraph of adjacent text. In the Vertical box, you can also turn on the Move With Text option; with this feature enabled, if you later move text that's adjacent to a frame to another location in the document, the frame moves along with the text. The Distance From Text boxes determine the amount of white space between the object and the surrounding text.

Text Wrapping   Mark one of the two diagram check boxes in this area to specify whether you want adjacent text to wrap around the frame.

Size   This area of the dialog box lets you change the dimensions of a frame. In the Width and Height list boxes, you can choose Auto, At Least, or Exactly. With At Least or Exactly, you can then enter a measurement value in the adjacent At boxes. Using Auto for either Height or Width causes the frame to make itself as high or wide as needed to hold the contents. Choose Exactly when you want the frame to assume the exact measurements you enter in the At boxes. At Least tells Word to set the frame to the minimum size you've specified by the values in the At boxes; you can then add text or graphics to the frame, and it will expand as needed beyond the minimum size.

Remove Frame   This button in the dialog box lets you remove a frame, while leaving the contents of the frame intact.

NOTE.   *As demonstrated in the exercises that follow, mouse users will find it far easier to locate and size a frame by dragging the frame around in the document, rather than using the Frame dialog box.*

Moving Frames

Once you have inserted a frame, you can easily move it to any location in a document. As with most moving and sizing tasks, it is easier to do this with a mouse than with keyboard keys. Here are the steps for mouse users to move a frame:

1. Turn on page layout view if it is not already on (Alt+V+P).

2. Place the insertion pointer on the border line of the frame. The mouse pointer changes into a four-headed arrow.

3. Click and drag the frame to the new location. As you drag the frame, a dotted line indicates its position. Release the mouse button, and the frame and its contents move to the new location.

Here are the steps for keyboard users to move a frame:

1. Turn on page layout view if it is not already on (Alt+V+P).

2. Using the arrow keys, position the insertion pointer inside the frame you want to move.

3. Select Frame Format (Alt+T+F).

4. In the dialog box that appears, specify the horizontal location you want for the frame, using an appropriate combination of entries in the Horizontal Position boxes. In the Relative To list box, indicate that the measurement you entered is relative to the margin, the page, or a column.

5. In the Vertical Position box, specify the vertical location you want for the frame, using an appropriate combination of entries. In the Relative To list box, indicate whether the measurement you entered is relative to the margin, the page, or a paragraph.

6. Select OK or press Enter.

For practice, try either set of the preceding steps to move a frame containing text to a different location in the document. (For this exercise, it does not matter where you put the frame.)

Sizing Frames

You can resize frames using the mouse or the keyboard. Mouse users can select the frame and drag the sizing handles. Keyboard users can select the frame and use the Format Frame command, entering the desired height and width measurements in the dialog box.

To resize a frame with the mouse,

1. Turn on page layout view if it is not already on (Alt+V+P).

2. If the sizing handles are not already visible, click anywhere in the frame you want to resize. Eight sizing handles appear on the edges of the frame.

3. Point to one of the sizing handles, and notice that the mouse pointer changes to a two-headed arrow.

4. Drag the handle to resize the frame as desired. Try dragging another handle.

To resize a frame using the keyboard,

1. Turn on page layout view if it is not already on (Alt+V+P).

2. Using the arrow keys, position the insertion pointer inside the frame you want to size.

3. Select Frame Format (Alt+T+F).

4. In the dialog box that appears, choose Exactly in the Width list box, and in the At box enter a width in inches for the frame. (To make the frame as wide as the object inside, choose Auto in the Width box.)

5. Choose Exactly in the Height list box, and in the At box enter a height in inches for the frame. (To make the frame as tall as the object inside, choose Auto in the Height box.)

6. Select OK or press Enter.

For practice, try resizing the frame containing the graph, using the steps outlined above. You might want to try selecting At Least in the Width and Height boxes, and other variations of frame dimensions, to see what happens.

Wrapping Text Around Frames

By default, Word wraps adjacent text around frames. You can turn this format trait on or off for a particular frame, by using the Text Wrapping option of the Format Frame command. It's easy—first turn on page layout view if it is not already on (Alt+V+P). Using the mouse or the arrow keys, place the insertion pointer inside the frame, and select Frame Format (Alt+T+F). In the Text Wrapping area of the dialog box that appears, choose Around (Alt+D) if you want text to wrap around the frame, or None (Alt+N) if you don't. Then select OK or press Enter to execute your choice.

Figures 11.9 and 11.10 show the difference when text wrapping is enabled or disabled. In Figure 11.9, the frame containing the graph has been placed in the center of the paragraph, and the Text Wrapping option is set to Around. In Figure 11.10, the frame is in the same location, but Text Wrapping is set to None. Note that only the graph frame is affected; in Figure 11.10, the text still wraps around the frame containing text, because Text Wrapping was not turned off for that frame.

Removing Frames

You can remove a frame only, and leave its contents intact, or you can delete both the frame and its contents.

Figure 11.9
Document with
frame, when Text
Wrapping is enabled

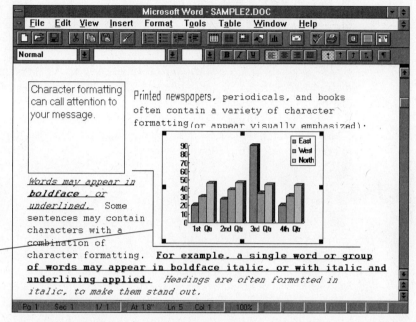

**Text wraps
around
frame**

Figure 11.10
Document with
frame, when Text
Wrapping is
disabled

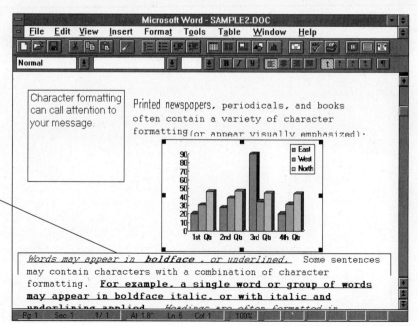

**Text does
not wrap
around
frame**

To remove a frame only, click in the frame, or use the arrow keys to place the insertion pointer within the frame. Select Format Frame (Alt+T+F), and choose Remove Frame in the dialog box. When you remove a frame and leave its contents intact, any borders applied to the frame will remain around the object.

To delete both the frame and its contents, use your preferred selection method to select the frame to be deleted (you need not select the contents, just the frame). Press the Del key.

You may want to experiment further with the use of frames within the SAMPLE2 document. When you are done, close the document without saving the changes; you will not need this modified version of the document.

The Organizational Tools of Desktop Publishing in Word

The various organizational tools that Word provides all help you to create documents with a desktop-published appearance. For the most part, these tools have been covered in earlier chapters of this text; however, it is the combination of these techniques, along with your ability to work with graphics, that will make the difference between an ordinary document and one that has a truly professional look. Word's organizational tools include columns, gutter margins, headlines and subheads, headers and footers, and the integration of graphics.

Before you attempt to apply desktop publishing techniques to any document, it is a good idea to sketch out on paper exactly how you want your document to look. It is much easier to pattern a document in Word after one that you've already designed on paper. This step also helps you avoid mistakes that may detract from the appearance of the finished document. You can often anticipate errors in overall layout because they are apparent in the paper-based sketch. Also, remember the Print Preview command (Alt+F+V). You can use this helpful tool to quickly get an accurate feel for the page design of your document.

Preparing, Proofing, and Printing the Text

Various options on the Format and Tools menus can aid in the preparation, proofing, and printing of text.

With some desktop publishing tasks, you must adjust the precise spacing between lines (called *leading* in typesetters' lingo), and between characters (called *kerning*) to achieve a particular result. As you learned in Chapter 4, Word lets you set spacing between lines with the Format Paragraph command, and spacing between characters with the Format Character command. The measurement options available for these commands allow you to be as precise in your settings as need be.

Keep in mind, also, the Format Page Setup command when you are laying out pages that are to be bound in book form, or printed and bound as double-sided pages. You can use the Gutter option in the Page Setup Margins dialog box to specify the "gutter" width needed for binding; use the Facing Pages option of the same dialog box when you want to make the margin adjustments needed to print double-sided pages. See Chapter 5 for details on these features.

Before you apply Word's desktop publishing capabilities to give your text that professional appearance, the text should be as close to perfection grammatically as is possible. A document that is littered with spelling or grammar errors takes on an amateur appearance, regardless of the time you've spent on layout or in adding graphics. Make the most of Word's Spelling, Grammar, and Thesaurus features on the Tools menu (detailed in Chapter 3) to minimize those language errors that have a way of creeping into a document.

Columns and Margins

With many documents, column arrangement becomes a significant part of desktop publishing design. One- and two-column layouts are the most popular, but you will often have many more than two columns. And with columnar text, there is a "visual" limit to keep in mind. As the number of columns increases, you approach a point where readability suffers. Readers don't see individual words, but rather phrases, or groups of words; hence, column width has a direct impact on readability. Overly wide columns make it difficult for the reader to follow phrases from line to line. Columns that are too narrow can also be hard to read, because the eyes must often jump lines in order to absorb a complete phrase.

Page margins, the number of columns, and the width between columns also have an impact, so choose these settings carefully. Point size, too, is significant, because it affects the number of columns. Small point sizes tend to work better in narrow columns, and wide columns generally need larger point sizes. Also, keep in mind that hyphenation helps reduce the jagged look of the right edge (the rag) of columns, especially in narrow columns. Use Word's Tools Hyphenation feature to help you with this task.

When working with columns in Word, remember that not all columns need be the same width if you set them up as side-by-side paragraphs using Word's table feature. (See Chapter 8 for details.)

Keep in mind the effects that page margins have on the space available for text in columns (as well as paragraphs), and on the overall design of your document. Wider margins result in a "lighter" document (Figure 11.11), and narrower margins create the "denser" appearance shown in Figure 11.12.

Figure 11.11
Print Preview of a
visually "light"
document with
wide page margins
and generous
space between
columns

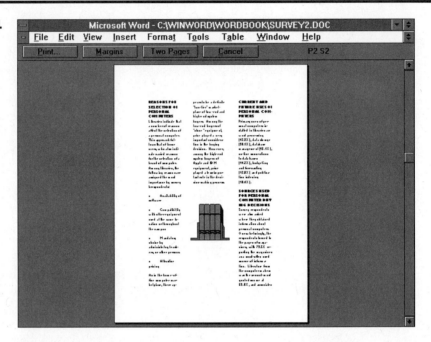

Figure 11.12
Print Preview of a
visually "dense"
document with
narrow page
margins and less
space between
columns

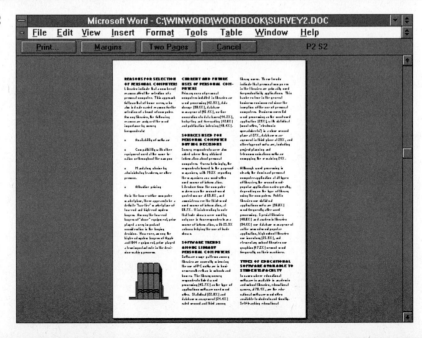

Headlines and Subheads

Headlines are vital in calling attention to your message. For this reason, they are commonly used throughout newsletters, magazines, advertisements, and brochures. You can differentiate your headlines from body text by setting the headlines in larger point sizes and different type styles. You can also emphasize headlines using borders or shading, or you can separate them from other text by means of white space or with rules (vertical or horizontal lines drawn with the Format Border command). Some things to avoid when designing headlines are all uppercase letters, and headlines that contain more than three lines (both tend to be hard to read). A typical headline might resemble this one:

386sx Power, 286 Price

Subheads let you add clarification to a headline. Within your text, subheads break up large, unwieldy expanses of text into smaller groups. These smaller units are visually and intellectually easier to follow. In the text below, a subhead has been added to the previous headline, to provide clarification:

386sx Power, 286 Price
PC Labs Tests 11 Complete Systems Under $1,600

Avoid a common blunder with subheads: Make sure the subhead is visually tied to the text that follows it. To do this, use the Format Paragraph command and set the Space Before Paragraph measurement to a value greater than the Space After Paragraph measurement. This will produce more space above the subhead than below it. In Figure 11.13, the subhead is too close to the prior text, and not close enough to the text that follows; the subhead thus appears disconnected from its related text. In Figure 11.14, the problem has been corrected by selecting the subhead and using Format Paragraph settings to increase the space before, and decrease the space after.

Figure 11.13

Subhead that is too far from its related text

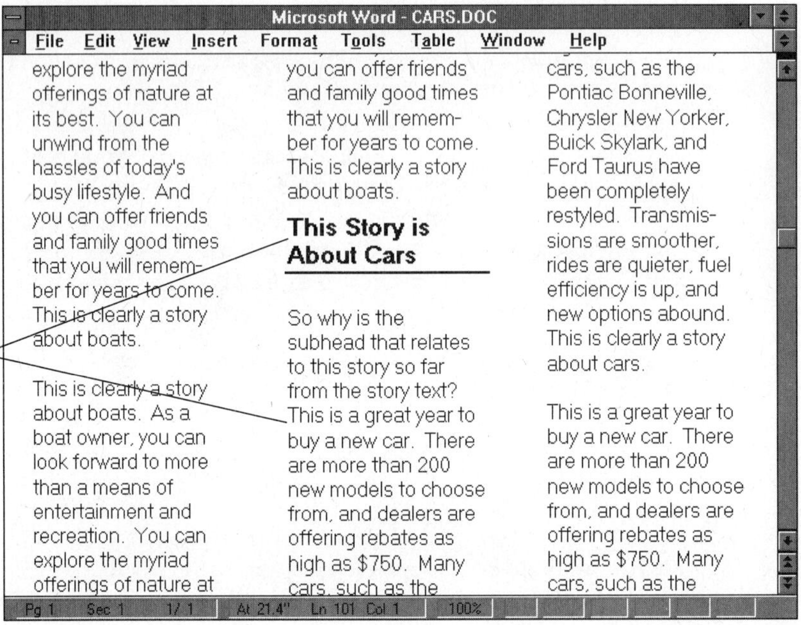

Subhead appears disconnected from related body text

Microsoft Word - CARS.DOC

File Edit View Insert Format Tools Table Window Help

explore the myriad offerings of nature at its best. You can unwind from the hassles of today's busy lifestyle. And you can offer friends and family good times that you will remember for years to come. This is clearly a story about boats.

This is clearly a story about boats. As a boat owner, you can look forward to more than a means of entertainment and recreation. You can explore the myriad offerings of nature at

you can offer friends and family good times that you will remember for years to come. This is clearly a story about boats.

This Story is About Cars

So why is the subhead that relates to this story so far from the story text? This is a great year to buy a new car. There are more than 200 new models to choose from, and dealers are offering rebates as high as $750. Many cars, such as the

cars, such as the Pontiac Bonneville, Chrysler New Yorker, Buick Skylark, and Ford Taurus have been completely restyled. Transmissions are smoother, rides are quieter, fuel efficiency is up, and new options abound. This is clearly a story about cars.

This is a great year to buy a new car. There are more than 200 new models to choose from, and dealers are offering rebates as high as $750. Many cars, such as the

Pg 1   Sec 1   1/1   At 21.4"   Ln 101   Col 1   100%

Figure 11.14

A properly positioned subhead and body text

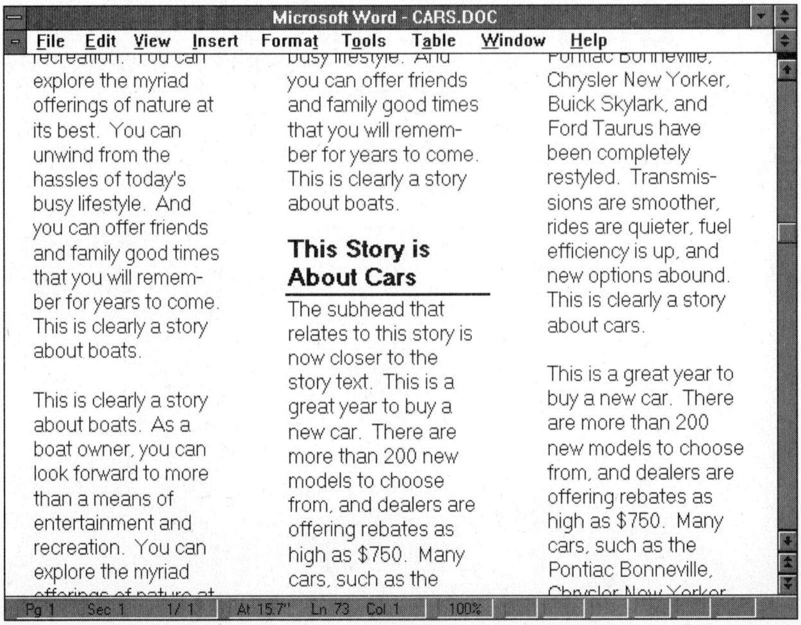

Microsoft Word - CARS.DOC

File Edit View Insert Format Tools Table Window Help

recreation. You can explore the myriad offerings of nature at its best. You can unwind from the hassles of today's busy lifestyle. And you can offer friends and family good times that you will remember for years to come. This is clearly a story about boats.

This is clearly a story about boats. As a boat owner, you can look forward to more than a means of entertainment and recreation. You can explore the myriad offerings of nature at

busy lifestyle. And you can offer friends and family good times that you will remember for years to come. This is clearly a story about boats.

This Story is About Cars

The subhead that relates to this story is now closer to the story text. This is a great year to buy a new car. There are more than 200 new models to choose from, and dealers are offering rebates as high as $750. Many cars, such as the

Pontiac Bonneville, Chrysler New Yorker, Buick Skylark, and Ford Taurus have been completely restyled. Transmissions are smoother, rides are quieter, fuel efficiency is up, and new options abound. This is clearly a story about cars.

This is a great year to buy a new car. There are more than 200 new models to choose from, and dealers are offering rebates as high as $750. Many cars, such as the Pontiac Bonneville, Chrysler New Yorker,

Pg 1   Sec 1   1/1   At 15.7"   Ln 73   Col 1   100%

Graphic Images

Word's ability to place graphics into frames (described earlier in this chapter) means that you have a great deal of flexibility when integrating graphics into text. You can also place a graphic image into the cell of a table, and then use Word's table formatting commands to control the location of the graphic. There is no "correct" method; use the techniques that feel most comfortable to you and that achieve the desired results.

You can use the sizing (scaling) and cropping techniques covered earlier in this chapter to add visual interest to many graphics. For example, you may be able to add interest to an illustration by purposely stretching it out of proportion, as in a stretched image of a dollar bill to convey an increase in buying power.

With graphics, the possibilities are endless. Remember that professionally published documents are often good sources of inspiration for your own effective graphics; you can get ideas for interesting graphic designs by examining publications that have abundant informational graphics, such as *USA Today, Time,* and *Newsweek*.

Graphs and Tables

Use the MS Graph utility (described in Appendix D) to design business graphs that can be inserted into Word documents. With Word's table feature (Chapter 8), you can design entire tables of data. Use a graph when you want the reader to see a visual representation of the underlying data, and a table when you want to emphasize the underlying data itself, rather than its visual representation. With tables that display business numbers, it is a good idea to visually set off any headings or column titles within the table, from the main contents of the table. You can do this by formatting the headings and titles, or by adding borders or shading, using the techniques outlined in Chapter 8.

Informational graphics (such as pie and bar charts) can go a long way in getting business information across to an audience of readers. Consider combining clip art, or drawings done in Windows Paintbrush or MS Draw, with business graphs done in an Excel or MS Graph spreadsheet. Figure 11.15 shows an example of how clip art can be combined with a business graph.

Using Service Bureaus

If optimum quality in printed output is a requirement for your product, you will probably need to utilize the services of a desktop publishing service bureau. Laser printers (which typically offer a resolution of 300 dpi, or dots per inch) are fine for most office documents, and for proofs used to make corrections while the document is still in the design process. However, for truly finished documents that are to be distributed to the public, you may want typeset quality. Most laser printers designed for use with personal computers cannot provide this type of printing quality; a higher resolution of 1200 dpi or greater may be needed. You can achieve such results by preparing the document using Word, and giving the final version (saved on disk) to a service bureau for final printing. (These service bureaus are listed under Desktop Publishing in the Yellow Pages.)

Figure 11.15
Clip art from
MS Draw combined
with graph created
in MS Graph

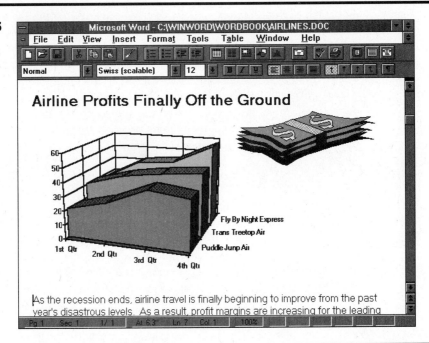

A service bureau may require you to print the file to disk using a specific format, such as PostScript; be sure to call ahead and determine how the agency can best utilize your Word documents.

Putting It All Together

The following pages contain examples of documents produced by Word for Windows (see Figures 11.16 through 11.23 at the end of this chapter), along with tips and hints on the particular tools used in Word to produce them. Included are a newsletter, a flyer, and a page from technical documentation. You can use the desktop publishing techniques described throughout this chapter to produce similar documents that meet your specific needs.

It has been said by the more cynical among us that desktop publishing software has made it possible for millions of people to produce very ugly documents with a minimum of effort. Perhaps this is somewhat correct, although advancing technology has given us such products as grammar checkers that offer advice on our prose, existing computer software is a long way from providing "layout checkers" that tell us when our document is badly organized, or in poor taste visually. Current incarnations of Word do not have the power (or insolence) to display a dialog box like this one:

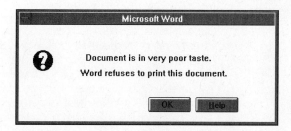

So it is up to you, the user, to build in the aesthetics—a challenging task, to be sure, since taste is a subjective matter in most arenas. For better or worse, here are some tips often mentioned by professionals in the publishing business:

■ Leave sufficient white space in your documents. A lack thereof results in a dense, cluttered look that can turn off your reader.

■ For the leading page of your document, choose one dominant visual element (like a headline), and organize the page around that element. Any other visual elements on the same page should be far reduced in emphasis, so they do not distract from the important element that is designed to get the reader's first attention.

■ Don't abuse fonts and type styles. Professional designers rarely produce a document that uses more than three type styles on a given page. A cardinal sin of desktop publishing is the mixing of different type styles on the same line of text; unless you are in the business of producing ransom notes, there is no good reason to do this.

■ When working with large amounts of text on a page, use subheads to visually break up the mass. This helps to lighten the page's appearance, as does the use of white space.

Finally, don't be afraid to borrow ideas from similar documents that look good in print. If you face the challenges of desktop publishing on a regular basis, there are numerous books available that cover desktop publishing from a design standpoint; much can be learned from such books.

Figure 11.16
Sample newsletter

In Focus

The Newsletter of Better Bifocals, Ltd.

NASA's new space shuttle Endeavour will carry the precision Cyclops 2001 contact lens into orbit, where it will be fitted onto the main lens of the Hubble telescope. The installation by US astronauts is planned for the upcoming December shuttle mission.

Issue 9

Better Bifocals Awarded Contract for World's Largest Contact Lens

Our company has received a contract from the US Government's National Aeronautics and Space Administration (NASA) to construct what will be the world's largest contact lens. This precision optical instrument will be fitted over the main imaging lens of the Hubble Space Telescope, to correct the problem of nearsightedness exhibited by the orbital eye in the sky.

Worldwide Sales Up for Prior Year

As the graph below illustrates, Better Bifocals posted record sales gains over the previous year. All of our hard-working employees can be proud of our sales results. While sales in Europe were down for the year, sharp upswings in sales in the US and the Far East more than compensated for lower European sales.

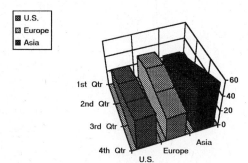

In This Issue...
Slim lenses for frail eyewear wearers and the very weight-conscious

Figure 11.17
Design techniques
used with sample
newsletter

Box around 'nameplate'
added witn Format
Borders command

Company logo created in
windows paintbrush and
pasted in from clipboard

Dutch Outline
Shadow font,
48 point

Scalable Swiss
font, 24 point

In Focus

The Newsletter of Better Bifocals, Ltd.

Horizontal
Rules added
with Format
Borders
command

Graphic pasted in
from MS Draw

Better Bifocals Awarded Contract for World's Largest Contact Lens

Our company has received a contract from the US Government's National Aeronautics and Space Administration (NASA) to construct what will be the world's largest contact lens. This precision optical instrument will be fitted over the main imaging lens of the Hubble Space Telescope, to correct the problem of nearsightedness exhibited by the orbital eye in the sky.

Worldwide Sales Up for Prior Year

As the graph below illustrates, Better Bifocals posted record sales gains over the previous year. All of our hard-working employees can be proud of our sales results. While sales in Europe were down for the year, sharp upswings in sales in the US and the Far East more than compensated for lower European sales.

NASA's new space shuttle Endeavour will carry the precision Cyclops 2001 contact lens into orbit, where it will be fitted onto the main lens of the Hubble telescope. The installation by US astronauts is planned for the upcoming December shuttle mission.

Table containing
two cells stores
side-by-side
paragraphs that
make up most of
this page

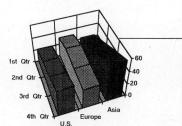

Graph created
and pasted in
from MS Graph

Issue 9

In This Issue...
Slim lenses for frail eyewear wearers and the very weight-conscious

Shadow border and shading
added with Format Borders
command

Figure 11.18
Sample advertising
flyer

Beads by Chani

Come and see for yourself Chani's unique

Custom Designed Jewelry.

Choose from among many different
semi precious stones that have been
hand–crafted into stunning sets
of necklaces with earrings.

Saturday
10 to
5 pm

On display will be original designs
in Rosequartz, Hematite, Fresh Water Pearls,
Tigereye, and Mother of Pearl.

PARTY ROOM
Refreshments will be served

Figure 11.19

Design techniques
used with sample
advertising flyer

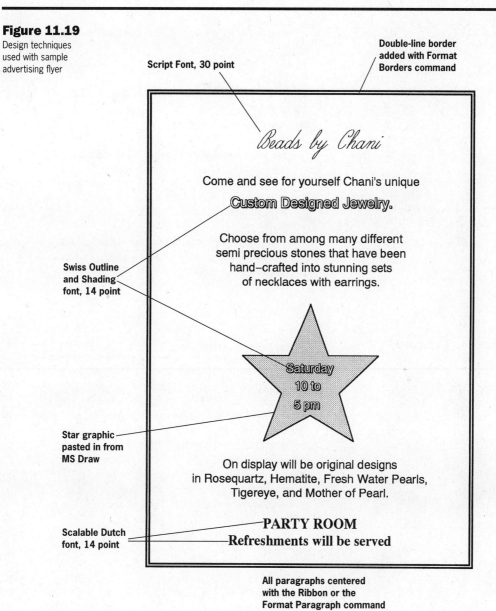

Script Font, 30 point

**Double-line border
added with Format
Borders command**

Beads by Chani

Come and see for yourself Chani's unique

Custom Designed Jewelry.

Choose from among many different
semi precious stones that have been
hand–crafted into stunning sets
of necklaces with earrings.

**Swiss Outline
and Shading
font, 14 point**

Saturday
10 to
5 pm

**Star graphic
pasted in from
MS Draw**

On display will be original designs
in Rosequartz, Hematite, Fresh Water Pearls,
Tigereye, and Mother of Pearl.

PARTY ROOM
Refreshments will be served

**Scalable Dutch
font, 14 point**

**All paragraphs centered
with the Ribbon or the
Format Paragraph command**

Figure 11.20
Sample of technical
documentation

Needed Supplies

To add a new computer to the company network, you
will need the following items:

(Obtain a workstation
disk from PC support, or

copy one following the
directions on page 17.)

1. The new computer, with an ARCNet adapter card
   already installed in one of the adapter slots.

2. A workstation boot disk (see "Creating A
   Workstation Boot Disk", this manual).

3. A network connector cable with a threaded–screw
   type connector on one end and a clamp–on type
   connector that matches the ARCNET adapter at
   the rear of the computer on the other end.

4. A wall outlet to connect the computer to.

Sources of Supplies

Item (a) should be supplied by our vendor, with the
ARCNet card already installed. (As of this writing,
our vendor is ABC Technology here in Detroit, phone
555–5555). The current standard workstation
configuration is the Supra Speedy 999 AT–compatible
computer, with 1 megabyte (MB) memory, single
1.2–megabyte floppy disk drive, monochrome
monitor, and ARCNet network adapter card. If the
Supra Speedy 999 is not available, any AT–
compatible computer with equivalent memory, floppy
disk, and monitor may be substituted.

Item (c), the cable, is also supplied by our vendor.
Make sure that the vendor knows which cable to ship,
as the firm's existing network installation uses the
older type of ARCNet cable, with different connectors
on the two ends of the cable. Newer types of ARCNet
cables have the same connectors on both ends, and
these will not work in the existing space.

Figure 11.21

Design techniques
used with sample
of technical
documentation

**Descriptive header
created with View
Header/Footer command**

**Dutch Scalable font,
16 point**

Mammoth Motors PC User Support Manual - Page 5

**Illustration pasted in
from MS Draw**

(Obtain a workstation
disk from PC support, or

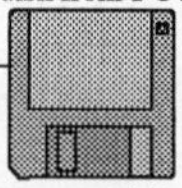

copy one following the
directions on page 17.)

**Art and comments
inserted into a frame;
frame is then placed
outside the main area
of text, at the desired
location.**

**Paragraphs for step-
by-step directions
were indented, and
numbered with
Bullets and
Numbering command.**

Needed Supplies

To add a new computer to the company network, you
will need the following items:

1. The new computer, with an ARCNet adapter card
   already installed in one of the adapter slots.

2. A workstation boot disk (see "Creating A
   Workstation Boot Disk", this manual).

3. A network connector cable with a threaded–screw
   type connector on one end and a clamp–on type
   connector that matches the ARCNET adapter at
   the rear of the computer on the other end.

4. A wall outlet to connect the computer to.

Sources of Supplies

Item (a) should be supplied by our vendor, with the
ARCNet card already installed. (As of this writing,
our vendor is ABC Technology here in Detroit, phone
555–5555). The current standard workstation
configuration is the Supra Speedy 999 AT–compatible
computer, with 1 megabyte (MB) memory, single
1.2–megabyte floppy disk drive, monochrome
monitor, and ARCNet network adapter card. If the
Supra Speedy 999 is not available, any AT–
compatible computer with equivalent memory, floppy
disk, and monitor may be substituted.

Item (c), the cable, is also supplied by our vendor.
Make sure that the vendor knows which cable to ship,
as the firm's existing network installation uses the
older type of ARCNet cable, with different connectors
on the two ends of the cable. Newer types of ARCNet
cables have the same connectors on both ends, and
these will not work in the existing space.

**Horizontal
rules created
with Format
Border
command**

Figure 11.22

Sample page from business report

REASONS FOR SELECTION OF PERSONAL COMPUTERS

Libraries indicate that a number of reasons affect the selection of a personal computer. This approach follows that of home users, who also indicate varied reasons for the selection of a brand of computer. Among libraries, the following reasons are assigned the most importance by survey respondents:

- Availability of software

- Compatibility with other equipment used at the same location or throughout the campus

- Mandatory choice by administrator, teachers, or other persons.

- Attractive pricing

As in the home-office computer marketplace, there appears to be a definite "two-tier" marketplace of low-end and high-end system buyers. Among the low-end buyers of "clone" equipment, price played a very important consideration in the buying decision. However, among the high-end system buyers of Apple and IBM equipment, price played a less-important role in the decision-making process.

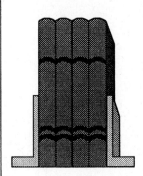

CURRENT AND FUTURE USES OF PERSONAL COMPUTERS

Primary uses of personal computers installed in libraries are word processing (42.9%), data storage (38.1%), database management (16.1%), on-line connections to data bases (14.2%), budgeting and forecasting (12.0%) and publication indexing (10.4%).

SOURCES USED FOR PERSONAL COMPUTER BUYING DECISIONS

Survey respondents were also asked where they obtained information about personal computers. Overwhelmingly, the respondents turned to the pages of magazines, with 73.5% reporting the magazines as a most-often used source of information. Literature from the computer makers was the second most quoted source at 63.0%, and associates

Figure 11.23

Design techniques used with sample page of business report

Format Columns command (or equivalent Toolbar icon used to set 3-column text for documents, and to add lines between columns.

REASONS FOR SELECTION OF PERSONAL COMPUTERS

Libraries indicate that a number of reasons affect the selection of a personal computer. This approach follows that of home users, who also indicate varied reasons for the selection of a brand of computer. Among libraries, the following reasons are assigned the most importance by survey respondents:

Paragraph bullets added with Tools Bullets and Numbering command, or with Bullets icon on Toolbar.

- Availability of software

- Compatibility with other equipment used at the same location or throughout the campus

- Mandatory choice by administrator, teachers, or other persons.

- Attractive pricing

As in the home–office computer marketplace, there appears to be a definite "two–tier" marketplace of low–end and high–end system buyers. Among the low–end buyers of "clone" equipment, price played a very important consideration in the buying decision. However, among the high–end system buyers of Apple and IBM equipment, price played a less–important role in the decision–making process.

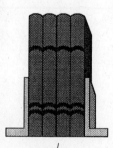

Art pasted in from MS Draw, inserted into a frame, and scaled to fit in column

CURRENT AND FUTURE USES OF PERSONAL COMPUTERS

Primary uses of personal computers installed in libraries are word processing (42.9%), data storage (38.1%), database management (16.1%), on–line connections to data bases (14.2%), budgeting and forecasting (12.0%) and publication indexing (10.4%).

SOURCES USED FOR PERSONAL COMPUTER BUYING DECISIONS

Survey respondents were also asked where they obtained information about personal computers. Overwhelmingly, the respondents turned to the pages of magazines, with 73.5% reporting the magazines as a most–often used source of information. Literature from the computer makers was the second most quoted source at 63.0%, and associates

12

Working with Styles and Templates

Formatting with Styles

Using Templates to Create Documents

WORD'S STYLES AND TEMPLATES ARE TOOLS YOU CAN USE TO more easily define the appearance of routinely produced documents to your liking. The first portion of this chapter discusses the use of styles; templates are covered in the second part of the chapter.

Formatting with Styles

You can simplify many of your formatting tasks by defining styles, which are collections of character and paragraph formatting codes stored under specific names. Styles not only save time that you might otherwise spend formatting your work, but also help maintain a consistent format for your documents. For instance, perhaps a typical set of paragraph formatting that you often use includes a half-inch left indent, a first-line indent, and a Times Roman font. If you define this set of formats to a style, you have a handy new tool that lets you apply all those formatting aspects to any paragraph in a document—with a single command.

One excellent use for a style is to format tables in a document, to give their headings and entries a consistent appearance throughout the document.

Besides making initial formatting easier to apply, styles offer another significant advantage when you are revising your documents. Change the formatting in a style, and all paragraphs in a document that are formatted with that style will also change—automatically. Suppose you decide to apply a border and shading to all paragraphs with a particular style. By changing the definition of the style to include the border and shading, you automatically add these new aspects to all paragraphs in all documents that use that style.

Putting Styles to Work

To put a style to work in your document, you must first define the aspects of the style and give it a name. You do this with the Format Style command. This step is done only once; once you have defined a style, it is saved as part of the active document's *style sheet*, which includes all the styles defined for that document, as well as Word's standard styles. (Word's standard styles are explained just below in "About the Predefined Styles.") You can also choose to save styles to a template. If you save a style to the default (NORMAL.DOT) template, the style becomes available to all documents you create in Word.

Once a style has been defined, you can apply it to any number of paragraphs in your document. As you will see, you can apply styles using the ribbon (with the keyboard or the mouse), or using the Format Style command.

TIP. *When the ribbon is visible on your workspace, you can see all the available styles displayed in the Styles box at the left side of the ribbon. Click on the Styles box to open it, or press Ctrl+S and use the ↓ key. You can then scroll through a list of all the styles made available by the template you are currently using.*

About the Predefined Styles

When you open a new document, certain predefined styles are made available for your use throughout that document. (As mentioned, the collection of styles available to a given document is called a style sheet.) The styles available will depend on which template you use when you open the document. For example, when you use the default Normal template, the styles listed in Table 12.1 are available. Additional styles may have been added to the Normal template used in your working environment, by you or other users, and will also be on the style sheet.

Table 12.1   **Styles Available in the Normal Template**

Style	Formatting
Normal	Font: Courier 12 point, Language: English (US), Flush Left (no indent)
Heading 1	Normal + Bold Underline, Space Before 1 line
Heading 2	Normal + Bold, Space Before 0.5 line
Heading 3	Normal + Bold, Indent: Left 0.25"

Note: The font used by your Normal style will probably differ, depending on the printer you have installed for use with Windows, and whether you have changed the default font with the Use As Default button in the Format Character dialog box. "Flush Left" means unindented paragraphs. "Space Before" means the line spacing that precedes the paragraph. These and other formatting descriptions also appear in the Description rea of the Style dialog box for the particular style.

In the foregoing table, notice that Word's heading styles used by the Normal template are based on the Normal style. For example, the Heading 1 style contains all formatting from the Normal style, plus boldface and underline, and the space before paragraphs is set to one line. This demonstrates an important point: *Styles can be based on other styles.* If you already have a style that contains much of the formatting you need, you can always define a new style based on the existing one. You cannot change the definition of any of the standard styles, but you can use them to create new ones.

All body text typed in the exercises of this book so far made use of the default Normal style. Some other examples of standard styles you have already seen are the ones that format outline headings, footnotes, and index entries.

Defining a Style

Word provides two methods for defining styles. You can use the Format Style command, enter a name for the new style, and then define the style by

choosing character and paragraph formatting from within the Style dialog box. Or, you can define styles "by example," that is, based on an existing paragraph that already has all of the desired formatting aspects applied. The "by example" method is faster, but the Format Style method makes it easier to see exactly what formatting elements you are working with. You can define up to 220 styles for a particular document.

Using Format Style to Define a Style

To define a new style using the Format Style command, choose Format Style (Alt+T+Y), and you'll see the Style dialog box (Figure 12.1).

Figure 12.1
Format Style dialog box

Enter style name or choose an existing name

Define shortcut key for a style

Style

Style Name: Normal

Shortcut Key
☒ Ctrl + ☒ Shift + Key:
Currently:

Description
Font: Swiss (scalable) 12 pt, Language: English (US), Flush left

Apply
Cancel
Define>>

Applies style in Style Name box to selected portion of document

Contains description of selected style

Expands dialog box to allow definition of a style

Because this dialog box can be used for applying styles as well as defining them, it contains a list box of available style names, a Shortcut Key definition area, and an Apply button. These elements of the dialog box will be covered later, in "Applying Styles." For now, let's concentrate on the Define button (Alt+D) that lets you define your style. When you select this button, the dialog box expands, to show the additional elements illustrated in Figure 12.2.

The expanded Style dialog box contains a special panel of Change Formatting buttons. These buttons let you establish the formatting elements for the style, by "connecting" you directly to the dialog boxes used by Word's formatting commands. For example, choosing the Character button displays the same dialog box as does the Format Character command; the Tabs button takes you to the Format Tabs dialog box, and so on. Make the desired changes to each required formatting element, and then choose OK to return to the expanded Style dialog box. (The only Change Formatting option that has not been covered earlier in this text is the Language button. This button brings up a dialog box that lets you change the language used by the Spelling, Thesaurus, and Grammar Checker utilities. Chapter 15 explains this Format Language command and its resulting dialog box.)

Once you have set up all the desired formatting for your style, you enter a name for the style in the Style Name box. Style names can be up to

For instructions on using Word's Spelling, Thesaurus, and Grammar Checker utilities, see Chapter 3.

If you change the definition of an existing style, it only affects the current document, unless you add the redefined style to the style sheet under a different name.

24 characters in length; you can use any characters, including spaces, but not the backslash. Then choose the Add button on the right of the dialog box to add the style to the document style sheet. (This Add button is a Change button if you are modifying an existing style.) When you have defined and added the style, you can choose Close from the dialog box to get back to your document. This defined style can then be applied to any selected paragraphs of a document, using the techniques covered under "Applying Styles" later in this chapter.

Figure 12.2

Expanded Style dialog box provides options needed to define a style

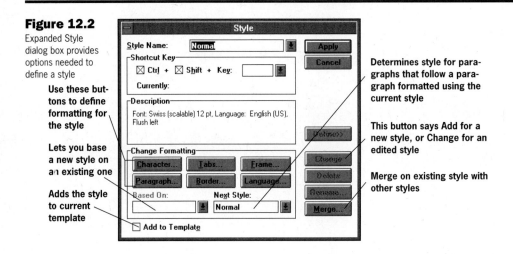

Use these buttons to define formatting for the style

Lets you base a new style on an existing one

Adds the style to current template

Determines style for paragraphs that follow a paragraph formatted using the current style

This button says Add for a new style, or Change for an edited style

Merge on existing style with other styles

Also at the right side of the dialog box are Delete, Rename, and Merge buttons. Choose Delete to remove a style from the style sheet. The Rename button displays another dialog box that lets you rename a style. The Merge button displays a dialog box that lets you merge styles with other templates or documents; its use is discussed later in the chapter, under "Merging Styles from Other Documents."

Finally, note the Add To Template check box at the bottom of the dialog box. Mark this box if you want to add the style you've defined to the current template. (If you are using the default Normal template, the style is added to that template and thus becomes *global*—available in all documents you create in Word.)

Here is the procedure to define a brand-new style, using the Format Style command:

1. Select Format and choose Style (Alt+T+Y).

2. In the Style Name text box, enter a name for the style. The name you enter overwrites the existing style name that's in the box (Normal is the default). (Remember—style names can be any combination of up to 24 characters, including spaces, but not the backslash.)

3. Choose the Define button (Alt+D) to expand the dialog box.

4. Use the Change Formatting buttons as needed, to assign the formatting you want to the style. For example, to set a one-inch left indent for the style, choose the Paragraph button, and enter **1"** for the left indent measurement in the Paragraph dialog box. Designate any other formatting by choosing the buttons to access the dialog boxes you need. Then choose OK. As you choose your formats, they are added to the Description area in the Style dialog box.

5. When you've specified all needed formats for the style, choose the Add button (Alt+A) to add the style to the document style sheet.

   NOTE. *The Add button becomes a Change button when you are creating your style based on an existing one, and its name appears in the Style Name box.*

6. If you want to create additional styles, enter a new name in the Style Name box, and repeat steps 4 and 5 for each additional style you want to create.

7. Select Close (or press Enter) to close the dialog box.

Creating a Style by Example

Probably the easiest way to create a style is to base the style on an existing paragraph that contains the desired formatting. Here are the steps to do this using a mouse:

1. Select the paragraph that contains the formatting on which you want to base the new style.

2. Click in the Style list box in the ribbon.

3. Enter a name for the new style. The name you enter overwrites the existing style name that's in the box.

4. Click anywhere outside the Style list box to create the new style and add it to the current style sheet.

Keyboard users can use these steps to create a style by example:

1. Select the paragraph that contains the formatting on which you want to base the new style.

To display the ribbon, choose Ribbon on the View menu (Alt+V+B).

To display the
ribbon, choose
Ribbon on the View
menu (Alt+V+B).

2. Press Ctrl+S to open the Style box in the ribbon. (If the ribbon is not turned on, you will see the prompt, "Which Style?" appear in the status bar.)

3. Enter a name for the new style. The name you enter overwrites the existing style name that's in the box.

4. Press Enter to create the new style and add it to the current style sheet.

Using the Based On and Next Style Options

The Based On list box of the Style dialog box lets you create a new style based on an existing one. (If the style you are defining is not based on any other style, this box will be dimmed and blank.)

When you base the definition of one style on another (existing) style, any change you make to the definition of the base style will cause a like change to the new style. For example, suppose you create a style called Alaska and assign it a 12-point Helvetica font, and then you create two new styles based on the Alaska style. Both the new styles will also use the 12-point Helvetica font. If you later change the font in the Alaska style, however, the font in both the Alaska-based styles will also change. (You can, of course, also change the two Alaska-based styles as needed.)

To base a new style on an existing one, type the name of the existing style into the Based On box, or choose an existing style name from the Based On list box, or select a paragraph that is formatted with the style that you want to use for the base style. Then proceed to create the new style as usual.

NOTE. *Remember that many styles are based on the default Normal style. Hence, any additions that you make to the Normal style will be reflected in all styles that are based on Normal.*

The Next Style box lets you specify a style that Word will automatically assign to the paragraph that follows the one being formatted with the current style. Typically, the next style will be the same as the current style, so that most successive paragraphs of a document have the same style. In some cases, however, you may find it useful to have Word assign a different style to the paragraph that follows the current one. An example of this technique is in a document that contains headings, which are usually formatted with a specific style. A heading is not normally followed by another heading, but rather by normal text. When you define the heading style, you could select Normal from the Next Style list box. Then, whenever you used that heading style, the next paragraph to follow would always automatically be formatted by the Normal style.

Assigning a Shortcut Key to a Style

As a time-saving feature, Word lets you assign shortcut keys to styles. If you know you are going to use a style regularly, assigning it to a shortcut key lets you more quickly and easily apply the style to selected text. By marking the Ctrl and Shift check boxes in the Shortcut Key area of the Style dialog box, create shortcut key-combinations using Ctrl or Shift or both, plus a letter or number key. The function keys can also be assigned as shortcut keys, without being combined with Ctrl or Shift. Keep in mind, however, that if you assign a function key for a shortcut key, you lose the use of the function key for its original purpose.

Here are the steps to assign a shortcut key to a style you have already defined:

1. Select Format Style (Alt+T+Y).

2. In the Style dialog box (look again at Figure 12.1), select the desired style in the Style Name list box (Alt+S).

3. To define the shortcut key, turn on or off the Ctrl and/or Shift check boxes as needed (in the Shortcut Key box). Then enter the desired key name in the Key box. (For example, to designate Ctrl+Y as the shortcut key for a style, mark the Ctrl check box, unmark the Shift check box, and enter **Y** in the Key box.)

4. Choose Apply or press Enter.

TIP. *If you want this shortcut key assignment to be saved to a template for use with other Word documents, use the Define button of the Styles dialog box to expand the dialog box, and turn on the Add To Template option.*

Applying Styles

After you have defined a style, you can apply that style to the paragraphs of your document, using the ribbon and the keyboard or mouse, or using the Format Style command.

The ribbon method is generally fastest. (If the ribbon is not visible, turn it on with the View Ribbon command, Alt+V+B.) Select the paragraphs to which you want to apply the style. Click on the down-arrow button next to the Style box in the ribbon, or press Ctrl+S. Then click on the name of the desired style in the list box (or use the ↓ key until the style is highlighted), and press Enter.

To apply a style using the Format Style command, select the paragraphs to which you want to apply the style. Choose Style on the Format menu (Alt+T+Y). In the Style Name box (Alt+S), click or highlight the desired style. Then choose the Apply button (or press Enter).

Tip. When applying a style to a single paragraph, you can just put the insertion pointer in the paragraph; Word considers it selected.

An Exercise in Defining and Applying a Style

Let's try creating a new style and applying it to the CHESS2 document you've worked with in previous exercises.

1. Open the CHESS2 document. (If you did not create this document earlier, you can use any document containing two or more paragraphs.)

2. Select Format Style (Alt+T+Y). When the Style dialog box appears, choose Define (Alt+D) to expand the dialog box.

3. In the Style Name text box (Alt+S), type **Chess 1** as a name for the new style. As you type, the current style name (Normal) is replaced by the name Chess 1. Notice, also, that Normal appears in the Based On box, because the new style is based on the existing Normal style.

4. In the Change Formatting button panel, choose Character (Alt+C) to display the Format Character dialog box. In the Fonts list box (Alt+F), choose any font other than the one you are currently using, and then choose OK.

5. When the Style dialog box reappears, choose the Paragraph button (Alt+P) to display the Format Paragraph dialog box. Set the Indentation From Left (Alt+L) value to 0.5"; set the First Line indent (Alt+F) to 0.5"; set the Line Spacing (Alt+I) to 1.5 Lines; and then choose OK.

At this point, your Style dialog box will resemble this one:

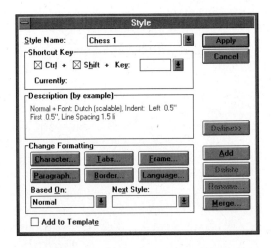

Notice that the Description box now lists the formatting changes you have made, including your selected font, the new paragraph indents, and the new line spacing.

6. Choose Add (Alt+A) to add the new style to the document style sheet.

7. Choose Close (or press Enter) to close the Style dialog box.

Now let's apply the new style to the first paragraph in the CHESS2 document.

8. Place the insertion pointer anywhere in the first paragraph of the CHESS2 document. (Word thus considers this paragraph selected.)

9. If the ribbon is not visible, turn it on with the View Ribbon command (Alt+V+B). Then click in the Styles list box of the ribbon (or press Ctrl+S).

10. Choose the Chess 1 style from the list of available styles. The paragraph with the insertion pointer assumes the style's formatting, as shown in Figure 12.3.

NOTE. *Remember that you can apply a style to any number of paragraphs, by selecting all the paragraphs first and then applying the style.*

Figure 12.3

Sample CHESS2 document with Chess 1 style applied to first paragraph

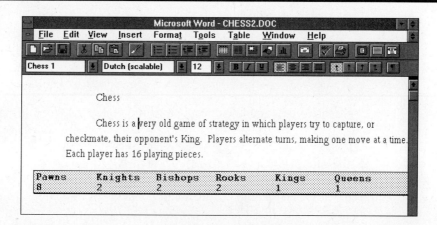

Merging Styles from Other Documents

Word lets you merge styles from other documents. This is particularly helpful when you are sharing documents and their formatting among other users. If a group of users can access the same styles, it helps to maintain consistency among the documents created by individuals in the group.

When you have an existing document or template file containing styles that you want to use in another document, you can do so with the Merge button in the expanded Style dialog box. First open the document that you want to format with the existing document's style sheet. Select Format Style

(Alt+T+Y), and choose Define (Alt+D). Then choose the Merge button (Alt+M). Here is the list box of files that appears:

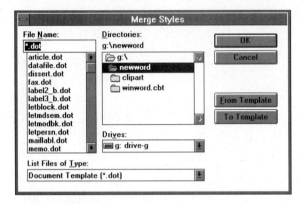

Choose the name of the other document or template that contains the desired style sheet. Then select the From Template button (Alt+F). Word offers helpful buttons on this style sheet selection screen that let you access another directory or drive to locate the desired file.

When you merge a style sheet with a document:

- Styles with identical names are merged; the new styles replace the old styles.

- Existing styles in the document with unique names are unchanged.

- New styles not already in the document are added to the document.

So be careful when you're merging a style sheet that contains names different from those in the document. You may want to use Format Style to rename some styles in the document to match or differ from the names in the incoming style sheet, to prevent conflict between the two sheets.

Word will warn you that the merging process replaces the current styles with like-named new styles. Choose Yes from the dialog box to complete the process of merging the styles. To return to the Styles dialog box, choose the Close button.

Using Templates to Create Documents

When your work involves many similar documents, sometimes you'll want to standardize more than just character and paragraph formatting elements. Word templates make it easy to collect styles and text together for application to memos, reports, and other documents that follow strict patterns.

Templates, like styles, provide a way to quickly tailor a Word document, but templates can accomplish even more than the character and paragraph formatting tasks of styles. Think of a template as a "model" that governs the overall format of the document you create. And, because you can easily copy styles into a template, you can make those styles instantly available whenever you are using that template. Templates can also contain "boilerplate" text for use in each variation of the document created with the template. For example, interoffice memos, though containing different text each time, usually have the same company name, date, to, from, and subject headings. In addition to styles and boilerplate text, templates can also contain glossaries (Chapter 13), macros (Chapter 14), and custom keyboard, menu, and toolbar assignments (Chapter 15).

When you create a new document with the File New command, Word always asks which template you want to use, and displays a list box of templates as part of the New dialog box, shown below. If you don't make a selection, Word uses the default template, NORMAL.DOT, to create the new document.

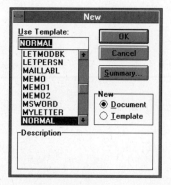

When you select a template by name from the Use Template list, your new document takes on all the format features belonging to that template. This includes any text stored in the template; any character, paragraph, and page layout formatting; and any styles you've added. Also, any macros, glossary entries, and keyboard, menu, or toolbar definitions stored in the template are available within the new document.

You can use any of Word's predefined templates, or you can create and save your own. In Chapter 2 of this text, you learned how to create a memo based on the MEMO1 template provided with Word. Take some time to examine the templates provided with Word; you may find some that will be useful in your work. They are summarized at the end of this chapter.

Since a template is a document, you use the same procedure to create and save a template as you do for a document. When you invoke the File

New command, Word lets you choose a button to specify whether you want to create a Document or a Template, as shown in the New dialog box above. Choose Template (Alt+T) and then OK, to tell Word that you are creating a new template. A blank document appears, and you can add whatever boilerplate text you want, along with formatting and styles, and then save the file with the File Save command.

You can also specify after you have created a file that it should be saved as a template. For example, if you have an existing boilerplate document on file, and you want to store it as a template, you can do so with the File Save As command. Open the file, select File Save As, and choose Document Template from the File Save As Type list box. A copy of the file is saved as a template, with the .DOT extension.

Creating and Applying a Template

To create a new template, perform the following steps:

1. Select File New (Alt+F+N).

2. In the New dialog box, mark the Template button (Alt+T), and choose OK (or press Enter).

3. Design your template. Start by inserting text or graphics; Word will automatically insert this same text and/or graphics in the same location of any new document created with this template.

4. Add any desired character, paragraph, section, or page layout formatting.

5. Create or apply any desired styles.

6. Define any needed glossary entries (Chapter 13) or macros (Chapter 14).

7. Select File Save (Alt+F+S).

8. In the File Name box, enter a name for the template, and choose OK or press Enter. (By default, Word saves all template files with a .DOT file name extension, unless you specify a different one.)

9. If prompted, you can enter summary information for the new template; then choose OK to close the Summary Info dialog box. (Word prompts you for summary information if the Prompt For Summary Info option is turned on under the Save category of the Tools Options command. See Chapter 15 for details.)

You can use a simple variation of the above steps to create a new template based on an existing one. Use the same File New command, and choose Template in the New dialog box. In the Use Template box, type or

Note. The addition of text, graphics, and formatting to a template need not be done in any particular order; you can define styles and glossary entries before entering text, or vice versa.

select the name of the existing template you want to use as a model for the new one; then choose OK. When you save this new template, be sure to give it a name different from its predecessor's.

Applying a Template

To apply a template to a document, you simply choose that template by name when you use Word's File New command. Any template (.DOT file) that you create will be available in the Use Template list box of the File New dialog box. (If you decide to save your templates with an extension other than .DOT, they will not appear in this list of template files, but you can always enter the template by name, including the extension, in the Use Template text box.)

Modifying an Existing Template

To modify an existing template, you simply open the template much the same way as you do a document. Select the File Open (Alt+F+O) command, and when the File Open dialog box appears, choose Document Template from the List Files of Type (Alt+T) dialog box. The files list box will then include only .DOT files, and you can click or highlight the name of the desired template, or type it into the File Name text box. Make the needed changes to the template, and save it again with the File Save command (Alt+F+S).

Customizing the NORMAL.DOT Template

Word's default template, NORMAL.DOT, is used to store all of Word's "global" document settings that are available for use in any document. Since NORMAL is the default template, it is worth spending some time to customize it so it will be of the most possible help to you. NORMAL is a template like all other templates, so you can modify it (and save the changes) as you would any other template, using the steps described above. Also, keep in mind the Use As Default check box present in some formatting command dialog boxes. This feature lets you change the defaults for the character font, the page setup, and the language used by the proofing tools, and save them to the NORMAL template.

- To change the default font, select Format Character (Alt+T+C), and choose the desired font and point size. Mark the Use As Default check box, and when prompted choose Yes to verify that this change should be stored to NORMAL.DOT.

- To change the default page setup, select Page Setup (Alt+T+U) and choose the desired setup options in the dialog box. Mark Use As Default and choose Yes to complete the process as described above.

- To change the default language used by the proofing tools (Spelling, Thesaurus, and Grammar), select Format Language (Alt+T+L) and specify the desired language. Mark Use As Default and choose Yes to complete the process as described above. (Note that you may need to purchase optional dictionaries in order to use a language other than U.S. English; see Chapter 15 for details.)

An Exercise in Creating and Applying a Template

In Chapter 2, you used one of Word's templates to design a memo; here, you'll create a template of your own. The following exercise helps you create your own business letterhead and store it as a template. You can then create documents based on that template, and they will automatically include your letterhead.

1. Select File New (Alt+F+N).

2. In the New dialog box, choose the Template button (Alt+T), and then choose OK (or press Enter). A blank document appears; notice that the document is titled "Template1."

3. On the first three lines of the document, type your name and address.

4. Select all three lines, and press Ctrl+E to center the text.

5. With the three lines still selected, choose Character from the Format menu (Alt+T+C). Pick a font that you like, and (if your printer supports it) a larger point size. Then turn on Bold, and choose OK.

6. Press Ctrl+End to move to the end of the document, and press Enter twice to insert blank lines.

7. Select File Save (Alt+F+S). When the Save As dialog box appears, notice that the existing file names shown in the list box are all template names (they have a .DOT file name extension).

8. Type **MYLETTER** in the File Name box; then choose OK or press Enter to save the template. (If prompted to add the summary information, do so, or you can bypass this dialog box by pressing Enter.)

9. Close the document with File Close (Alt+F+C).

You can now create documents based on the MYLETTER template. Simply choose File New (Alt+F+N), select MYLETTER from the Use Template list box, and choose OK. The result will be a new document, already containing your letterhead, ready for you to enter text.

Word's Templates

This chapter gives you an idea of what you can do with styles and templates; a detailed discussion of all the possibilities could fill another book by itself. You can obtain more ideas for creating your own styles and templates by examining the sample templates provided with Word, and the styles stored in each. In addition to these, you'll find many other uses for templates—for example, to create sales brochures, invoices, forms, legal briefs, and contracts.

Table 12.2 provides a brief description of Word's templates; for more details, refer to "Document Templates" in the *Microsoft Word User's Guide*.

Table 12.2   Sample Templates Included with Word for Windows

Global Template	Contains Formats For
NORMAL.DOT	Serves as the basis for documents when you do not specify a particular template
Letters	
LETBLOCK.DOT	Block-style letter
LETMODBK.DOT	Modified block-style letter
LETMDSEM.DOT	Modified semiblock-style letter
LETPERSN.DOT	Personalized version of a modified block-style letter
Memos	
MEMO.DOT	Business memo
MEMO1.DOT	Standard memo
MEMO2.DOT	Stylish memo
Reports	
REPSTAND.DOT	Business report using portrait orientation
REPLAND.DOT	Business report using landscape orientation
REPSIDE.DOT	Business report with sideheads (headings printed to the left of the text)
Labels	
LABEL2_B.DOT	Two-across mailing labels
LABEL3_B.DOT	Three-across mailing labels

Table 12.2   **(Continued)**

**Other
Documents**

DATAFILE.DOT	Used with Print Merge data files
FAX.DOT	Fax cover sheet
OVERHEAD.DOT	Overhead projection presentations
PROPOSAL.DOT	Formal business proposal
ARTICLE.DOT	Article manuscripts
DISSERT.DOT	Academic dissertations
TERM.DOT	Academic term papers
PRESS.DOT	Press release
MAILLABL.DOT	Mailing label formats

Using Glossaries

Creating and Editing
Glossaries

Printing Glossary Entries

Specifying a Location for
Storing Glossary Entries

Using the Spike to Collect
and Move Text and
Graphics

GLOSSARIES IN WORD ARE STORED ABBREVIATIONS THAT CORRE-
spond to selected text and/or graphics. You can save text that you
use often—such as a signature block, a telephone number, a product name, or a company name, address, and logo—to a glossary
entry with a short name. Then you can insert that text or graphic into a document as often as needed by typing just the glossary name. Think of glossary
entries as a kind of shorthand, or as somewhat similar to entries you paste in
from the Clipboard—with one significant difference: Clipboard entries are
stored temporarily, in your computer's memory, but glossaries can be stored
permanently, in templates.

TIP. *Glossaries are excellent for typing popular medical or legal terms, scientific phrases, hard-to-type foreign phrases, common headings and salutations,
and proper names with difficult spellings. Another excellent use for glossary
entries is to store the formats of column headings and sample entries for a
table you frequently use.*

Creating and Editing Glossaries

This section shows you how to store, insert, and edit your glossary entries
using the Edit Glossary command and the F3 Glossary key. Later in the chapter, you'll see how to print and organize your glossaries, and learn about the
handy Spike feature.

Storing Text or Graphics as a Glossary Entry

To create a glossary entry, first select the desired text and/or graphic that is
to be stored in the glossary. Then choose the Edit Glossary (Alt+E+O). This
command is dimmed in the Edit menu unless glossary entries already exist,
or unless you have selected some text. The Glossary dialog box is shown in
Figure 13.1.

Figure 13.1

Glossary entry
dialog box

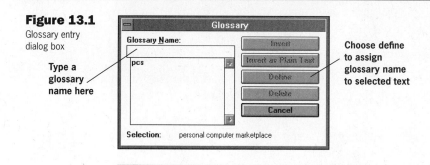

Type a
glossary
name here

Choose define
to assign
glossary name
to selected text

Type the name for the glossary entry into the Glossary Name text box. Names for glossaries can be up to 31 characters long, and you can include spaces. It makes sense to use names that are easy to remember, and at the same time easy to type.

Once you have selected the glossary item and typed its name, the Define button becomes available in the dialog box. You use this button to accept the selected text as the definition for the name you've typed. When you choose Define (Alt+D), the dialog box vanishes, and your selection is stored as a glossary entry. The selected text in the document is not affected; a copy of it is placed in the current template when you exit Word, as explained later in "Specifying a Location for Storing Glossary Entries."

TIP. *If you want a glossary entry to be available whenever you use Word, open a document using the default NORMAL template, and then create the entry. When you exit, Word lets you save the glossary entry to the NORMAL template.*

Inserting Text or Graphics from a Glossary Entry

After you've stored desired text and/or graphics as a glossary entry, it's a simple matter to insert that entry at any location in any document, simply by referring to the glossary name. There are two ways to do so: You can type the glossary name and then press the Glossary key (F3). Or you can choose the Edit Glossary command, type the glossary name (or choose it from the list box), and then choose either the Insert or the Insert as Plain Text button (explained later). The Glossary key method is generally faster, but there are two good reasons for using the Edit Glossary command—it lets you insert a glossary entry without formatting, and it lets you find a glossary name that you've forgotten. We'll look at both these processes shortly.

Whenever you know the name of a glossary entry and you want to insert the glossary entry along with its original formatting, use the Glossary key (F3). Here are the steps:

1. Position the insertion pointer in the document at the point where you want to insert the contents of the glossary entry. Make sure the insertion pointer is either at the start of a line, or is preceded by a space.

2. Type the name of the glossary entry at the insertion point.

3. Press the Glossary (F3) key. Word replaces the glossary name you've typed with the full text and/or graphics of the glossary.

If you can't remember the name of the glossary entry, or you want to change its formatting in the current document, use the Edit Glossary command as outlined on the following page.

1. Position the insertion pointer in the document at the point where you want to insert the contents of the glossary entry.

2. Select Edit and choose Glossary (Alt+E+O).

3. Type the name of the glossary entry in the text box, or select the glossary entry from the list box.

4. To insert the glossary entry as it was originally formatted, choose the Insert button (Alt+I). Or, to insert the glossary entry without any formatting, choose the Insert As Plain Text button (Alt+T).

NOTE. *If you choose the Insert As Plain Text button in the Glossary box, the text of the inserted glossary entry adopts the formatting of the text around it. You can then change the formatting as desired.*

An Example of the Use of Glossaries

Suppose you must routinely type the name and address of a company into various business letters. You can store that name and address in a glossary entry, and recall it at any time by typing the glossary name and then pressing the F3 key. Here's how this can be done:

1. Open a new document with File New (Alt+F+N, then OK).

2. Type the following text, pressing Enter after each line:

```
Terminally Tiny Tacos
1414 Arlington Blvd
Arlington, VA 22030
```

3. Highlight all three lines of text. Press Ctrl+E to center the address box, and then Ctrl+B to add boldface.

4. With the selection still highlighted, choose Edit Glossary (Alt+E+O).

5. In the Glossary Name text box, type the abbreviation **coname**; then choose Define (Alt+D). The dialog box disappears.

6. With the address block still highlighted, press Del to erase it; in Step 7 you'll reinsert it from the glossary entry.

7. Now assume you are starting to create a new document, and you want to use the glossary entry to duplicate the address block. With the cursor at the start of the document, type **coname** and press Glossary (F3). Word automatically replaces the glossary name you've typed with the actual name and address.

Editing Glossary Entries

To edit existing glossary entries, you insert them into a document, select and revise the glossary text within the document, and then use the Edit Glossary command to replace the revised glossary entry under the same glossary name. (Edit Glossary also lets you delete and rename glossary entries.) Let's try this:

1. Insert the glossary entry into a blank space in a document.

2. Make the desired changes to the contents of the glossary entry.

3. Select the entire entry, which includes the text and/or graphics you changed.

   TIP. *If you want to include paragraph formatting in the revised glossary entry, make sure you include the paragraph mark when you select the entry. You can make paragraph marks visible by selecting Tools Options (Alt+O+O), choosing View from the Category list, and turning on Paragraph Marks (Alt+M) in the dialog box. Mouse users can also click on the Paragraph button in the Toolbar.*

4. Choose Glossary on the Edit menu (Alt+E+O).

5. In the Glossary Name box, type or select the *original* name of the revised glossary entry.

6. Choose Define (Alt+D).

7. When Word asks if you want to redefine the original glossary entry, select Yes (Alt+Y).

Deleting a Glossary Entry

To delete a glossary entry that is no longer needed, select Edit Glossary (Alt+E+O), and choose the Glossary Name for the entry that you want to delete. Choose the Delete button (Alt+L), and then the Close button (tab to Close, then press Enter).

NOTE. *You cannot use the Edit Undo command to undo the deletion of a glossary entry.*

Renaming a Glossary Entry

You can also change the name of a glossary entry. To do this you'll need to delete the existing glossary name; then, while the Glossary dialog box is still open, define the same entry under a new glossary name, using the normal process for creating a glossary entry.

Printing Glossary Entries

An option available in the File Print command dialog box lets you print a document's glossary entries. When you choose this option, Word prints the names and contents of all glossary entries available to the active document, in alphabetical order.

To print your glossary entries, choose Print on the File menu (Alt+F+P). In the Print dialog box that appears, click to open the Print list box (or press Alt+P), and choose Glossary. Choose the OK button, and the glossary entries are printed.

Specifying a Location for Storing Glossary Entries

Tip. When you use a template other than NORMAL.DOT, be sure to store your glossary entries *globally* when prompted by Word. Then you'll be able to use them from any document. For more details on templates, see Chapter 12.

Where your glossary entries are stored depends on two things: whether you are using the default template (NORMAL.DOT), and the settings you've entered in the File Template command dialog box.

When you use the NORMAL template, glossary entries are stored there. As you exit Word, you are asked if you want to store glossary entries created during that work session to the NORMAL template; answer Yes to store the glossary entries, or No to discard them.

When you use a template other than NORMAL.DOT, then the storage location for new glossary entries depends on the settings in the Template dialog box that appears when you choose the File Template command:

Notice the Store Macros and Glossaries area:

- If Prompt for Each New is marked (the default), Word asks you where you want the glossary entry saved as you are creating the entry. That inquiry gives you a choice of saving the glossary entry globally (in NORMAL.DOT), or in the current template.

- If you choose the With Document Template option, Word saves new glossary entries in the template you are using with the current document.

- If you choose Global, Word saves new glossary entries to the NORMAL template file. All glossary entries saved to NORMAL are "global" in nature, meaning they are available from any document in Word.

Using the Spike to Collect and Move Text and Graphics

Word also provides a special type of glossary entry called the Spike. Like normal glossary entries, the Spike stores text and graphics. The contents of the Spike, however, are not limited to one specific selection of text or graphics; rather, the Spike "collects" what you store there. Each time you add selected text or graphics to the Spike, your selection is incorporated with what is already there. With the Spike, you can collect data from a number of different locations in the document, and insert the data as a group in another location. You can insert the data once and empty the Spike, or keep the data in the Spike so you can insert it again elsewhere.

To store text or graphics in the Spike, first select the item, and then press the Spike key (Ctrl+F3). The selected item is removed from the document and placed in the Spike. Repeat this process for all additional items to be added to the Spike.

To empty the contents of the Spike into a document, first position the insertion pointer at the desired location, and then press the Unspike key (Ctrl+Shift+F3). The contents of the Spike appear at the insertion pointer, and the Spike is emptied. Or, to keep the contents of the Spike intact, type the word **spike** at the location where you want the data inserted, and press Glossary (F3). The contents of the Spike replace the word **spike**, but the Spike is not emptied.

Macros and Word

MACROS ARE RECORDED COMBINATIONS OF KEYSTROKES AND CER-tain mouse actions. Macros can automate many of the tasks you normally perform manually, keystroke by keystroke, within Word. In a macro you can record a sequence of keyboard and mouse entries, and link them to a single key-combination. Later, you "play back" the recorded keystroke sequence by pressing the assigned key-combination (or by choosing the macro by name from a list). When the macro is played back, Word performs as if you had manually executed the operations contained within the macro. When your work involves the production of daily reports or the performance of any repetitive tasks, you can often save many keystrokes by creating a few macros. And you can add customized commands or Toolbar options based on macros; how to do so is covered in Chapter 15.

Tip. Repetitive operations that involve a long sequence of menu or dialog box selections are excellent candidates for macros.

At first glance, macros may seem similar to glossary entries (described in Chapter 13), but there are significant differences. Glossary entries can repro-duce text and graphics at any location in a document. Macros can also simu-late typing, but they can do much more. Macros can perform menu and dialog box selections, which cannot be done with glossary entries. For example, if you routinely print two copies of a certain weekly report, you can create a macro that opens the report file, executes the File Print com-mand, and marks the dialog box options needed to send two copies of the report to the printer. Later in this chapter, you will find an example to try so you can see how a macro can be used.

About the Location of the Macro Commands You will use two com-mands when performing most macro operations: Record Macro, and Macro. Keep in mind that these commands may be found on one of two menus, depending on whether or not a document is open in Word. When a docu-ment is open, you will find the Record Macro and Macro commands on the Tools menu. When no document is open, however, these two commands appear on the File menu instead, because with no document open, the File and Help menus are the only menus available in Word. The discussions of this chapter focus on macro use within documents and therefore refer to the Tools Macro and Tools Record Macro commands.

Recording a Macro

The easiest way to create a macro is by *recording* it. To do this, you turn on Word's macro recorder with the Tools Record Macro command, enter a macro name or accept the default name in the Record Macro dialog box, choose OK, and then perform the actual keystrokes for the desired actions to be recorded.

NOTE. *You can also create macros by writing them from scratch, using Word's macro editor and the WordBasic programming language built into Word. You can find complete instructions for manual creation of macros in your Word for Windows User's Guide.*

Before you begin to record macros, note this important limitation of the macro recorder: You cannot record mouse actions within the text of a document (such as text selection). When you are recording a macro, the mouse pointer becomes a transparent arrow, and if you attempt to use the mouse within the document, Word just beeps. You *can* record the mouse actions for selecting menu options or choosing dialog box settings. If you want to select text as part of a macro, however, you must use the keyboard to do so.

Here are the steps to record a macro:

1. In an open document, select Tools Record Macro (Alt+O+R). Or, if no document is open, select File Record Macro (Alt+F+R). The Record Macro dialog box appears, as in Figure 14.1.

The Record Macro Name text box contains a default name for the macro, which you can change to any name you want. Macro names can be up to 32 characters in length, and must start with a letter. Use any combination of letters or numbers, but you cannot use spaces, or characters other than letters or numbers. In the Description box, you can add an optional description of what the macro does, up to 255 characters. The Shortcut Key option can also be used to assign a shortcut key-combination to a macro, as explained later in "Assigning Shortcut Keys to Macros."

Figure 14.1
The dialog box for recording a macro

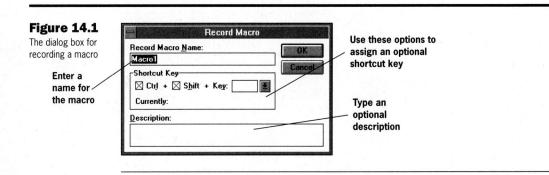

Enter a name for the macro

Use these options to assign an optional shortcut key

Type an optional description

2. In the Record Macro Name box, type a name for the macro (or you can leave the default name as is). Add a description if you want, by pressing Alt+D and typing the description. Also, assign the shortcut key if desired.

3. Choose OK. If the status bar is turned on, the letters REC will appear there to tell you that Word is ready to record the macro.

4. Perform the actions you want the macro to execute when it is played back.

5. Choose Tools Stop Recorder (Alt+O+R). (When you are recording a macro, the Record Macro command becomes the Stop Recorder command.)

6. If you are working with Record Macro in an open document, and using a template other than the default NORMAL template, a dialog box appears asking where you want to store the macro. Choose the specific template by name in the dialog box, or choose As Global if you want the macro to be available to all Word documents. (For more details on this subject, see the next section, "Specifying a Location for Storing Macros." For more about templates, see Chapter 12.)

Tip. If you are using a template other than NORMAL.DOT, be sure to store your macros globally when prompted by Word, if you want to be able to access them from any document.

Tip. Check your Word keyboard template to see what keys are unassigned, so you can quickly pick an unused key-combination for your macro. Note that all Ctrl+Shift key-combinations are unassigned, so you may want to use any of these.

Assigning Shortcut Keys to Macros

Word lets you assign shortcut key-combinations to the macros you record. You can use Shift, Ctrl, or both, along with a letter, number, or function key (F2 through F12). Word also lets you assign the Ins and Del keys, alone or with Ctrl and/or Shift. (However, it's probably not the best choice to assign a macro to either Ins or Del alone, since you would no longer be able to use those keys for their normal editing functions.) As an example of a shortcut key, you might assign a key-combination of Ctrl+Shift+P to a macro that prints two copies of the current document. Once the key-combination is assigned, you can press Ctrl+Shift+P to play back the macro.

WARNING! *Word lets you assign most keys to macros—even if they are already assigned to another function by default. For example, Ctrl+B normally applies boldface to selected text, or turns on boldface for typed text. You are allowed to assign Ctrl+B to a macro, but if you do, you lose the ability to employ that key-combination for the boldface formatting task. So before reassigning any key or key-combination that is already otherwise in use, be sure that you are willing to give up your option to use that key for that function. Most tasks that are assigned to key-combinations have Toolbar or menu equivalents, so you may feel comfortable giving up a Ctrl+key combination for use with a macro.*

To assign a shortcut key for a macro, use the Shortcut Key options in the Record Macro dialog box. Simply turn on the Ctrl and/or Shift check boxes as appropriate, and enter the name of the letter, number, or function key to use as the other part of the key-combination. (You can type the name of the key, or you can choose it by name from the list box.) As an example, consider the illustration in the dialog box shown here:

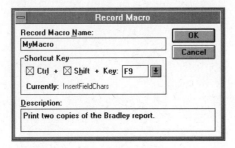

In this case, the Ctrl and Shift check boxes are turned on, and F9 is chosen in the Key text box. Thus the Ctrl+Shift+F9 key-combination is assigned as the shortcut key that will execute the MYMACRO macro. The Currently: line in the Shortcut Key box shows the task that will be performed by the assigned key.

Specifying a Location for Storing Macros

Where macros are stored depends on two things: whether you are using the default NORMAL template, and the settings you choose in the Template dialog box that appears when you choose File Template (Alt+F+T).

When you are using the default template, macros are stored there. When you exit Word, you are asked if you want to store the macros you've created during that session to the NORMAL template; you can answer Yes to store the macros, or No to discard the macros.

When you are using a template other than NORMAL, the storage location for new macros depends on the settings in the Template dialog box. This dialog box appears when you choose File Template, as shown here. Notice the Store New Macros and Glossaries box:

- If Prompt for Each New is turned on (the default), Word will ask you where you want to store the macro when you create it. (The Macro dialog box that appears gives you a choice of saving the macros globally in NORMAL.DOT, or in the current template.)

- If you select In Template, Word saves new macros in the template you are currently using.

- If you choose As Global, Word saves the new macros to the NORMAL template. Global macros saved to NORMAL are available from any document in Word. (For more information on templates, see Chapter 12.)

Playing a Macro

If you've assigned your macro to a shortcut key, as described in the foregoing section, you can simply press that key-combination to play back the macro. Another way to execute a macro is with the Tools Macro command. Select this command, and a Macro dialog box appears, where you specify by name the macro you want to run. Here are the steps:

1. Choose Tools Macro (Alt+O+M). The Macro dialog box appears, as shown in Figure 14.2.

2. Type the name of the desired macro in the Macro Name box, or choose it by name from the list box. (If you do not see the macro you want, select the Global Macros option button in the Show area of the dialog box (Alt+G). When Template Macros is selected, only those macros based on the current template are visible in the list box. You'll learn more about these options in the section just below.)

3. Choose Run (Alt+R), and Word executes the steps of the chosen macro.

About the Macro Dialog Box Options

The Macro dialog box shown in Figure 14.2 contains various options that will be useful as you work with macros. Once you've entered or chosen a macro name to run, all the command buttons at the right side of the dialog box become available. Also, if you entered any description of the macro when you created it, that text appears in the Description box.

The five command buttons are fairly self-explanatory: Run, Edit, Cancel, Delete, and Rename. Choose Run to execute the chosen macro. The Edit button lets you edit a macro using WordBasic (this process is not covered here; see your Word documentation for instructions). The Cancel button closes the dialog box without running the macro. The Delete button deletes the selected macro from the template in which it is stored, and the Rename button lets you give the selected macro a new name.

Figure 14.2
The dialog box for playing back a macro

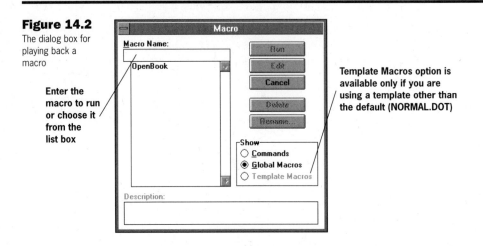

Enter the macro to run or choose it from the list box

Template Macros option is available only if you are using a template other than the default (NORMAL.DOT)

The Show options determine what macros are visible in the list box. If Global Macros is selected, the list box displays all macros that have been stored with the NORMAL template, and are therefore available to all Word documents (as explained in the earlier section, "Specifying a Location for Storing Macros"). If Template Macros is selected, you'll see listed only the macros that have been stored with the current template; Template Macros is unavailable if you are currently in a document using the NORMAL template. If the Commands button is selected, the macros that control Word's menu commands are listed. You won't need to use the Commands option unless you want to customize the operation of Word's menus (see Chapter 15).

An Example of Creating and Running a Macro

Many of you typically need to see as much of the Word workspace as possible, and you therefore turn off the Toolbar, ruler, and ribbon. This is a good example of how a macro can help execute a repetitive task: You can create a macro to carry out the commands necessary to set up your workspace. Let's do this:

1. First turn on your ribbon, ruler, and Toolbar if they are not already on (use Alt+V to open the View menu, and choose the appropriate commands).

2. Select Tools and choose Record Macro (Alt+O+R).

3. In the Record Macro dialog box, type **morespace** in the Record Macro Name text box, as a name for this macro.

4. Since Ctrl+Y is not otherwise used by Word, it would make a good short-cut key. In the Shortcut Key area, press Alt+H to unmark the Shift check box, and leave the Ctrl check box turned on. Tab over to the Key box, and type the letter **Y**. Notice that the designation, "Currently: unassigned," appears in the Shortcut Key box, telling you that the key-combination you have chosen is not used for anything else.

5. Press Alt+D to move to the Description field, and type

   ```
   Turns off ribbon, ruler, and Toolbar.
   ```

6. Choose OK.

7. Select View and choose the Toolbar option (Alt+V+T) to turn off the Toolbar.

8. Select View and choose the Ribbon option (Alt+V+B) to turn off the ribbon.

9. Select View and choose the Ruler option (Alt+V+R) to turn off the ruler.

10. Select Tools and choose Stop Recorder (Alt+O+R) to complete the recording of the macro.

11. Use the appropriate commands of the View menu (Alt+V) to turn the ribbon, ruler, and Toolbar back on. Then run the macro by pressing Ctrl+Y, and watch these three screen elements get turned off by Word.

Creating Macros that Run Automatically

Word makes certain names available for you to assign to macros that you want to run automatically when a certain event occurs. Automatic macros are stored in the NORMAL template. Listed here are the five automatic macro names, and the event that will automatically run the macro you've assigned to those names.

Macro Name	Action That Runs Assigned Macro
AutoExec	Word is started
AutoExit	You exit Word
AutoOpen	File Open command is chosen
AutoNew	File New command is chosen
AutoClose	Current document is closed

For example, if you name a macro AutoExec, that macro will run every time you start Word. If you name a macro AutoNew, that macro will run whenever you choose the New command from the File menu. A macro named AutoClose, which runs whenever the current document is closed, will also run whenever you exit Word or Windows *before* closing a Word document (since Word automatically closes documents when you quit Word or Windows).

TIP. *An excellent use for an AutoOpen macro is to automatically change to your favorite subdirectory of Word files. Create a macro with Tools Record Macro, name it AutoOpen, and while recording it, make the usual selections in the File Open dialog box to switch to your favorite directory. After switching directories, choose Cancel in the File Open dialog box, and stop recording the macro.*

A Note About Macros and Customizing Word

Keep in mind that macros that you use often can be added as options on your Word menus. You can also add favorite macros as icons on the Toolbar. You'll find complete details on these processes in Chapter 15, "Customizing Word."

15

Customizing Word

BY TAKING ADVANTAGE OF THE MANY WAYS IN WHICH YOU CAN CUS-
tomize Word, you can modify the program to match your specific
word processing needs. Word offers a great deal of flexibility in
this area; you can change the design of the menus and/or the Toolbar, and you can assign your own hotkeys and speed-keys to perform specific
tasks. Many of Word's defaults and preferences can be altered, such as
whether table grid lines or nonprinting characters are shown, whether
backup copies are made automatically when you save documents, and what
unit of measure appears in the dialog boxes. The first portion of this chapter
teaches you how to use the Tools Options command to change the overall
preferences of Word. The second half of the chapter demonstrates how you
can customize the menus and the Toolbar.

Using the Tools Options Command

The Tools Options command is your key to customizing options in eleven different categories used to control the behavior of Word. Select Tools Options
(Alt+O+O), and then select one of the eleven Options dialog boxes; the
Options box for the View category is shown in Figure 15.1. As you choose
different categories, the dialog box changes accordingly. Each Options dialog
box contains two parts: the list box of category icons on the left, and the
Options panel for the selected category in the main part of the box.

When you first choose Tools Options during a new Word session, the
View category is the default selection in the Category list box, and the View
options are displayed in the main part of the dialog box. In subsequent Word
sessions, the category displayed will be the one last chosen.

Figure 15.1

Tools Options
dialog box for the
View category

Here is the procedure for changing the options in any category:

1. Select Tools Options (Alt+O+O).

2. From the Category list box at the left side of the Options dialog box, select the desired category icon. Use the mouse and the scroll bar, or press Alt+C and use the arrow keys to highlight the desired category icon.

3. In the main Options panel, turn on or off the desired options, or enter values to specify the settings that you want as defaults in Word. Details on the options for each category are provided in the remaining paragraphs of this section.

4. Select any other category icons in the list box and change their settings as needed.

5. When you have made all desired changes to all categories, choose OK to close the dialog box and place the settings into effect.

View Category

The View category of the Tools Options dialog box is shown in Figure 15.1. The options in this category let you control different aspects of the Word screen's appearance, such as whether scroll bars are visible, and whether tabs, spaces, and paragraph markers appear as visible characters.

Window Options   Window options determine whether the following features are enabled or disabled in the Word workspace.

Horizontal Scroll Bar and Vertical Scroll Bar   Turn on these options to display the horizontal and/or vertical scroll bars. The horizontal scroll bar appears along the bottom of the workspace, and the vertical scroll bar appears on the right of the workspace.

Status Bar   Turn on this option if you want the status bar to be visible at the bottom of the workspace. If the horizontal scroll bar is turned on, it will appear above the status bar.

Style Area Width   This option controls the width of the style area at the left side of the workspace, where style names are listed. You can either type in a value (inches or centimeters), or click on the scroll box arrows to increase or decrease the measurement.

Show Text With Options

The Show Text With options determine how Word displays text and its related elements.

Table Grid Lines   Turn this option on to have Word display dotted grid lines between the rows and columns of a table. The grid lines do not print, but are a visual aid in determining the cell boundaries.

Text Boundaries   When this option is turned on, Word displays dotted boundary lines around text elements such as headers and footers, and frames containing text when in page layout view. The dotted lines do not print, but are a visual aid in determining the text boundaries.

Picture Placeholders   With this option enabled, Word displays rectangles in place of graphics. Turn on this feature to speed up Word's display performance when you are working with documents that contain graphic images; scrolling will go faster because Word does not have to redraw the graphics.

Field Codes   When this option is turned on, Word displays the codes of any fields in the document, rather than the results of the fields.

Line Breaks and Fonts as Printed   Turn this on to have Word display line breaks and fonts as they will appear when printed.

Nonprinting Characters Options

Turn on any of the following options to tell Word to make these nonprinting characters visible:

- **Tabs** displays tabs as right-pointing arrows.

- **Spaces** represents spaces with space marks, which are small dots.

- **Paragraph Marks** shows the beginning of new paragraphs (created by pressing Enter) with paragraph symbols, new lines (created by pressing Shift+Enter) with newline markers (an arrow pointing down and left), and end-of-cell markers (small circles) in tables.

- **Optional Hyphens** displays nonbreaking hyphens, or optional hyphens that you add with Ctrl+Hyphen and that Word adds when you use Tools Hyphenate.

- **Hidden Text** makes hidden text visible, by showing the text with a dotted underline to indicate that it is normally hidden.

- **All** displays all nonprinting characters.

Tip. You can print hidden text by choosing the Hidden Text option in the Print category of the Options dialog box.

General Category Options

When you select Tools Options and choose the General category, the dialog box shown in Figure 15.2 appears. Use the various options in this dialog box to set your defaults for typing and navigation keys.

Figure 15.2

General options

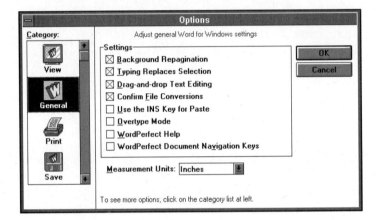

Background Repagination   Turn this on to have Word repaginate documents as needed in the background (when you are not typing or editing documents). With very long documents, pagination can slow down Word's performance. You can turn this option off and then use the Tools Repaginate Now command to force repagination of a document as desired. (Note that repagination also happens automatically whenever you print a document.)

Typing Replaces Selection   When this setting is turned on, Word replaces selected text with newly typed text. Otherwise, newly typed text pushes selected text to the right.

Confirm File Conversions   When this option is turned on, Word asks for confirmation of the file type (by displaying a list box of file types) when you open a foreign file within Word. When the option is turned off, Word selects what it guesses to be the appropriate file type and makes the conversion without asking for confirmation.

Use the INS Key for Paste   Turn this on when you want to use the Insert key as a shortcut for the Edit Paste command. Pressing Ins will insert the contents of the Clipboard at the insertion pointer.

Overtype Mode When this setting is turned on, Word replaces existing text with the characters you type. (Note that you can switch between Insert mode and Overtype mode at any time by pressing the Ins key, if the Use INS Key for Paste option is not turned on.)

WordPerfect Help When this is on, Word lets you access commands using the WordPerfect command key sequences. Depending on what you choose in the dialog box that appears in response to the Help WordPerfect Help command, Word either displays a help box showing the Word equivalent of the WordPerfect key, or translates the WordPerfect key into a Word command.

WordPerfect Document Navigation Keys When this is on, Word accepts your use of navigation keys from WordPerfect, and responds with the equivalent Word keyboard action.

Measurement Units Use this list box to choose the desired unit of measurement to appear on the ruler, in dialog boxes, and for margins and tab settings. The default is inches, but you can change it to centimeters, points, or picas.

Print Category

When you select Tools Options and choose the Print category, the dialog box shown in Figure 15.3 appears. There are four groups of options: Printing Options, Envelope Options, Options for Current Document Only, and Include with Document options.

Figure 15.3

Print options

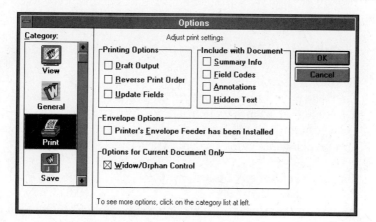

Printing Options

Note. The options in the Print category are also available through the Options button in the Print dialog box.

Draft Output   When this is on, Word uses the printer's draft mode for printing. Many printers (especially dot-matrix printers) can print faster in draft mode; formatted characters may appear as underlined, and pictures appear as empty frames. For this option to work, your printer must support draft printing; some printers do not.

Reverse Print Order   Turn on this option to reverse the normal order of printed pages. Word normally prints from the beginning page of a document (or the first specified page in a group of pages), and continues to the last page.

Update Fields   Turn on this option to tell Word to update all fields before printing a document.

Include With Document Options

Summary Info   Turn this on when you want Word to print the information stored in the Summary Info dialog box whenever you print a document. The summary information is printed on a separate page.

Fields Codes   When this is turned on, Word prints the codes of any fields in the document, rather than the results of the fields.

Annotations   Turn this on when you want Word to print any annotations in the document, on a separate page at the end of the document. When you turn on this option, the Hidden Text option (see below) is automatically enabled because annotations are stored as hidden text.

Hidden Text   This tells Word to print all hidden text in the document.

Envelope Options

Only one option for envelope printing is available: Printer's Envelope Feeder has been Installed. Turn this on if you are printing envelopes, but your printer does *not* have an automatic envelope feeder and you must therefore manually insert the envelopes.

Options for Current Document Only

Only one feature is available: Widow/Orphan Control. This option, when on, prevents the printing of a single line of a paragraph at the top or bottom of the page. (For widow/orphan control to work, a paragraph that is split by a page break must have more than three lines either before or after the page break.)

Save Options

The Save category lets you specify the default options used by Word when you are saving files. When you select Tools Options and choose the Save category, the dialog box shown in Figure 15.4 appears.

Figure 15.4
Save options

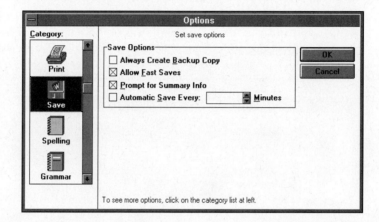

Always Create Backup Copy   Turn this on when you want Word to create a backup copy whenever you save a document. The backup copy is assigned the current file name, with a .BAK extension. Note that Word does not allow fast saves (see below) if you turn on the Always Create Backup Copy option.

Note. You can also access the Save options by choosing the Options button in the Save As dialog box.

Allow Fast Saves   When this is enabled, Word can often save documents faster than usual, by performing a fast save whenever possible. With a fast save, Word does not always update the entire file; instead, changes to an existing document are added to the end of the disk file. As the file grows in size, Word will occasionally perform a normal (full) save. If you turn off this option (or if you turn on Always Create Backup Copy), Word always performs a full save.

Prompt for Summary Info   Turn this on if you want Word to display the Summary Info dialog box when you save a document for the first time. As summary information, you can enter a title, subject, author name, keywords, and comments. (You can also enter summary information at any time via the File Summary Info command.)

Automatic Save Every *n* Minutes   When this is turned on, Word performs an automatic save of the document after a specified interval has passed. The default value for this feature is 10 minutes; in the Minutes text box you can enter any desired number to change the interval.

Spelling Options

The Spelling category contains options for the default dictionaries and rules used by the Tools Spelling command. When you select Tools Options and choose the Spelling category, the dialog box shown in Figure 15.5 appears.

Figure 15.5

Spelling options

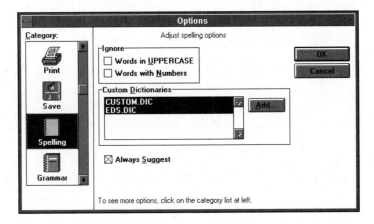

Note. The Spelling options can also be accessed by choosing the Options button in the Spelling dialog box.

Two options appear in the Ignore area of the dialog box: Words in UPPERCASE, and Words with Numbers. Choose an option to tell Word's Spelling utility to skip all words typed in all uppercase letters, or all words containing numbers. If Ignore Words in UPPERCASE is turned on, Word will ignore words typed in uppercase, but will still check words that have been set to uppercase using the All Caps or the Small Caps character format option.

The Custom Dictionaries list box lets you choose the custom dictionaries that you want Word to use during the spell-check; you can select up to four dictionaries. In the list box, Word displays all files with a .DIC file name extension that are in the current directory, the Word directory, and the Spelling path as defined by the WIN.INI file. Use the Add button in this box to add a new custom dictionary.

The Always Suggest check box, when marked, tells Word to display suggested spellings each time an unknown word is found during a spell-check. (Even when this option is off, you can use the Suggest button that appears in the Spelling dialog box to display a list of suggestions.)

Grammar Options

The Grammar category contains the options for the default dictionaries and style rules used by the Tools Grammar command. When you select Tools Options and choose the Grammar category, the dialog box shown in Figure 15.6 appears.

Figure 15.6

Grammar options

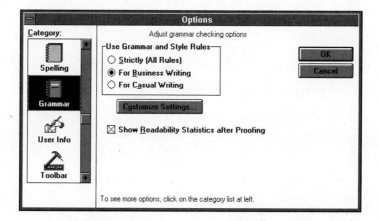

Note. You can also access the Grammar options by choosing the Options button in the Grammar dialog box.

The buttons in the Use Grammar and Style Rules area let you control the level to which Word checks grammar in your document. If you turn on Strictly, Word applies all rules of grammar and style contained in the Grammar utility. Select For Business Writing, and Word applies fewer grammar and style rules, as appropriate for business correspondence. The For Casual Writing level is more flexible yet, and applies the fewest categories of grammar and style rules.

Choose the Customize Settings button to bring up another dialog box that lets you customize the settings used by the three grammar-checking levels (Strictly, For Business Writing, and For Casual Writing). In this dialog box, you can specify which rules are used during a grammar-check, by marking the grammar and style rules you want each level of checking to apply. You can also use the list boxes in the Catch area of this dialog box to change how Word addresses split infinitives, consecutive nouns, and prepositional phrases during a grammar-check. The Explain button lets you display another dialog box that offers an explanation of the available Grammar and Catch choices; tab to or click on the option you want to read about, and then choose the Explain button. When you've made all the desired choices in the Customize Grammar Settings box, choose OK (or press Enter) to return to the Grammar category Options box.

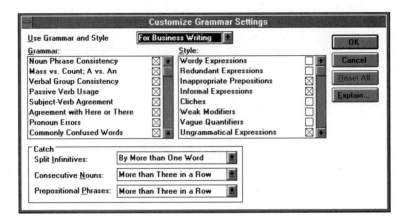

One last option, the Show Readability Statistics After Proofing check box, remains for the Grammar category. Mark this box to tell Word to display an information box after a grammar-check is completed, showing various readability statistics for the document. These statistics tell you how many words, characters, paragraphs, and sentences are in your document, and show several calculated readability indexes.

User Info Options

The User Info category includes the default user information, such as user name and address. (Word stores this information for the first time when the program is installed.) When you select Tools Options and choose the User Info category, the dialog box shown in Figure 15.7 appears.

Figure 15.7
User Info options

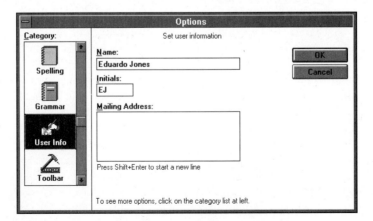

Enter your name in the Name text box; this name then appears by default under Author Name in the Summary Info dialog box. In the Initials box, enter the initials that you want Word to use when inserting annotations. For Mailing Address, enter the address you want Word to use as a return address when addressing envelopes with the Create Envelope command. Press Shift+Enter after typing each line.

Toolbar Options

Use the Toolbar category to customize the main Toolbar to contain the commands you use most. You can change the icons used for various Toolbar operations, or you can assign your macros to new Toolbar icons. For specifics on customizing your Toolbar, refer to "Customizing Word's Toolbar" later in this chapter.

If you are using a template other than the default (NORMAL.DOT) template, Word displays a dialog box that gives you a choice of storing changes to the current template, or to the global (NORMAL) one. If you are using the global template, changes are stored there.

When you select Tools Options and choose the Toolbar category, the dialog box shown in Figure 15.8 appears.

In the Tool to Change list box, you can select the Toolbar icon that you want to change or delete. This list box is a vertical representation of the icons in the Toolbar. To add a new icon, you'll choose it from the Button box.

In the Show area, you'll choose Commands or Macros to display all Word commands, or all macros currently available, in the Commands/Macro list box in the center of the screen. Use that list box to associate a command/macro with an icon, as explained in the stepped procedure later in this section. The Description box recaps the Word command/macro that you select in the Command/Macros list box.

At the right side of the Toolbar Options dialog box are command buttons titled Change, Close, Reset Tool, and Reset All. Use the Change button to replace the button in the Tool to Change box with the new button you select from the Button list box. Use Reset Tool to reset the selected button to its definition in the global (NORMAL) template. Use Reset All to restore Word's original Toolbar configuration.

The two Context options, Global and Template, determine whether your Toolbar changes apply to the global (NORMAL) template, or to another template. If you are currently using the NORMAL template, the Global option is automatically selected, and the Template option is dimmed.

Figure 15.8

Toolbar options

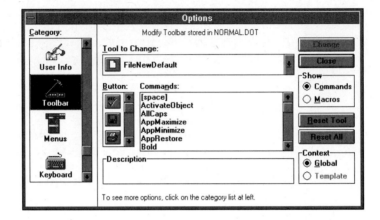

Menus Options

Use the Menus category to customize Word's menus. You can change the names of menu commands, delete them, or add your own commands that are associated with your macros. For specifics on customizing your menus, refer to "Customizing Word's Menus" later in this chapter.

Word stores any changes you make to the menus in the current template; if you are not using a specific template, changes are stored in the default template. If you are using a template other than NORMAL, Word lets you choose whether to store your changes to the current template or to the global (NORMAL) template.

When you select Tools Options and choose the Menus category, the dialog box shown in Figure 15.9 appears.

In the Menu list box, you'll choose the menu containing the commands you want to modify; for example, to add a new command to the File menu, first choose &File from the Menu list box. In the Menu Text box, you'll type the name of a new menu command, or select an existing menu command from the list box, to modify or delete.

You can specify a hotkey to activate a command, by placing an ampersand (&) in the command name, positioned in front of the character that will serve as the hotkey. For example, to add a command called Open Book to the File menu, and make the hotkey for that command Alt+F+B, first select &File in the menu box, and then enter Open &Book in the Menu Text box. (Finally, you will need to select a macro to associate with the new command, so Word will know what to do when you choose that command or hotkey.)

Figure 15.9

Menus options

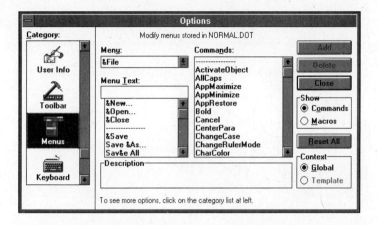

In the Show area, you'll choose Commands or Macros to display all Word commands, or all macros currently available, in the Commands/Macros list box in the center of the screen. Use that list box to associate the command that appears in Menu Text with a specific Word command/macro (as explained in the stepped procedure later in this section). The Description box recaps the Word command/macro that you select in the Commands/Macros list box.

At the right side of the Menu Options dialog box are command buttons titled Add, Delete, Close, and Reset All. Use the Add button to add the command in the Menu Text box to the menu shown in the Menu box. Use Delete to remove the command shown in the Menu Text box from its assigned menu. Use Reset All to restore Word's original menu configuration.

The two Context options work as explained previously for Toolbar options.

Keyboard Options

Use the options in the Keyboard category to customize Word's shortcut key assignments. Word stores any changes you make to the keyboard assignments in the current template; if you are not using a specific template, changes are stored in the default (NORMAL) template. If you are using a template other than NORMAL, Word lets you choose whether to save your changes to the global template, or to the current template.

When you select Tools Options and choose the Keyboard category, the dialog box shown in Figure 15.10 appears.

In the Shortcut Key area, enter the key-combination you want to modify. Mark the Ctrl and/or Shift check boxes as needed, to specify the beginning of the key-combination. Then enter a letter, number, or other key by name in the Key box, or choose a key from the list.

Figure 15.10

Keyboard options

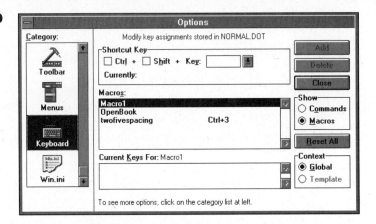

In the Show area of the dialog box, you'll choose Commands or Macros to display all Word commands, or all macros currently available, in the Commands/Macro list box in the center of the screen. Use that list box to associate the designated shortcut key with a specific Word command or a macro. The Current Keys For box will show the keyboard sequence currently assigned to the command or macro that is highlighted in the Commands/Macros list box.

At the right side of the Key Options dialog box are command buttons titled Add, Delete, Close, and Reset All. Use Add to add the Shortcut Key assignment to the command or macro selected in the Commands/Macros list box. Use Delete to cancel the key assignment selected in the Current Keys For box. Use Reset All to restore Word's original key assignment configuration.

The two Context options work as explained previously for Toolbar options.

WIN.INI Options

Use the WIN.INI category options to customize the settings in your WIN.INI file. (This file is read by Word at startup, and controls certain aspects of Word's operation.) The contents of your WIN.INI file are fairly complex, and for the most part are beyond the scope of this book. For more information about the file and how the options in this dialog box apply, refer to Appendix C of your Word documentation.

When you select Tools Options and choose the WIN.INI category, the dialog box shown in Figure 15.11 appears. Here is a brief description of each element in the dialog box:

- **Application** Use this list box to type or select the Windows application you want to modify.

- **Startup Options** After selecting the desired application, use this list box to choose the startup options you want to specify for Windows.

- **Option** This box contains the option that is currently selected under Start-up Options. You can also type the name of the startup option into this box, if it does not appear in the Startup Options list.

- **Setting** If the setting you want for this option isn't shown in the Startup Options box, type it in this text box.

- **Set**, **Delete**, and **Close** These buttons are located at the right side of the dialog box. Use Delete to delete the selected startup option; use Set to establish the setting you specify in the Setting box; and use Close to close the dialog box.

Figure 15.11
WIN.INI options

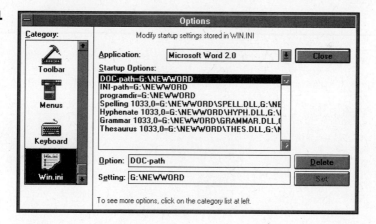

Customizing Word's Menus

Word lets you redesign its menu structure as extensively as you desire. You can change each and every command available throughout the Word menus, if you want to. You can add custom commands and menus to do the tasks that you perform on a regular basis. You'll use the Menus category of the

Tools Options command to do all this. As usual, you can save your custom menus to be used globally, or with a particular template, as explained later in "Saving your Toolbar, Keyboard, and Menu Changes."

The following procedures show how to add and remove commands and macros from the menus. After the steps is an exercise that demonstrates the addition of a custom command (for capitalizing letters in a text selection) to Word's Format Menu.

Adding a Command or Macro in a Menu

To add a command or a macro to Word's menus, follow these steps:

1. Select Tools Options (Alt+O+O).

2. From the Category list box (Alt+C), select Menus.

3. From the Show box, choose either Commands (Alt+O) or Macros (Alt+M), as appropriate.

4. In the Menu list box (Alt+U), select the command menu that will be affected.

5. From the Commands/Macros list box, choose the command or macro you want to add.

   NOTE. *If you want to rename the command or macro, select the existing name in the Commands/Macros list, select the Menu Text box, and then type in the new name. To assign a hotkey to your new menu entry, you must type an ampersand (&) before the desired hotkey letter of the entry in the Menu Text box. If you wish to add a separator line to the end of the menu, choose the dotted line that appears at the top of the Commands/Macros list.*

6. Select Add (Alt+A). The command/macro you added is appended to the bottom of the menu.

7. Repeat steps 3 through 6 for each command or macro you want to add to the menu.

8. Select Close (or press Enter).

Removing a Command or Macro from a Menu

To remove a command or a macro from Word's menus,

1. Select Tools Options (Alt+O+O).

2. From the Category list box (Alt+C), select Menus.

3. From the Menu list box (Alt+U), select the menu that contains the command or macro you want to remove.

4. From the Menu Text list box (Alt+T), select the command or macro you want to remove.

5. Choose Delete (Alt+D), and then Close (or press Enter).

Resetting the Menus to Word's Default Configuration

You can easily reset any customized menus to the default menu configuration provided by Microsoft. Select Tools Options (Alt+O+O), and from the Category list box (Alt+C), select Menus. Choose the Reset All button (Alt+R), answer Yes in the dialog box that appears, and then select Close (or press Enter).

An Exercise in Adding a Menu Option

The following exercise takes you through the steps to add a menu choice that will change a text selection in a Word document to all capital letters. For this example, you will add to the Format menu a command called AllCaps, which performs this capitalization operation.

1. Select Tools Options (Alt+O+O).

2. From the Category list box (Alt+C), select Menus.

3. From the Show box, choose Commands (Alt+O).

4. From the Menu list box (Alt+U), select Format.

5. From the Commands list box (Alt+N), choose AllCaps.

6. Choose the Add button (Alt+A); then choose Close (or press Enter).

Now open the Format menu (Alt+T), and you will see that the AllCaps command has been added. You can try the effects of the new command by opening a document, selecting some text, and choosing the AllCaps command from the menu.

Customizing Word's Toolbar

As with the menus, you can also customize Word's Toolbar. You can add icons to do tasks that you perform often, or remove icons that you rarely or never use. You can also change the appearance of the icons; Word provides a number of extra icons in addition to the ones that you see on the standard

Toolbar. You can save your custom Toolbar to be used globally, or with a particular template, as explained later in "Saving your Toolbar, Keyboard, and Menu Changes."

The following procedure shows how you can add or remove commands or macros from the Toolbar. At the end of the section is an exercise that demonstrates the addition of a custom icon (for printing the current page of a document) to the Toolbar.

Adding or Changing a Command or Macro on the Toolbar

To add a command/macro to the Toolbar, or change the command/macro associated with a particular icon, follow these steps:

1. Select Tools Options (Alt+O+O), and from the Category list box (Alt+C), select Toolbar.

2. In the Show box, choose Commands (Alt+O) to add or change a command on the Toolbar, or Macros (Alt+M) to add or change a macro.

3. From the Commands/Macros list box choose the command or macro you want to add or reassign.

4. If you are adding a new icon, choose it from the Button list box.

5. In the Tool to Change list box, choose the space where you want to place the new icon. (The list box is a vertical duplicate of the Toolbar.) Or, if you are reassigning an existing icon, choose that icon.

6. Choose the Change button (Alt+A).

7. Repeat steps 2 through 6 for each command or macro icon you want to add or change.

8. Select Close (or press Enter) to close the Toolbar options dialog box.

Removing a Command or Macro from the Toolbar

You remove a command or macro from the Toolbar by removing the icon, and replacing it with a space. To replace a Toolbar icon with a space, follow these steps.

1. Select Tools Options (Alt+O+O), and from the Category list box (Alt+C), select Toolbar.

2. In the Tool to Change list box, select the icon you wish to remove.

3. In the Show box, choose Commands (Alt+O) if it is not already chosen. (Or, to remove one of your customized buttons, you might need to choose Macros.)

4. In the Commands list box, select the first entry, [space].

5. Choose the Change button (Alt+A), and then Close (or press Enter) to close the Toolbar options dialog box.

Resetting the Toolbar to Word's Default Configuration

You can easily reset a customized Toolbar to the default Toolbar arrangement provided by Microsoft. Select Tools Options (Alt+O+O), and from the Category list box (Alt+C), select Toolbar. Choose the Reset All button (Alt+E), then select Close (or press Enter).

For more information about macros, refer to Chapter 14.

An Exercise in Adding a Toolbar Icon

Perhaps you often find it necessary to print the current page of the document you are working on, and you want a Toolbar icon that runs a macro to perform this task. First you must create the macro to print the current page of a document; here are steps to do so:

1. Turn on your printer, and open any document.

2. Select Tools and choose Record Macro (Alt+O+R).

3. Choose OK (or press Enter) to accept the default name assigned to the macro. (Unless you have created other macros during this session, this name will be Macro1.) If you're using a template other than NORMAL, a dialog box will ask you how you want to store the macro (in the current template, or globally).

4. Select File and choose Print (Alt+F+P).

5. Choose Current Page (Alt+E), and then OK (or press Enter) to print the current page.

6. Select Tools and choose Stop Recorder (Alt+O+R).

With the macro recorded, you can now assign it to a Toolbar icon. Follow these steps:

7. Select Tools Options (Alt+O+O), and from the Category list box (Alt+C), select Toolbar.

8. In the Show box, choose Macros (Alt+M).

9. From the Macros list box (Alt+S), select the name of the macro you just created (unless you have created other macros during this session, it will be Macro1).

10. From the Button list box (Alt+B), pick an icon you like that is not already being used by the Toolbar.

11. In the Tool to Change list box (Alt+T), choose a space where you want to place the new icon (for this exercise, it does not matter what position you choose).

12. Select the Change button (Alt+A), and then Close (or press Enter) to close the dialog box.

With the document still open and your printer turned on and ready, click or select the new icon. Word responds by printing the current page of the document.

Saving Your Toolbar, Keyboard, and Menu Changes

When you exit Word after making changes to the Toolbar, keyboard assignments, or menu structure, Word automatically asks you if the changes should be saved to the current template. If you are using a template other than NORMAL, the changes will be saved to that template; otherwise, the changes are saved to NORMAL. If you wish to save your changes to a template different from the one currently in use, you must "attach" that template with the File Template command. Choose File Template, and from the Template dialog box select the template to which you want to save your new menu, key assignment, or Toolbar customization. If you want the custom items to be available throughout Word (globally), attach them to the NORMAL template.

Using the Format Language Command

The Spelling, Grammar, and Thesaurus utilities available from Word's Tools menu are designed to work with different languages. You can pick the language that Word uses with these utilities, by using the Format Language command.

NOTE. *Before you can use the Spelling, Grammar, or Thesaurus proofing tools with other languages, you must install the required language proofing files. For information on obtaining these files, contact your software dealer, or call Microsoft Customer Support (the telephone number for your country is printed on the software registration card).*

When you select Format Language (Alt+T+L), the Language dialog box appears, as shown here:

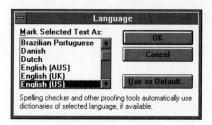

In the Mark Selected Text As list box (Alt+M), select the language you need to apply, and then choose OK. Your document will then be checked (when you invoke the Tools Spelling, Grammar, or Thesaurus commands) using the appropriate foreign-language dictionaries. If you want to make the selected language the default language for use with the proofing tools, select that language from the list box (Alt+M), choose the Use as Default button (Alt+U), and answer Yes in the dialog box that appears.

16

Finding and
Managing Files

The Find File Dialog Box

*Using Find File to Search
for Files*

ONE ISSUE ASSOCIATED WITH ANY SIZABLE DOCUMENT PROCESSING operation is that of file management. As you create more documents, it generally gets more difficult to keep track of where specific information is stored. Within a remarkably short period of time, you can easily compile dozens or even hundreds of documents on your hard disk. Personal computer users connected to file servers on a network face the same problem, compounded by the number of other users on the network.

Word offers a powerful tool—the Find File command on the File menu—that assists you in finding and managing your documents. (You were first introduced to Find File in Chapter 4.) With Find File, you can search for a document based on its contents, or based on an entry you made in the Summary Info dialog box. Word normally prompts you for the summary information (title, author name, subject, keywords, and comments) when you save a document for the first time, as described in Chapter 4. If you supply this helpful summary information, you can later use the Find File command to locate files based on a search of that information. Using the summary information is a significant help in searching, but Word's Find File command does not limit you to that technique. You can also search for a document based on its contents, although this is a considerably slower way to go.

TIP. *Don't overlook the importance of the summary information for a file. If you take a moment to fill it in when you first save the file, many of your file management tasks will be simplified. See Chapter 4 for details.*

You can perform all the usual file management tasks using the Find File command options, including deleting files, copying files, and printing multiple files. And a Preview feature lets you quickly examine the contents of files without opening them.

The Find File Dialog Box

The first time you choose Find File during a session, Word takes a moment to examine the files on your hard disk. Then you'll see the Find File dialog box, shown in Figure 16.1. If you are using Find File for the first time ever, the File Name list box contains all files with a .DOC extension. If you have already used Find File, Word displays all files that meet the last search criteria you specified. The Paths Searched line at the top of the screen reflects the drive and directories for the files listed, and the Sorted By line tells you the current sort criteria.

In the Content display box appears a preview (in normal view) of the document that is currently highlighted in the File Name box. Select another file, and its contents appear in the Content box. Files in foreign formats are shown without formatting and graphics. If you see something other than the document contents in the Content box, it means the Find File options have been changed. You can change this display back to the file contents, or to several other formats, by choosing Options (Alt+T) from the Find File dialog box and turning on the arrangement you want. You'll read more about this later, in "Using the Find File Options."

Figure 16.1

The Find File dialog box

File preview shown here; can display file summary info, or document statistics

List of files found appears here

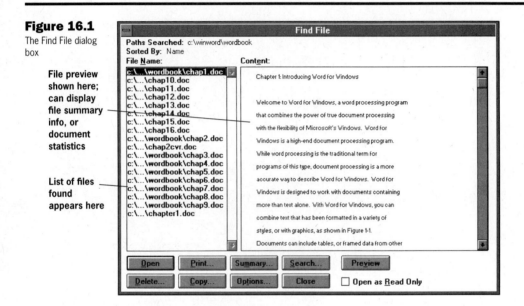

At the bottom of the dialog box is a panel of command buttons; most of these are fairly self-explanatory. Open opens the selected file, Print prints the selected file, and Summary displays the Summary Info dialog box for the selected file. The Search button is used to start a search for a file (this topic is discussed shortly). The Preview button is used with graphic image files, to display the image stored in the file. (Graphic images are not automatically displayed in the Content box; you must use the Preview button to display them.) The Delete button deletes the selected file, and the Copy button copies a file to a new file name. The Options button displays another dialog box (also discussed shortly) that lets you determine how files in the list box are sorted and how they are displayed in the Content box. As usual, the familiar Close button is used to close the Find File dialog box.

The Open as Read Only check box is used to open a file in a read-only state, in which Word does not allow edits to be saved to that same file name.

Using Find File to Search for Files

As its name implies, a major role for the Find File command is to locate files for you. The summary information for a file is a significant aid to effectively locating a particular file, and your searches will be more productive if you have completed the Summary Info dialog box for all your saved files. As mentioned, you can also search based on the contents of a file, but this is a slower method, especially if you are searching a large number of files.

Here are the steps to use Find File to locate a file, based on either summary information or contents:

1. Select File and choose Find File (Alt+F+F).

2. Choose Search (Alt+S) to display the Search dialog box, shown in Figure 16.2.

Figure 16.2

Search dialog box

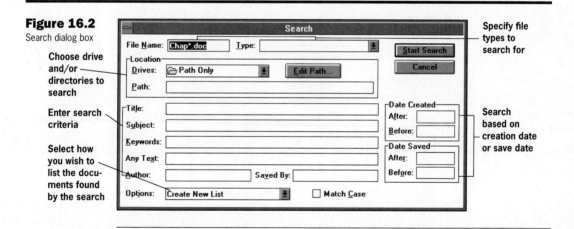

Choose drive and/or directories to search

Enter search criteria

Select how you wish to list the documents found by the search

Specify file types to search for

Search based on creation date or save date

3. In the Type box (Alt+T), select a file name extension to indicate the type of file you want to find.

Typically, you'll want to find document files, but Word does not limit you in this area; you can select all files (*.*), Word documents (.DOC), Word templates (.DOT), Windows Metafiles (.WMF), or Windows Bitmaps (.BMP). Or you can specify an extension, or even a specific file name of your own choosing, by typing it into the File Name text box (Alt+N). For example, entering *.BAT in the File Name box limits the search to all files with a .BAT extension.

4. Use the Location box to specify which drives and directories you want Word to search. If you need to add to the search path, select the Edit Path button, and then choose additional directories from the list of

directories that appears. The names of the additional directories then appear in the Path text box.

Now it's time to really get specific. To narrow your file search, enter search criteria in any of the remaining text boxes within the Search dialog box.

- Use the Title, Subject, Keywords, and Author boxes when you have supplied these data in the summary information of the files in your Word directories. You can enter partial words and phrases in these boxes; for example, if you enter Report in the Title box, Word might find documents that have Weekly Production Report and Reporting Procedures entered as the Title in their Summary Info dialog box.

- The Date Created and Date Saved boxes let you search based on a creation or save date. Type these dates in the same date format set for the Windows Control Panel.

- The Saved By box lets you search based on the name of the person who last saved the file; Word obtains this name from the Tools Options User Info.

- The Any Text box (Alt+X) can be used to tell Word to search the contents of the document itself, looking for the text that you enter in the box. Using Any Text to search for files is somewhat slow, as Word must search through the entire document text itself, rather than just in the summary information. But if you cannot remember any summary information (or, worse yet, if you haven't used the Summary Info feature in your files), the Any Text box may be your only hope of finding a specific document. Just type in the text you want to locate.

  NOTE. *If you allow fast saves when you save your documents (see Chapter 2), Word may not be able to locate a document based on what you enter in the Any Text box. If you routinely search for files based on Any Text, turn off fast saves. Select Tools Options, choose Save from the Category list, and turn off Allow Fast Save.*

- Word normally ignores letter case during a search. If the case of the search text is important, mark the Match Case (Alt+C) check box.

Once you've entered your search criteria, tell Word how to handle the results of the search:

5. In the Options box (Alt+I), specify whether you want to use the existing list of files (in the Find File screen) as the basis for the search, or whether you want to create a new list of files. Normally, you'll want to leave this at the default of Create New List, so the search will be based on all files meeting your criteria. To search only within the current list, choose Search Only In List. To search the existing list and add any matching found files to that list, choose Add Matches To List.

6. When the terms of your file search are set, choose the Start Search button (Alt+S).

Word performs the search based on the criteria you have provided, and all files matching your search criteria will appear in the Find File screen's File Name list box (or be added to the list already there), as shown in Figure 16.3. You can highlight the name of any of these files to preview their contents, or you can use any of the command buttons at the bottom of the screen to perform the desired file management operation.

Figure 16.3

The File Name list in the Find File dialog box contains files located after the search is completed.

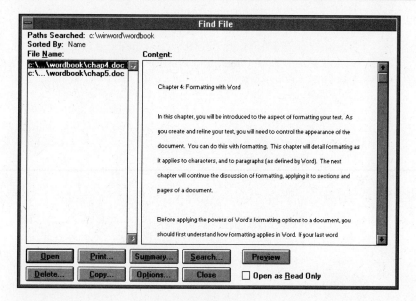

Using the Find File Options

When you click on Options in the Find File dialog box (or press Alt+T), this dialog box appears:

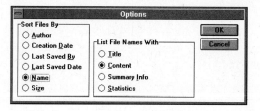

Use these Find File options to determine how the files in the File Name list box are sorted, and what information appears in the Content box. Select a button under Sort Files By to designate an arrangement for the file list in the File Name box (by author, creation date, the name of the person who last saved the file, the date last saved, file name, or file size). Select a button under List File Names With to choose what is displayed in the Content box for each located file. You can display the contents of the Title box from the Summary Info dialog box; or a preview of the actual contents of the file; or all the summary information; or the document statistics. The name of the Content box will change accordingly.

After making your option selections, choose OK or press Enter to return to the Find File dialog box.

Selecting Multiple Files for Printing, Copying, or Deleting

Another significant benefit offered by the Find File command is that it lets you perform file management operations on multiple files. For example, if you want to print a number of files, you can do so using a single operation in Find File. In contrast, if you were to use the File Print command for this task, you would need to open and print each file, one at a time.

To work with multiple files, first use the Find File dialog box to list and select the files you want to work with. Then choose the Open, Print, Copy, or Delete buttons as needed.

Mouse users can select multiple files in the Find File dialog box as follows:

1. Click on the name of the first file to be selected.

2. Hold down the Ctrl key, and click on each additional file name you want to select.

Keyboard users can select multiple files in the Find File dialog box as follows:

1. Use the ↑ or ↓ keys to highlight the name of the first file to be selected.

2. Press Shift+F8.

3. Use the arrow keys to move the dotted-line selection box to the next desired file name, and press the Spacebar.

4. Repeat Step 3 for each file you want to select.

To print the selected files, select the Print button. In the Print dialog box, choose the desired printing options (detailed in Chapter 6), and choose OK to print the documents.

To delete the selected files, select the Delete button. Word displays a dialog box asking you to confirm that you want to delete the files. Choose Yes to proceed, or No to cancel.

To copy the selected files, select the Copy button. Word displays a dialog box asking for the path name to which you want the files copied. Enter the path (you can enter a floppy drive identifier, such as A:), and choose OK to copy the files to the desired destination.

A P P E N D I X   A

Installing Word

Word for Windows comes with several disks that you'll need to install the program on your computer's hard disk. Before you begin installation, it's good idea to protect your original disks from accidental erasure by placing a write-protect tab over the notch on the edge of the disk, or, if you have 3 ¼-inch disks, by pushing the plastic locking button so the small square is open.

Your computer needs to meet certain hardware requirements before it will run Word for Windows properly. The following are the minimum requirements.

Hardware Requirements

The following hardware is needed to use Word for Windows 2.0. Note that a mouse is not required, but is highly recommended.

- IBM PC/AT or higher, or IBM PS/2 (model 50 or higher), or equivalent IBM-compatible computer (using the 80286 processor or higher)

- 1 megabyte of memory or more

- IBM EGA, VGA, Hercules graphic card, or other graphics cards compatible with Microsoft Windows, version 3.0 or above

- Hard disk or network file server

- One floppy disk drive

- MS-DOS or PC-DOS, version 3.0 or above

- Microsoft Windows, version 3.0 or above

Installation

Follow these steps to install Word for Windows:

1. Start Windows in the usual manner. (Note that you cannot install Word or run Word in real mode; you must use the standard or enhanced mode of Windows.)

2. Insert the Word Setup disk in drive A.

3. Open the Windows File menu (Alt+F) and choose Run.

4. In the Run dialog box that appears, enter **a:setup** and choose OK (or press Enter).

Word's installation process will begin. Follow the directions that appear on the screen to complete the installation. Here are some of the questions and prompts you'll see:

- Word will ask in which directory you want to install the program; Word suggests C:\WINWORD as a directory name. You can accept this default name, or you can enter any drive and directory name you wish.

- If the directory name entered in the dialog box does not exist, Word will create the directory for you; however, you must answer Yes in the dialog box that states "The specified path does not exist." When you have specified a directory, choose Continue (Alt+C) to continue with the installation.

- Word provides the opportunity to install selective parts of the program. For example, you can choose to install the program without the help files or the tutorial.

- By choosing Custom Installation when prompted, you can select which optional features of the program you want to install by checking options in a dialog box that appears. If you are new to Word for Windows, it's best not to choose Custom Installation until you're sure which features you'll need. During the installation process, Word will check to make sure you have sufficient disk space to install the program. If you install Word with no optional features, approximately 6 megabytes of disk space will be needed. If you install Word with all optional features, approximately 15 megabytes of disk space will be needed.

- Throughout the installation process, Word will prompt you when it needs another disk. Just remove the disk in the drive and insert the one Word asks for.

When the installation process is complete, you will be returned to the Windows desktop. A new program group containing Word will have been added to the desktop; click on the Word icon in that program group to start Word.

APPENDIX B

Command References

This appendix provides three handy command reference aids. You'll find two tables summarizing commands accessed from the keyboard and an illustrated guide to Word for Windows's menu structure.

Table B.1 **Keyboard Commands**

**Insertion Pointer
Movement**

Left Arrow	One character to the left
Right Arrow	One character to the right
Up Arrow	One line up
Down Arrow	One line down
Ctrl+Left Arrow	One word to the left
Ctrl+Right Arrow	One word to the right
End	To the end of a line
Home	To the start of a line
Ctrl+Up Arrow	One paragraph up
Ctrl+Down Arrow	One paragraph down
Page Down	Down one window
Page Up	Up one window
Ctrl+Page Down	To the bottom of a window
Ctrl+Page Up	To the top of a window
Ctrl+Home	To the end of a document
Ctrl+End	To the start of a document

Text Selection

Shift+Left Arrow	Select left character
Shit+Right Arrow	Select right character
Shift+Up Arrow	Select prior line
Shift+Down Arrow	Select next line

Text Entry

Enter	Start new paragraph
Shift+Enter	Start new line
Ctrl Enter	Insert hard page break

Table B.1   **(Continued)**

Text Entry

Ctrl+Shift+Enter	Insert column break
Hyphen	Insert normal hyphen
Ctrl+Hyphen	Insert optional hyphen
Ctrl+Shift+Hyphen	Insert nonbreaking hyphen
Ctrl+Shift+Spacebar	Insert nonbreaking space

Deletions

Del	Delete character to the right of insertion pointer
Backspace	Delete character to the left of insertion pointer
Ctrl+Del	Delete word to the right of insertion pointer
Ctrl+Backspace	Delete word to the left of insertion pointer

Character Formatting Keys

Ctrl+F2	Increase point size
Ctrl+Shift+F2	Decrease point size
Shift+F3	Change case
Ctrl+Spacebar	Remove formatting
Ctrl+A	All capital letters
Ctrl+B	Bold
Ctrl+D	Double underline
Ctrl+F	Change font
Ctrl+H	Hidden text
Ctrl+I	Italic
Ctrl+K	Small capital letters
Ctrl+P	Change point size
Ctrl+U	Underline
Ctrl+W	Underline words, but not spaces
Ctrl+Equal sign	Subscript
Ctrl+Plus sign	Superscript

Table B.1   (Continued)

**Paragraph
Formatting Keys**

Ctrl+1	Single-spaced lines
Ctrl+2	Double-spaced lines
Ctrl+5	One-and-one-half spaced lines
Ctrl+E	Center lines
Ctrl+L	Left-align lines
Ctrl+R	Right-align lines
Ctrl+J	Justify lines
Ctrl+Ø	Close space before paragraph
Ctrl+O	Open space before paragraph
Ctrl+Q	Remove paragraph formatting from selected text

Table B.2   Function Key Commands

COMBINATION KEY	F1	F2	F3	F4	F5	F6	F7
Normal	Help	Move	Glossary	Repeat Command	Go To	Next Pane	Spelling
Shift	Help Pointer	Copy	Toggle Case	Rept Find/ Go To	Go Back	Previous Pane	Thesaurus
Ctrl		Grow Font	Spike	Close Doc Window	Restore Doc Window	Next Window	Move Doc Window
Ctrl+Shift		Shrink Font	Unspike		Insert Book-mark	Previous Window	Update Source
Alt	Next Field	Save As		Close Word Window	Restore Word Window	Next Window	
Alt+Shift	Previous Field	Save				Previous Window	

Table B.2 **(Continued)**

COMBINATION KEY	F8	F9	F10	F11	F12
Normal	Ext. Selection	Update Field	Menu	Next Field	Save As
Shift	Shrink Selection	Toggle Field	Button Bar for Special Pane	Previous Field	Save
Ctrl	Size Doc Window	Insert Field	Maximize Doc Window	Lock Field	Open
Ctrl+Shift	Column Selection	Unlink Field	RulerMode	Unlock Field	Print
Alt		Minimize Word Window	Maximize Word Window		
Alt+Shift		Double-click on Field			

Figure B.1

Word for Windows's menu structure

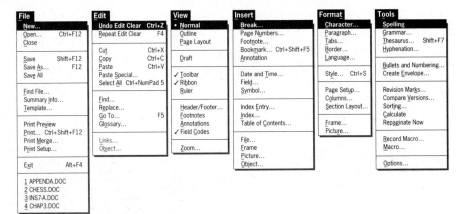

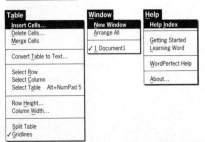

A P P E N D I X   C

Using Microsoft Draw

Microsoft Draw for Windows (MS Draw) is a drawing application that you can use to create pictures which can be placed in your Word documents. Use MS Draw to create corporate logos, business illustrations, or artwork that emphasizes a point in your document. You can also import existing graphic images into MS Draw and edit those images. Once you complete a drawing, the File Update command in MS Draw lets you insert that drawing into your Word document. To use MS Draw you need a mouse.

Starting MS Draw

To start MS Draw from within Word, click on the Draw icon in the toolbar, or choose Insert Object (Alt+I+O) and select Microsoft Drawing from the dialog box that appears. In a moment, an MS Draw window will appear (Figure C.1). The parts of the MS Draw window are illustrated in the figure. The *drawing area* is where you create your image using tools selected from the *Toolbox*. You can enhance a drawing with colors chosen from the *Color Palette*. The *menu bar* presents many options you can use while working with a drawing. For example, it enables you to manipulate selected objects and add text to your drawing.

All drawing takes place within the Draw window. As with all windows, you can move or size the window using the usual techniques.

You can create a drawing in the MS Draw window, or you can import an existing drawing (using the File Import Picture command) and modify it. Once you have completed the drawing, you can use the File Update command to insert the drawing into a Word document. When you save the document, the drawing is saved along with it.

Using the MS Draw Toolbox

You draw your image by choosing the various drawing tools from the MS Draw Toolbox, and drawing (with the mouse) in the drawing area. For example, you could draw a line by first clicking on the line tool, then clicking and dragging in the drawing area.

The Toolbox contains nine drawing tools, as shown in Figure C.2. You select a tool by clicking on it. When you click on a tool, any tool used previously is deselected. Also note that while you are in the drawing area, the mouse pointer changes when you select a different tool.

Figure C.1

MS Draw Window

Menu bar

Toolbox

Drawing area

Color Palette

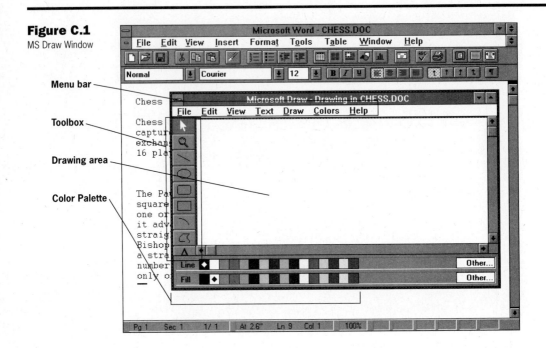

Figure C.2

Toolbox drawing tools

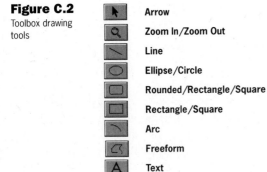

Arrow

Zoom In/Zoom Out

Line

Ellipse/Circle

Rounded/Rectangle/Square

Rectangle/Square

Arc

Freeform

Text

Here are brief descriptions of what each tool can do. Try each one to become familiar with how it works:

- *Arrow*   Use this tool to manipulate objects. Click on the Arrow icon, then click and drag an object to the desired location.

- *Zoom In/Zoom Out*   Use the Zoom In/Zoom Out tool to change a drawing's magnification. (Note that you can also do this from MS Draw's View menu.) Click on the Zoom In/Zoom Out icon, then place the pointer where you want to zoom in or out. To zoom in (increase magnification by one level), click on the mouse. To zoom out (decrease magnification by one level), press and hold the Shift key and then click. Each click of the mouse button will increase or decrease magnification by one level.

- *Line*   To draw a line, click on the Line tool, and then place the pointer where you want the line to begin. Hold down the mouse button and drag the mouse to draw the line; release the mouse button to end the line. You can force a line to maintain an angle to the nearest 45 degrees as you draw it; to do this, hold the Shift key down as you draw the line. To draw a line from its center point, hold the Ctrl key down as you draw the line. To draw a line from its center point while forcing it to match the nearest 45 degree angle, press and hold Shift and Ctrl as you draw the line.

- *Ellipse/Circle*   Use this tool to draw ellipses or circles. Click on the Ellipse/Circle icon, then place the pointer at one corner of an imaginary rectangle or square that will contain the circle or ellipse you wish to draw. Hold down the mouse button and drag to draw the circle or ellipse; release the mouse button when done.

  To draw a circle, hold the Shift key down as you drag the mouse. To draw a circle from its center, hold Ctrl and Shift down as you drag the mouse. To draw an ellipse from its center, hold the Ctrl key down as you drag the mouse.

- *Rounded Rectangle/Square*   The Rounded Rectangle/Square tool allows you to draw rectangles and squares with rounded corners. Click on the Rounded Rectangle/Square icon, then place the pointer at one corner of the rectangle or square you wish to draw. Hold down the mouse button and drag to draw the rectangle or square; release the mouse button when done.

  To draw a rounded rectangle from its center, hold the Ctrl key down as you drag. To draw a square with rounded corners, hold the Shift key down as you drag. To draw a rounded square from its center, hold the Ctrl and Shift keys down as you drag.

■ *Rectangle/Square*   Use the Rectangle/Square tool by clicking on the Rectangle/Square icon, and then placing the pointer at one corner of the rectangle or square you wish to draw. Hold down the mouse button and drag to draw the rectangle or square; release the mouse button when done.

To draw a rectangle from its center, hold the Ctrl key down as you drag. To draw a square, hold the Shift key down as you drag. To draw a square from its center, hold the Ctrl and Shift keys down as you drag.

■ *Arc*   Use this tool to draw arcs. (In MS Draw, arcs are drawn as 90-degree sections of circles or ellipses.) To draw an arc that is part of an ellipse, click on the arc icon, then place the pointer where you want one end of the arc to begin. Hold the mouse button down and drag to draw the arc. The quadrant of the ellipse that the arc will be drawn upon (upper left, lower left, and so on) is controlled by the direction in which you drag the mouse. When done drawing, release the mouse button.

To draw an arc that is part of a circle, hold the Shift key down as you drag the mouse. You can change the arc angle from the standard 90 degrees by selecting the arc, then choosing Edit Arc from the Edit menu. Control handles will appear at the ends of the arc; drag the control handles to reshape the figure.

■ *Freeform*   You can draw freehand shapes with this tool. Click on the Freeform icon, then place the pointer where you want the figure to begin, and hold down the mouse button. In a moment, the pointer will change to a pencil shape. While holding the mouse button, drag the pointer to draw freehand. Release the mouse button when done drawing. Note that instead of just dragging the mouse, you can click and drag to add straight line sections to the freehand shape. As you click and drag, you add straight sections; if you drag without clicking repeatedly, you add freehand sections.

■ *Text*   Use the Text tool to add text objects to your drawings. A text object contains a single line of text. First, select the desired font, point size, and alignment for the text from the Text menu. Then, click on the Text tool. Click in the drawing area where you want the text to begin, and an insertion pointer will appear. Type the desired text. (Remember that you are limited to a single line; if you want more than one line of text in a drawing, you must create a separate text object for each line.) When you are done typing, press Enter or Esc, or click anywhere outside the text object.

Selecting and Editing Objects

MS Draw is an object-oriented drawing package, so everything you add to a drawing is an object. You must select an object in order to perform certain drawing and editing tasks. Once an object is selected, you can copy it to other locations, move it, change its size, or delete it.

To select an object, click on it with the mouse. You can also select an object by clicking on the Arrow tool and dragging a selection marquee (a dotted-line border which appears as you drag) to completely enclose the object.

To select multiple objects, click on the Arrow tool. Then, click and drag a selection marquee completely around the desired objects.

Delete an object by selecting it and pressing Del. To move an object, select it and then drag it with the mouse. To resize an object, select it, then drag on one of the resize handles (the small black squares that appear when the object is selected). To copy an object, select it, then choose Edit Copy. Click anywhere in the drawing area and choose Edit Paste to insert the copy of the selected object. You can then drag the copy to the desired location.

Adding Colors to Your Drawing

The Color Palette provided by MS Draw (see Figure C.1) lets you add color to your drawings. (Remember that your hardware must support color for it to be displayed or printed.) The Color Palette can be turned on or off with the Show Palette command in the Colors menu; if your Color Palette is not visible, choose Colors Show Palette (Alt+C+P) to display it.

The Color Palette provides two types of colors: line and fill. Line colors are used for lines, text, and pattern foregrounds. Fill colors are used to fill in interiors (such as the interior of a rectangle or an ellipse).

Set the desired color by clicking on the appropriate color in the Color Palette; the top row of colors establishes the line color and the bottom row of colors establishes the fill color. A diamond-shaped indicator appears at the currently selected color.

To change the color of an existing object, first select that object; then, choose a new color from the Color Palette.

To set a new default color, first click on the Arrow tool to make sure no objects are selected. Then choose the desired color from the Color Palette.

The MS Draw Menus

The menus provided by MS Draw let you perform various tasks when you are drawing an image. The menu choices are briefly described in Table C.1. For additional details, refer to your MS Draw documentation.

Table C.1   MS Draw Menu Choices

Command	Purpose
File Menu	
File/Update	Updates the drawing in the Word document
File/Import Picture	Imports a graphics file into the MS Draw window
File/Exit and Return	Closes the MS Draw window, and returns to the Word document
Edit Menu	
Edit/Undo	Cancels last operation
Edit/Cut	Cuts selected item, and moves it to the Clipboard
Edit/Copy	Copies selected item to the Clipboard
Edit/Paste	Places contents of Clipboard in drawing
Edit/Clear	Deletes selection
Edit/Select All	Selects all objects in the drawing area
Edit/Bring to Front	Places selected objects in front of all others
Edit/Send to Back	Places selected objects behind all others
Edit/Object	Edits text characters, or edits freeform or arc
View Menu	
View/25%, 50%, 75%	Reduces drawing to a percentage of its original size
View/Full Size	Restores drawing to actual size
View/200%, 400%, 800%	Enlarges drawing to a percentage of its original size
Text Menu	
Text/Plain	Changes text style to plain (no enhanced formatting)
Text/Bold	Changes text style to bold
Text/Italic	Changes text style to italic
Text/Underline	Changes text style to underline
Text/Left	Aligns text to left
Text/Center	Centers text
Text/Right	Aligns text to right
Text/Font	Changes font
Text/Size	Changes point size

Table C.1   **(Continued)**

Command	Purpose
Draw Menu	
Draw/Group	Groups selected objects
Draw/Ungroup	Ungroups selected group
Draw/Framed	Draws an outline around selected object
Draw/Filled	Fills interior of selected object
Draw/Pattern	Chooses one of seven fill patterns
Draw/Line Style	Chooses a style for line type or width
Draw/Snap to Grid	Snaps objects to nearest grid point
Draw/Show Guides	Shows horizontal and vertical guides (grids)
Draw/Rotate/Flip	Rotates or flips selected object
Colors Menu	
Colors/Show Palette	Displays Color Palette at bottom of drawing area
Colors/Edit Palette...	Changes, adds, or deletes colors from palette
Colors/Add Colors from Selection	Adds colors of selected object to palette
Colors/Get Palette...	Selects and opens an existing Color Palette
Colors/Save Palette...	Saves current Color Palette

Quitting MS Draw

To exit from MS Draw, choose Exit and Return from the File menu (Alt+F+X). If you have made any changes to the drawing and the document has not been updated with the latest version of the drawing, Word will display a dialog box like the following:

Choose Yes (Alt+Y or Y) from the dialog box to update the document, and the MS Draw window will close.

Inserting a Drawing into a Word Document

Insert a drawing created in MS Draw into a document by performing the following steps:

1. Create or open the Word document where you want to place the drawing.

2. Place the insertion pointer at the desired location for the drawing.

3. Choose File Update (Alt+F+U) from the MS Draw menu bar. The drawing is inserted into the Word document at the insertion pointer.

You can close the MS Draw window by choosing Exit and Return from the File menu (Alt+F+X), or by pressing Alt+F4 (Close Application Window). The drawing can be saved as a part of the document, using Word's File Save or File Save As command. If you later want to make changes to the drawing while you are in the Word document, double-click on the drawing within the Word document and the MS Draw window will open, containing the existing drawing.

Importing Graphics Files into MS Draw

Use the Import Picture command from the File menu to import graphic files created in other programs, such as Corel Draw or Windows Paintbrush. You can then edit the image while in MS Draw. To import a file, perform the following steps:

1. Select File Import Picture (Alt+F+I). The Import Picture dialog box appears.

2. From the Directories list, choose the drive and/or directory that contains the file you want to import.

3. In the Files list box, choose the desired file by name. If a file is in a format that MS Draw cannot import, it will not be visible in the list box.

4. Click on OK. MS Draw will disassemble the image, and paste it into the window as a multiple selection of objects.

APPENDIX D

Using Microsoft Graph

Microsoft Graph for Windows (MS Graph) can be used to create business graphs and charts. (Note that Microsoft interchangeably uses the terms *graph* and *chart* to mean business graphs.)

When MS Graph is first started, two windows appear over your Word document, as shown in Figure D.1. One window, called the Datasheet window, contains sample numeric data in a table. The other window contains a sample chart based on the sample data in the datasheet window. When you replace the sample data with your own data, MS Graph redraws the chart based on your data. You can use various commands within MS Graph to change the type of chart displayed.

Figure D.1

An MS Graph Datasheet window and Chart window

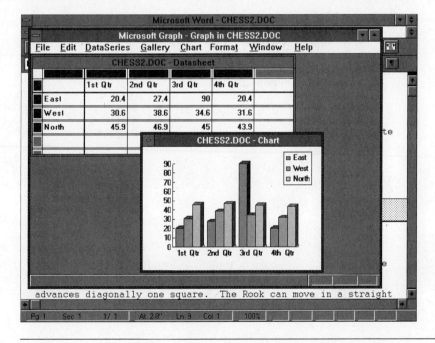

You can insert a chart created by MS Graph into a Word document with the File Update command in MS Graph. You can cut, copy, or move the chart within your Word document, just as you can move any other object in your documents. The chart is automatically saved when you save the document in Word.

Parts of a Chart

The chart in Figure D.1 is typical of a business chart. It consists primarily of *markers* that represent the data contained in the datasheet. In Figure D.1 the markers are shaded vertical bars. However, the appearance of the markers varies, depending on the type of chart you select. In a bar chart, the markers appear as columns; in a line chart, the markers appear as lines. The markers in a pie chart appear as wedges of the pie.

With the exception of pie charts, all charts have two axes: a horizontal axis, called the *category axis*, and a vertical axis, called the *value axis*. A chart also can contain *gridlines*, which provide a frame of reference for the values that appear on the value axis. A chart can also contain a *legend* that indicates which data the markers represent.

Creating a Chart in MS Graph: An Overview

You can create a chart and insert it into a document by performing the following steps (remember, you can get help at any time by pressing F1):

1. Create or open the Word document in which you want to place the chart.

2. Place the insertion pointer at the desired location for the chart.

3. Start MS Graph by clicking on the Graph icon in the toolbar or choosing Insert Object (Alt+I+O), then selecting Microsoft Graph from the dialog box that appears. The MS Graph Datasheet window and Chart window will appear. You can move and size these windows if you wish.

4. Type your data directly into the Datasheet window (see the following section, "Entering Data in the Datasheet Window," for details).

5. Format the numbers as desired. (Select the cell or cells you want to format and choose Format Number. In the Number dialog box that appears, select the desired format and choose OK. See "Formatting Data in the Datasheet Window" for details.)

6. Use the Gallery menu options to select the desired type of chart. Add any other objects (such as legends or chart gridlines) with options in the Chart menu.

7. When the chart is completed, choose File, Update (Alt+F+U). The chart is inserted into the Word document at the insertion pointer.

You can close the MS Graph windows by choosing Exit and Return from the File menu (Alt+F+X), or by pressing Alt+F4 (Close Application Window).

If you later want to make changes to the chart, double-click on the chart within the Word document, and the MS Graph windows containing the existing chart will open.

Entering Data in the Datasheet Window

The easiest way to enter data is to type it directly into the cells of the datasheet. An alternate method for entering data is to select a cell and press F2; a dialog box appears, and you can enter or edit data in this box. Choose OK when you're done, and the data is placed into the cell.

Enter a name for each *data series*, a label for each *category*, and a number for every value that is to be plotted in the chart. If your data series are arranged by rows, enter the series names in the first column, and enter the category labels in the first row. In the sample of a datasheet shown in Figure D.2, the series are arranged by rows, and the resulting chart appears in the lower right.

Figure D.2

Chart resulting from data series arranged by rows

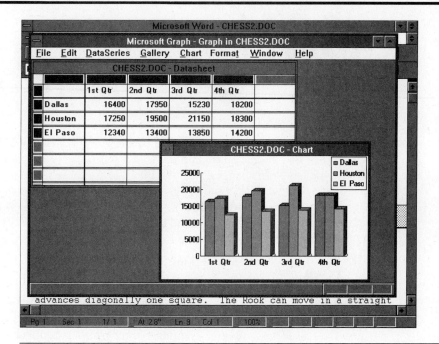

If your series are arranged by columns, enter the series names in the first row, and enter the category labels in the first column. In the example shown in Figure D.3, the series are arranged by columns, and the resulting chart appears in the lower right.

Figure D.3

Chart resulting data series arranged by columns

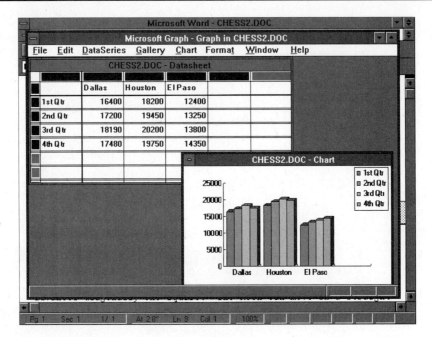

When you enter data into the Datasheet window, MS Graph automatically creates a bar chart based on the values you enter (unless the default chart type has been changed with the File, Set as Default Chart command). When you include text in the cells—labels to the left of the values, headings above the values, or both—MS Graph uses the text to add labels and a legend to the chart. In Figure D.1, the labels (East, West, and North) in the first column of the Datasheet are used in the legend that appears in the chart. The headings (1st, 2nd, 3rd, and 4th Quarter) that appear above the values are used as labels in the chart.

You can move around in the datasheet with the cursor keys, or by clicking in a cell with the mouse. If a column is too narrow to accommodate your data, you can widen it. Just click on a cell in the desired column (or move to the cell with the cursor keys), choose Format Column Width, enter the desired width in the dialog box that appears, and choose OK (or press Enter).

Formatting Data in the Datasheet Window

You can format the numbers that you have entered in the datasheet. The format that you apply to the numbers is used by MS Graph to determine the type of tick marks that appear on the chart axes. As an example, if you use a format that includes dollar signs for the numbers entered in the datasheet, MS Graph will place dollar signs before the numbers that appear along the vertical axis.

If you do not choose a specific number format, MS Graph displays the numbers using a default format called General format. The General format displays numbers with as much precision as possible. If a number is too wide to fit in a cell, General format causes the number to be displayed using scientific notation.

To change the format of the numbers in the datasheet, follow these steps:

1. Select the cell or cells that you want to format.

2. Choose Format Number (Alt+T+N).

3. In the Number dialog box that appears, select the desired number format.

4. Click on OK (or press Enter).

Adding Legends and Other Formatting

You can add a legend to a chart at any time with the Chart Add Legend command (Alt+C+C). You can move the legend by clicking on it and dragging it to the desired location. Once you have added a legend, the name of the command changes to Delete Legend. You can use this command (Alt+C+L)to remove the legend from the chart.

Selecting Desired Chart Types

Once you have entered your numbers in the datasheet, MS Graph displays the default chart type. You can change the chart type with the Gallery command. Twelve different chart types are available from the Gallery menu. You can also customize a chart by selecting options available from the Chart menu.

To change the chart type, perform these steps:

1. Open the Gallery menu (Alt+G).

2. Choose the desired type of chart.

3. In the Chart Gallery dialog box that appears, choose the desired style for the chart.

4. Click on OK, or press Enter.

To change the type of a customized chart, perform the following steps:

1. Choose Format Chart (Alt+T+C).

2. In the Chart Type box, choose the desired chart type.

3. If multiple chart formats are available, choose the desired format in the Data View box.

4. Click on OK, or press Enter.

About Pie Charts

Because pie charts show the relationship between parts and a whole, you can plot only a single data series in a pie chart. If you enter more than one row or column of data in the Datasheet and choose Pie as the desired type of chart, MS Graph uses the data in the first row or column to build the chart. All additional data is ignored. (As noted below, The DataSeries command determines whether the chart is based on a row or a column.)

When working with pie charts, use the DataSeries command to tell MS Graph whether the chart should be drawn based on a data series stored in rows or a data series stored in columns. Open the DataSeries menu (Alt+D) and choose Series in Rows if your data series is stored in the row; choose Series in Columns if your data series is stored in the column.

Exiting from MS Graph

To exit from MS Graph, choose Exit and Return from the File menu (Alt+F+X). If the document has not been updated with the latest version of the chart, MS Graph will display a dialog box asking if you want to update the graph. Choose Yes (Alt+Y) from the dialog box to update the document, and the MS Graph windows will close. The chart can be saved along with the document using Word's File Save or File Save As command.

If you work with business graphics often, experimenting with all of the features of MS Graph may be well worth your time. A detailed explanation of all features and options of MS Graph is beyond the scope of this book; if you want to learn more about MS Graph, refer to the MS Graph documentation supplied by Microsoft.

INDEX

C

Calculate command, 21

caret (^), 60

centering text, 110-111

.CGM file name extension, 263

Character dialog box (figure), 96

characters. *See also* fonts
- boldfacing, 96, 98
- color of, 95, 96
- copying formatting, 103
- formatting, 94-103
- italic, 96, 98-99
- nonprinting, 11, 339
- point size of, 95, 100-101
- spacing of, 95
- special, searching for, 60-61
- subscript, 95, 101-102
- superscript, 95, 101-102
- underlining, 96, 98

charts
- creating in MS Graph, 382-386
- inserting into Word documents, 274-276, 381, 382

check boxes, 14

Clipboard, 34-37, 275-276
- moving/copying text with, 56-57
- viewing contents of, 35

Close key (Ctrl+F4), 15

collapsing outlines, 211-214

columns
- creating, 142-143
- side-by-side, 198, 285
- in tables, 190-191

Columns icon, 10, 142

Column Width command, 190-191

Column Width dialog box (figure), 190

command buttons, 13

commands
- customizing menus, 352
- list of, 369-372
- removing from menus, 352

Comments field, 232

Compare Versions command, 21, 85-86

Compare Versions dialog box (figure), 85

Computer Graphics Metafile, 263

Control menu, 8

Convert Text to Table command, 198

Copy command (Ctrl+Ins), 17, 35, 56

Copy icon, 10, 35

copying
- character formatting, 103
- paragraph formatting, 117
- text, 56-58
- using Clipboard, 34-37, 56-57
- using hotkeys, 57-58

Copy key (Shift+F2), 56, 57

Create Date field, 231

Create Envelope command, 21, 171-172

cropping graphic images, 272, 273

Ctrl+Del (Cut), 56

Ctrl+F3 (Spike), 324

Ctrl+F4 (Close Window), 15

Ctrl+F5 (Restore Window), 15

Ctrl+F6 (Next Window), 87

Ctrl+F7 (Move Window), 15

Ctrl+F9 (Insert Field), 225, 254

Ctrl+F11 (Lock Field), 231

Ctrl+Ins (Copy), 56

Ctrl+Shift+F3 (Unspike), 324

Ctrl+Shift+F5 (Insert Bookmark), 80

Ctrl+Shift+F10 (Ruler Mode), 120